THE POST-COMMUNIST ERA

Also by Ben Fowkes

COMMUNISM IN GERMANY UNDER THE WEIMAR REPUBLIC

RUSSIA AND CHECHNIA: The Permanent Crisis

THE DISINTEGRATION OF THE SOVIET UNION

THE RISE AND FALL OF COMMUNISM IN EASTERN EUROPE

The Post-Communist Era

Change and Continuity in Eastern Europe

Ben Fowkes
Senior Lecturer in History
University of North London

First published in Great Britain 1999 by
MACMILLAN PRESS LTD
Houndmills, Basingstoke, Hampshire RG21 6XS and London
Companies and representatives throughout the world

A catalogue record for this book is available from the British Library.

ISBN 0–333–69203–9

 First published in the United States of America 1999 by
ST. MARTIN'S PRESS, INC.,
Scholarly and Reference Division,
175 Fifth Avenue, New York, N.Y. 10010

ISBN 0–312–22368–4

Library of Congress Cataloging-in-Publication Data
Fowkes, Ben.
The post-communist era : change and continuity in Eastern Europe /
Ben Fowkes.
    p.   cm.
Includes bibliographical references and index.
ISBN 0–312–22368–4
 1. Europe, Eastern—History—1989–   2. Post-communism—Europe,
Eastern.   I. Title.
DJK51.F69   1999
947'.0009'045—dc21   99–13906
                                                                                                 CIP

© Ben Fowkes 1999

All rights reserved. No reproduction, copy or transmission of this publication may be made without written permission.

No paragraph of this publication may be reproduced, copied or transmitted save with written permission or in accordance with the provisions of the Copyright, Designs and Patents Act 1988, or under the terms of any licence permitting limited copying issued by the Copyright Licensing Agency, 90 Tottenham Court Road, London W1P 0LP.

Any person who does any unauthorised act in relation to this publication may be liable to criminal prosecution and civil claims for damages.

The author has asserted his right to be identified as the author of this work in accordance with the Copyright, Designs and Patents Act 1988.

This book is printed on paper suitable for recycling and made from fully managed and sustained forest sources.

10 9 8 7 6 5 4 3 2 1
08 07 06 05 04 03 02 01 00 99

Printed and bound in Great Britain by
Antony Rowe Ltd, Chippenham, Wiltshire

Contents

Preface vi
List of Abbreviations viii

1 Introduction: Mapping Out the Theme 1
2 The Inheritance of the Past and the Revolutions of 1989 9
3 History Changes Gear: the Transition in East-Central Europe 23
4 Hesitant Beginnings in South-Eastern Europe: a 'Balkan Lag'? 59
5 National Minorities and Ethnic Conflict 76
6 The Economic Underpinnings: Tearing down the Old, Building up the New 109
7 The Shock of the New: Social Consequences and Costs of Transition 132
8 The Middle Years: Drifting towards the Millennium 150

Appendix: Statistical Tables 189
Notes 200
Index 226

Preface

It is somewhat ambitious, and perhaps also foolhardy, to attempt a presentation of the most recent decade in the history of Eastern Europe which does justice to the variety and complexity of events and yet retains the virtue of brevity. This book was originally even more ambitious; it began as a study of post-communist transition in general. As time went on, however, I became more and more deeply convinced that what was happening in the newly independent countries of the former Soviet Union was so different from developments further west that a separate study would be required. That vast Eurasian landmass, stretching from Moldova to Mongolia, remains so strongly marked with the imprint of the communist past, so hesitant and inconsistent in its economic and political reforms, so subject to extremes of social misery, political instability and ethnic conflict, that it is doubtful whether one can speak of a transition process at all. There is plenty of drama, certainly, and plenty of action, but the actors are repeating the same lines, and, instead of moving forward, they are running on the spot. It seemed impossible to give these points the detailed attention they deserved within the compass of a single slim volume. The present work, therefore, has a more modest aim. It can be seen as Part 1 of a two-part story.

What I have tried to produce here is an account of the *domestic* evolution of the Eastern European countries, conceived broadly so as to take into account the interplay of economic and social changes and politics. I have omitted the story of reunited Germany, as it seems to me to belong to the West (although I have made some comments on the privatization process there). Questions of international relations, which bulk large in some works on this and related themes, have not been treated in any detail. I therefore summarize them here. In the last decade Russia has withdrawn from Eastern Europe, although maintaining a watching brief over the fate of its minorities in the Baltic; the states of Eastern Europe, left to themselves, aspire almost without exception to enter the North Atlantic Treaty Organization (NATO) and the European Union (EU); they will get there eventually, some sooner, some later; the division between the West and the East of Europe will gradually become merely geographical. As for relations between the countries of the region, they have been friendly and uneventful, except where affected by minority questions (which are treated in Chapter 5). Even in this area, a spirit of compromise and co-operation has largely prevailed (except in former Yugoslavia).

My general conclusion is optimistic. The crisis of transition has by and large been weathered. At the same time, it would be wrong to ignore the many political and economic vicissitudes suffered by Eastern Europe since 1989, and, although the stagnation of the 1980s has been replaced by movement everywhere, in some cases the precise direction of this movement remains uncertain.

The compilation of evidence for a book like this does not present a problem. Generally politicians have been open about their aims, and discussions have taken place in public. This is a change from the previous era. There may have been hidden agendas, but I have not generally speculated about them, in the absence of positive proof. The modest purpose of this book is to present a clear view of what has happened in the decade, politically and otherwise, and to show how this has affected the people of the region. The main obstacle in the way of this endeavour is the difficulty of making sense of the mass of facts which pour down upon the observer from one week to the next. I hope I have at least succeeded in summarizing the main lines of development.

I should like to thank the institution where I work, the University of North London, for allowing me a period of sabbatical leave, during which part of this project was completed; I should also like to thank Bülent and Kyril for helpful comments on aspects of Balkan history.

BEN FOWKES

List of Abbreviations

ÁPV Rt.	Állami Privatizációs és Vagyonkezelő Részvénytársaság
AS – BZNS	Aleksander Stamboliyski Bălgarski Zemedelski Naroden Săjuz (Aleksander Stamboliyski Bulgarian Agricultural People's Union)
AWS	Akcja Wyborcza Solidarności
ÁVÜ	Állami Vagyonügynökség
BBIOST	*Berichte des Bundesinstituts für Ostwissenschaftliche und Internationale Studien*
BBWR	Bezpartyjny Blok Wspierania Reform (Non-Party Bloc in Support of Reform)
BNS	Blocul Naţional Sindical
BSP	Bălgarska Sotsialisticheska Partiya (Bulgarian Socialist Party)
BZNS – NP	Bălgarski Zemedelski Naroden Săjuz – Nikola Petkov
CDR	Convenţia Democratică din România (Democratic Convention of Romania) (Convenţia Democrată Română [Romanian Democratic Convention])
CDU	Christlich – Demokratische Union
CIS	Commonwealth of Independent States
CITUB	Confederation of the Independent Trade Unions of Bulgaria
CJE	*Cambridge Journal of Economics*
CMEA	Council for Mutual Economic Assistance
CPCS	*Communist and Post-Communist Studies*
ČMKOS	Českomoravská komora odborových svazů
CNSLR-Frăţia	Confederaţiu Naţională a Sindicatelor Libere din România – Fraţia (National Free Trade Union Confederation of Romania – Brotherhood)
ČSKOS	Česká a slovenská konfederace odborových svazů
ČSSD	Česká strana sociálně demokratická (Czech Social Democratic Party)
DPS	Dvizenie za prava i svobodi (Movement for Rights and Freedoms)
DPSCG	Demokratska Partija Socijalista Crna Gora (Democratic Socialist Party of Montenegro)
EAS	*Europe-Asia Studies*

List of Abbreviations

EBRD	European Bank for Reconstruction and Development
EC	European Community
EEPS	*Eastern European Politics and Societies*
EFTA	European Free Trade Association
ESWM	Együtteles-Spolužitie-Wspólnota a Mad'arská l'udová strana (Coexistence, Coexistence, Coexistence and Hungarian People's Party)
FDSN	Frontul Democrat Salvării Naţionale (Democratic Front of National Salvation)
FIDESZ	Fiatal Demokraták Szövetsége
FKGP	Független Kisgazda-, Földmunkás-és Polgári Párt
FSN	Frontul Salvării Naţionale (National Salvation Front)
FT	*The Financial Times*
GDP	Gross Domestic Product
GNP	Gross National Product
HDZ	Hrvatska Demokratska Zajednica
HSD-MS	Hnutí za Samosprávnou Demokracii Moravy a Slezska (Movement for Self-Governing Democracy of Moravia and Silesia)
HSLS	Hrvatska Socijalno-Liberalna Stranka
HSP – 1861	Hrvatska Stranka Prava – 1861
HZDS	Hnutí za demokratické Slovensko
IMF	International Monetary Fund
IFOR	Implementation Force
JCS	*Journal of Communist Studies*
JNA	Jugoslovenska narodna armija
KDNP	Keresztény demokrata Néppárt
KDU-ČSL	Křesťanská a demokratská unie – Československá strana lidová (Christian and Democratic Union – Czechoslovak People's Party)
Keesing's	*Keesing's Record of World Events*
KLD	Kongres Liberalno-Demokraticzny (Liberal Democratic Congress)
KPN	Konfederacja Polski Niepodległej (Confederation for an Independent Poland)
KSČ	Komunistická strana Československa
KSČM	Komunistická strana Čech a Moravy (Communist Party of Bohemia and Moravia)
KUK	Konfederace umení a kultury
LDDP	Lietuvos Demokratine Darbo Partija
LDK	Lidhja Demokratike e Kosovës

x   List of Abbreviations

LNNK	Latvijas Nacionāli Konservātivā partija/Latvijas Nacionāla Neatkaribas Kustiba (Latvian National Conservative Party/Latvian National Independence Movement)
LVP	Latvijas Vienības Partija (Party of Latvia's Unity)
MATAV	Magyar Távközlés Részvénytársaság
MD	*Le Monde Diplomatique*
MDF	Magyar Demokrata Forum
MIÉP	Magyar Igazság és Élet Párt
MKDH	Mad'arské Krest' ansko-demokratické Hnutie
Moct-Most	*Moct-Most: Economic Policy in Transitional Economics*
MOL	Magyar Olaj- és Gázipari Részvénytársaság
MSZMP	Magyar Szocialista Munkáspárt
MSZOSZ	Magyar Szakszervezetek Országos Szövetsége
MSZP	Magyar Szocialista Munkáspárt
NATO	North Atlantic Treaty Organization
NDH	Nezavisna Država Hrvatska
NDP	Narodna Demokratska Partija (National Democratic Party)
NKVD	Narodnyi Komissariat Vnutrennikh Del (People's Commissariat for Internal Affairs)
NLR	*New Left Review*
NSZZ–Solidarność	Niezależny Samorządny Związek Zawodowy 'Solidarność' (Independent Self-Governing Trade Union Solidarity)
ODA	Občanská demokratická aliance (Civic Democratic Alliance)
ODS	Občanská demokraticka strana
ODS–KDS	Občanská demokratická strana a Křest' ansko-demokratická strana (Civic Democratic Party and Christian Democratic Party)
ODU	Občianská demokratická únia
OE	*Osteuropa*
OECD	Organization for Economic Cooperation and Development
OF	Občanské Forum
OH	Občanské Hnutí
OPZZ	Ogólnopolski Porozumienie Związków Zawodowych (All Poland Trades Unions' Alliance)

List of Abbreviations

OSCE	Organization for Security and Co-operation in Europe
P of PC	*Problems of Post-Communism*
PDP	Partija za Demokratski Prosperitet
PDS	Partei des demokratischen Sozialismus
PDSH	Partia Demokratike të Shqipërisë
PDSR	Partidul Democrăţiei Sociale din România (Social Democratic Party of Romania)
PHARE	Poland, Hungary, Assistance to the Commonwealth of Independent States
PL	Porozumienie Ludowe (Peasants' Alliance)
PNL	Partidul Naţional Liberal
PNTCD	Partidul National Tărănesc Creştin şi Democrat
PPSH	Partia e Punës e Shqipërisë
PRM	Partidul România Mare
PSL	Polskie Stronnictwo Ludowe
PSM	Partidul Socialist al Muncii
PSSH	Partia Socialiste e Shqipërisë (Socialist Party of Albania)
PUNR	Partidul Unităţii Naţionale Románe
PZPR	Polska Zjednoczona Partia Robotnicza
RECE	*Revue d'Études Comparatives Est–Ouest*
RFE/RLRR	*Radio Free Europe/Radio Liberty Research Report*
ROAD	Ruch Obywatelski Akcja Demokratyczna
ROP	Ruch Odbudowy Polski
SD	Stronnictwo Demokratyczne
SDA	Stranka demokratske akcije (Party of Democratic Action)
SDL'	Strana demokratickej l'avice (Party of the Democratric Left)
SDRP	Socjaldemokracja Rzeczpospolitej Polskiej
SDS	Săjuz na demokratichnite sili
SDS	Srpska Demokratska Stranka
SED	Sozialistische Einheitspartei Deutschlands
SHIK	Shërbimi Informetiv Kombëtar (National Information Service)
SIS	Slovenská Informačná Služba (Slovak Information Service)
SKJ	Savez Komunista Jugoslavije
SLD	Sojusz Lewicy Demokratycznej
SNS	Slovenská Národna Strana
SOE	*Südosteuropa: Zeitschrift für Gegenwartsforschung*
SOEM	*Südosteuropa Mitteilungen: Vierteljahresschrift der Südosteuropa Gesellschaft e.V.*

List of Abbreviations

SPD	Sozialdemokratische Partei Deutschlands
SPR-RSČ	Sdružení pro Republiku – Republikánská strana Československa (Association for the Republic – Republican Party of Czechoslovakia)
SPR – VRS	Sdružení pro Republiku – Vlastenecká Republikánská Strana (Association for the Republic – Patriotic Republican Party)
SPS	Socijalistička Partija Srbije
SS	Soviet Studies
SWB EE	Summary of World Broadcasts, Part 2, Eastern Europe
SZDSZ	Szabad Demokraták Szövetsége (Alliance of Free Democrats)
SZUP	Služba za zaštitu ustavnog poretka
TACIS	Technical Assistance to the Commonwealth of Independent States
Transition (OMRI)	Transition: Events and Issues in the Former Soviet Union and East-Central and Southeastern Europe
Transition (WB)	Transition: the Newsletter about Reforming Economies
Transitions (OMRI)	Transitions: Changes in Post-Communist Societies
TSLK	Tevynes Sajunga (Lietuvos Konservatoriai) (Homeland Union, Conservatives of Lithuania)
UB	Urząd Bezpieczeństwa
UD	Unia Demokratyczna (Democratic Union)
UDMR	Uniunea Democrată Maghiară din România
UNHCR	United Nations High Commission on Refugees
UNTAES	United Nations Transitional Administration in Eastern Slavonia
UP	Unia Pracy
USD	Uniunea Social Democrată
USRP	Unia Socjaldemokratyczna Rzeczpospolitej Polskiej
UW	Unia Wolności
VJ	Vojska Jugoslavije
VMRO-DPMNE	Vnatreshna Makedonska Revolucionerna Organizacija – Demokratska Partija za Makedonsko Nacionalno Edinstvo
VPN	Verejnost proti násiliu
VR	Vatra Românească
ZChN	Zjednoczenie Chrześcijańsko-Narodowe

ZS	Związek Solidarność (The Solidarity Union)
ZSL	Zjednoczone Stronnictwo Ludowe
ZRS	Združenie robotníkov Slovenska

1 Introduction: Mapping Out the Theme

Any discussion of the process of transition in the post-communist lands is bound to raise problems of definition. The concept of the 'post-communist lands' is in itself not particularly problematic. No one doubts that over a large geographical area covering the eastern part of Continental Europe and the northern part of Asia the communist experiment came to an end at the turn of the 1980s (though there is still room for discussion about the political and economic persistence of communist structures over much of the former Soviet Union, particularly Central Asia). But problems arise with any attempt to subdivide the area. The term 'Eastern Europe' has traditionally been used for the western part of the communist world. It would be very convenient if we could divide the area neatly in two, defining 'Eastern Europe' as the part which came under *indirect* Soviet rule after 1945, as opposed to 'the former Soviet Union', which was directly ruled from Moscow.[1]

But we cannot. There are more complex and historically based divisions to be taken into account; moreover, they often overlap. Many of the inhabitants of 'Eastern Europe' are unhappy about the term; they find it rather insulting, as it brings with it overtones of backwardness and divergence from the advanced West. The Czechs in particular consider the term inapplicable to them. Some Hungarians take the same view; but not all of them, as is shown by the example of the sociologist Elemér Hankiss, who entitled his book *East European Alternatives*.[2] Writers in the West have adopted many different strategies for dealing with this problem. Some (for example P.G. Lewis[3]) heroically transfer the whole of Eastern Europe into Central Europe. Even Dr Lewis, who is a specialist on Poland, is unable to stick to this geographically inappropriate solution: his maps of the area are explicitly labelled 'Eastern Europe'! Joseph Rothschild has a different solution: he refers to 'East-Central Europe'.[4] This is also inappropriate, because it excludes the Balkan countries, which are very much present in his excellent account. In 1992 I wrote: 'it may well happen in the future that the term "Eastern Europe" falls out of use'.[5] This prediction has been fulfilled to some extent, but not in the specialist journals published in the West, which have often retained the words 'Eastern Europe' or 'East Europe' in their titles.[6] As Larry Wolff has pointed out[7] the idea of Eastern Europe 'is deeply embedded in the history of two centuries'. It cannot simply be erased.

In view of this, the most rational approach is to retain 'Eastern Europe' as an overarching geographical definition, and to use the term 'East-Central Europe' to embrace Poland, Hungary, the Czech Republic and Slovakia, with the possible addition of the three ex-Soviet Baltic countries of Estonia, Latvia and Lithuania and the two northernmost ex-Yugoslav states of Slovenia and Croatia. The former German Democratic Republic (GDR), or East Germany, was rightly assigned to East-Central Europe before 1989, but the reunification of Germany in 1990 altered the picture. It automatically entered the European Union and became a part of Western Europe. Henceforward, to use Claus Offe's striking image, while 'other countries had to repair their sinking ships while still at sea, the GDR was refitted in the Federal German dry dock'.[8] The story of this refit, interesting though it is, will therefore largely be excluded.

The remaining states of Eastern Europe can be described as 'the Balkans', or 'South-Eastern Europe'. These two terms, used interchangeably, include Romania, Bulgaria, Albania and the south of former Yugoslavia. Greece belongs here too, but is excluded for a number of specific historical reasons (no period of communist rule; membership of the European Union) although these marks of differentiation will surely decline in importance as the communist epoch fades into the past.[9]

The division outlined above is largely geographical. But the continuing importance and impact of historical factors might suggest various other divisions:

1. former Soviet lands and the rest;
2. the older three-way division into former Habsburg, former Russian and former Ottoman territories; and
3. the still older religious division between historically Roman Catholic or Protestant lands, on the one hand, and lands with an Orthodox or Muslim tradition, on the other.

All these ways of dividing Eastern Europe reflect genuine differences, the impact of which continues to be felt.

Further east, in the Eurasian landmass beyond the rivers Niemen and Pruth, we meet with other problems of definition. 'Member of the CIS (Commonwealth of Independent States)' would seem at first glance a suitable description for former Soviet countries, but not all of them are members of this organization. The three Baltic countries did not join, and are hardly likely to do so in the future: they were also clearly divided from the rest by their relatively short period under direct Soviet rule (from 1944 to 1991), although the same point can be made about Moldova, much of Belarus and parts of Ukraine, which are all CIS members. In contrast, it should not be forgotten that the Baltic states have a fairly long history of association with the Russian Empire before 1917. They all have ethnic Russian minorities. They are geographically close to Russia and retain strong economic links with their eastern neighbour. The members of the CIS all have economic and cultural connections with Russia in common, as well as a longer, and an unbroken, history of subordination to the Russian Empire and then the Soviet Union. The Russians regard their CIS neighbours as the 'near abroad', and there have been tendencies in the mid-1990s towards the emergence of a Moscow-centred informal empire on the former Soviet space.[10] Even in dealing with the CIS, however, there are divisions between Europe and Asia, between west and east, between more independent and more subservient members, to be taken into account. So the quest for a *definition* inescapably becomes a process of establishing historical, cultural and geographical *dividing lines*.

For the purposes of the present work, the author has drawn a line that is in part arbitrary, although it has some historical basis, between the former Soviet Union and Eastern Europe. None of the countries of Eastern Europe were ever incorporated directly into the Soviet Union; this theoretical independence is not of negligible importance, because it meant that direct Russian influence was weak. The chronological difference between 1917 and 1945 is also important; Eastern Europe's pre-1945 traditions were still living and did not need to be artificially resuscitated after 1989; whereas the upheavals of the decades after 1917 in the Soviet lands were both deep going and long lasting, so that there were no living links with the pre-revolutionary epoch. The three Baltic states occupy an intermediate position between the two extremes.

The other problem associated with the theme of this book is the much-criticized term 'transition'. A transition implies both a starting point and an objective, an ultimate goal. The starting point can be defined with a fair degree of clarity. It is the communist regimes and systems in what turned out to be their dying days – the late 1980s. The final goal, however, is extremely hazy, given that the ideal 'capitalist' or 'free market' society with fully democratic institutions has never existed and probably never will. Moreover, even if we take the end point of the transition as some variant on the 'actually existing Western capitalism' of the 1990s, that too is problematic, since Western capitalism has itself undergone sweeping changes. The model itself has to be seen as an ideal type rather than some particular, concretely existing system.

Not everyone sees the goal of transition as hazy and blurred. Some writers – one could call them the teleologists – see the history of post-communist societies as moving in a definite direction; to them historical development possesses a definite underlying purpose, and an overall coherence, with the move towards liberal democratic polities being underpinned by the emergence of a progressive and healthy market-based economy. Teleological observers admit the existence of counter-vailing factors, such as ethnic conflicts, or particularly stubborn survivals of the communist epoch, whether in politics, economics or psychological attitudes, but they see them as essentially partial and transitory obstacles on the way to the millenium. In the long run, it is said, these will be overcome; indeed, in many cases, it is claimed, they have been overcome already.

A less teleologically biased view, however, would indicate that this view is far too optimistic. The period of post-communist transition, now and for the future, is characterized by the uncontrolled play of numerous political, social, economic and cultural forces; it is the 'New World Disorder', to use Kenneth Jowitt's striking phrase.[11] The one constant here is an absence: a lack of organized intervention into the Brownian movement of the human atoms which have been freed from their molecular bonds by the disintegration of communism. After all, in principle at least (though less and less in practice in its later years) communism was an all-embracing system of politics, economics, ideology and cultural production from which people could only disentangle themselves by emigration or revolution. That system has gone, and its replacements can exercise only minimal control.

Hence the objective of this book is to identify the chaotically intermingling forces of the post-communist transitional epoch, and portray their complex interplay on the regional and national levels. It is essential to treat the transition at a national level because one of the features of the post-communist chaos has been the almost complete absence of any overarching international organization. The collapse of the old organizations, the Council for Mutual Economic Assistance (CMEA) (known in the West as Comecon) and the Warsaw Pact (which were themselves expressions of the *pax Sovietica*), has been accompanied by a rise in national egoism. There is not yet a *pax Americana*. It may come; but the new organizations (such as the Visegrád group) are regional and fragile and the old ones (the United Nations, the European Union, NATO) have so far failed to replace their Soviet rivals

THE EMERGING PICTURE IN EASTERN EUROPE

It will help to clarify matters if we seek to identify the main elements in the present situation. They are, firstly, the distortions inherited from a malfunctioning socialist[12] system, such as a 'shadow economy' of extra-legal economic activity, and a deeply rooted psychology of irresponsibility both towards the state and one's fellow human beings. The latter phenomenon grew out of the paradox that communism, instead of bringing people together as intended, actually atomized them and destroyed any sense of community; the resultant mixture of egoistic individuals was held together by sheer force and terror, so that once the pressure was removed the mixture fell apart. Secondly, we have seen the re-emergence of a number of features of the pre-communist inheritance: ethnic divisions, formerly suppressed, have now resurfaced more strongly; and there has been a resurgence of religious belief, less repressed but certainly not encouraged under communism, although the results of this religious revival have not always been negative (as well as sometimes reinforcing inter-ethnic hatred, it has also given rise to a sense of moral responsibility and placed some limits on the crude self-interest of the search for individual advantage characteristic of the free market). The third element is the market economy itself, not just the domestic economy, but the irruption of uncontrolled market forces from the more advanced economies outside the former communist sphere.

The entry of superior, or equivalent but cheaper, foreign products naturally leads, under conditions of free competition, to the destruction of local industries and deprives millions of people of their livelihoods. They have often been unable to find alternative employment, given the lack of opportunities for retraining and the well-nigh universal decline in industrial activity. By 1997 fifteen million people were out of work in Eastern Europe (and these numbers were very unevenly distributed). Many of the unemployed were wandering around their countries, sleeping in the main railway stations, begging, and existing at the margins of society. They were not the only people to suffer the costs of transition. '50 million new poor and growing inequality' is how Branko Milanovic summed up the situation in 1994 in the World Bank's newsletter *Transition*.[13] We shall examine this situation in more detail in Chapter 7.

It would, however, be wrong to paint too gloomy a picture of the impact of market forces. There is a positive side. For some there have been opportunities. It is precisely a feature of the post-communist chaos that the strong, the energetic, the young, those possessing special skills, have a chance to rise far above their fellow citizens. Figures for changing income distribution are eloquent on this point. This new bourgeoisie has a number of components. Alongside people who have genuinely and honestly made their own way there are the scions of the old *nomenklatura* who have benefited from communist-era connections; and there are criminal elements, members of the burgeoning Mafia.[14] The Mafia is acknowledged as a problem even in Poland, which is in general one of the most progressive post-communist societies. Some free market theorists, with a commendable concern to be consistent and perhaps a touch of desperation, see the Mafia as an economically healthy aspect of the new situation. What the post-communist world needs is the formation of private capital; the fortunes built up by the Mafia will not be buried in vaults but used to promote economic growth. In fact, at least in Russia, this proposition is of doubtful validity, for the simple reason that fortunes made there tend to be transferred abroad immediately.

Although they have become much stronger since the fall of communism, the mafiosi are not a new force. They belong very much to 'late socialism', as do the ex-members of the *nomenklatura*,[15] who have also largely been able to come to terms with the new post-communist situation and take advantage of market forces. In many cases the latter have even been able to reposition themselves on the political spectrum and retain power in free elections.

The emerging picture is thus very different from the various scenarios dreamed of by the anti-communist dissidents of the 1980s, the makers of the revolutions of 1989 and 1991, who appeared to have triumphed in those golden moments when the collapse of communism was thought to herald the coming of a new world order. The dissident movements of the 1980s, it should be recalled, were distinguished by the positive character of their goals: they were not merely anti-communist. They wanted to build up a civil society in which the citizens of a country would organize themselves collectively to participate in political life, overcoming the passivity and apathy induced by long years of communist oppression. The dissidents' victory was shortlived. 'Civil society' soon turned out to be a mirage; instead of co-operation there was a chaotic war of all against all. The former dissidents were excluded from power one by one and the machine politicians took over. Now only

Václav Havel remains in place, in his position of lonely eminence as President of the Czech Republic.

The former dissidents shared a commitment to democratic values in the full sense, not hedged about by considerations of political advantage or national *realpolitik*. Their removal has contributed to, although it has not caused, both a rise in corruption and a reversion to authoritarianism. The privatization process has been accompanied by insider dealing on a large scale and repeated financial scandals; there has been a partial return to the censorship of the media which was one of the paramount features of the old system, and one of the main targets of dissident attack. When one thinks of the strong pressure exerted from outside, by Western governments and Western institutions, in *favour* of democratic practices (especially through embargoes and the imposition of financial penalties on offenders) it is significant that many ruling politicians of both 'right' and 'left' in the post-communist world feel able to ignore Western advice and defy Western pressure: one thinks of Sali Berisha in Albania, Vladimír Mečiar in Slovakia and Ion Iliescu in Romania until they lost power, and, among those still in power, Franjo Tuđman in Croatia, Slobodan Milošević in Serbia, Boris Yeltsin in Russia, and a whole series of leaders in Transcaucasia and Central Asia.

The final element in the new situation is the changed international system, characterized by the collapse of Soviet, and, consequently, Russian power, the hegemony of the United States and the subordinate hegemony of the EU. The entry of the countries of Eastern Europe into the EU is not, however, a magical Open Sesame to success and reintegration. The one example of integration so far is a case in point: the unification of the former German Democratic Republic with the Federal Republic of Germany. Despite the unique financial effort made by the West German state to ease the transition, the result in the short term has been a collapse of East German industry, severe unemployment and continuing stagnation. Admittedly, the other former communist states will probably do better than this, because those that qualify for entry have already undergone most of the pains of transition in the last eight years. A new dividing line will open up, however, between the qualifying states and the rest; this will go to reinforce the existing and historically based tripartite division between East-Central Europe,[16] the Balkans and the former Soviet Union.

The structure of the present book reflects these contrasts. It also reflects the interplay between the comparative approach and the study of specific nations or areas. There are clearly many respects in which each nation, or state, studied here is unique; but there are equally many features they share, which make it absurd to abandon the attempt at comparison. The continuing presence of the communist past, the instability of democracy and the rise of charismatic dictators or semi-dictators, the tendency for extremes of nationalism to develop (sometimes as part and parcel of a process of 'nation-building'), the problem of economic transition, the inheritance of relative backwardness, the cultural changes consequent on a fuller integration into the Western (or to put it less prejudicially the modern) global cultural sphere, all these features cry out for comparative treatment.[17] But at the same time, no comparative treatment can be undertaken without a clear awareness of the sequence and the interconnection of events at the level of the nation state. In the chapters that follow, I shall endeavour to do justice to both requirements.

2 The Inheritance of the Past and the Revolutions of 1989

A LEGACY OF BACKWARDNESS

The historical backwardness of Eastern Europe, in the economic sense, has been defined briefly by Kochanowicz as consisting in certain features which prevailed until the nineteenth century: 'low population density; low urbanization; a major economic role for the landed aristocracy; and labour obligations for the serfs'.[1] These comments apply to the whole of the region, though there was already a certain distinction by the start of the fifteenth century between a more advanced East-Central Europe and a less advanced East and South. Daniel Chirot has pointed out that the backwardness of the whole of Eastern Europe (except Bohemia, which some have argued does not properly belong in the region at all[2]) arose long before the twentieth century, and in fact before the industrial revolution of the early nineteenth century in Western Europe. Eastern Europe began to be differentiated from the West during the later Middle Ages, as a result of the failure of its agriculture to develop, and of the late development and long persistence of serfdom in the East.[3] Within that general picture, the development of East-Central Europe began to diverge from that of Eastern Europe proper, because the lands of Poland, Bohemia and Hungary were closer geographically to the West and tended therefore to adapt to match their advanced neighbours. East-Central Europe began to occupy an intermediate position, possessing 'some Western traits' but subject to only 'shallow' Western influence.[4]

Like Eastern Europe, South-Eastern Europe fell behind the West after the Middle Ages, but for different reasons. The Balkan economies were based on small-scale peasant farming rather than the big landownership (the system of *latifundia*) which prevailed further north. This was a result of the Ottoman conquest of the fourteenth and fifteenth centuries, which destroyed the position of the native aristocracy. The subsequent predominance of small peasant farms did not assist economic growth. Moreover, the Ottoman state created the conditions for continuing agricultural stagnation in the Balkans, by establishing a command economy in grain, supplemented by taxes to pay for a series of wars with the Habsburg Empire. For the next three centuries there was a complete absence of population growth in South-Eastern Europe.[5] Later on, in the nineteenth century, sharp political and economic contrasts emerged within the Balkan peninsula itself. Just as, further north, there was an economic gap between East-Central Europe and Eastern Europe, with the former much closer to Western levels, so in the south a gap opened between the independent states of Serbia, Bulgaria, Greece and Romania on the one hand and the surviving parts of the Ottoman Empire (such as Bosnia and Albania) on the other. The independent states enjoyed an average per capita national income of 250–300 francs per annum; areas still under Ottoman rule only 150 francs.[6] The reason for this difference in income was the failure of the Ottoman lands to match the strong growth in agricultural productivity and exports achieved by the independent states in the second half of the nineteenth century. The economic divergence between north and south was superimposed on existing religious and cultural differences, especially in the lands which became Yugoslavia, where Roman Catholic, more urbanized Croatia was at one end of the scale, and largely Muslim, rural Kosovo at the other, with Orthodox Serbia somewhere in the middle.

Eastern Europe's historical economic backwardness had a number of political, social and cultural concomitants. These naturally varied according to the region under consideration, so that generalizations are likely to be riddled with exceptions. One may tentatively assert, however, that politically Eastern Europe was marked by a lack of democratic traditions and a tendency towards authoritarianism, socially by the domination of landowning and bureaucratic elites, and culturally by deeply traditional values covered by a very thin veneer of Western-influenced intellectual life. These features of the situation were hardly changed by the brief inter-war period of independence. The new post-1918 rulers of Eastern Europe were interested, not in radical change, but in 'security, survival and state-building'.[7]

Despite the above, it is important to note that some qualifications are in order for specific countries of East-Central Europe. Independent Czechoslovakia could hardly be said to have lacked a democratic political culture after 1918. In Poland, too, democratic traditions were present beneath the crust of the authoritarian regime that took over in 1926. In Hungary the rule of the gentry elite, though undemocratic, did not exclude lively and free parliamentary debate. These points have a bearing on the kind of politics that resurfaced after the fall of communism.

Economic divergences within Eastern Europe, and between Eastern Europe and the more advanced West, remained in existence during the inter-war era. Using an average of the performance of six leading European countries[8] between 1926 and 1934 as a benchmark index of 100, respective levels of national income were Czechoslovakia 57, Hungary 45, Yugoslavia 41, Poland 35, Bulgaria 32, and Romania 30.[9] What is surprising, and must be counted as a tremendous failure of communist policies of forced industrialization, is that the gap indicated by these figures was not affected by the breakneck industrial development put in hand by Stalin and his imitators. In relation to the West the communist era in fact brought a slight worsening of the overall position, despite the frantic efforts made to 'catch up'. Andrew Janos makes this comment: 'Whatever methodological assumptions we make, Communist economies were drifting downward from the relative position that their countries had held in the world economy prior to World War II'.[10]

In relation to each other, the position of each country was roughly the same in the 1980s as it had been a hundred years before: in terms of Gross Domestic Product (GDP) per capita, and using Austria as a benchmark, with an index of 100, the figures were the GDR 59, Czechoslovakia 55, Hungary 41, Bulgaria 37, Yugoslavia 36, Poland 27,[11] and Romania 20.[12] These figures show two things: the region was marked by persistent relative backwardness, and, within that, the economic gap between the north and the south still existed.

There was also considerable political diversity in communist Eastern Europe. Once the initial forced uniformity of the Stalin years had been brought to an end, and despite the underlying threat of Soviet intervention, the policies of the region's rulers developed in different directions. By the end of the communist era, Poland, Hungary and Yugoslavia lay at the liberal end of the spectrum, the GDR, Czechoslovakia and Bulgaria were ruled by conservative dogmatists, and Romania and Albania were dictatorships plain and simple.

These differences had a considerable impact on the manner and mode of the transition from communism, as we shall see.

THE STARTING POINT

Before considering the transition from communism we need to sketch out the starting point, to adumbrate the main features of the situation in the communist world in the 1980s. We shall look in turn at politics, society, the economy and the intellectual and cultural atmosphere.

In politics the situation can be summed up quite simply: a single party, the communist party, ruled unchallenged.[13] One might say that Eastern Europe had a holiday from politics between 1947 and 1989; further east, the holiday has lasted longer. Elections took place, but did not decide anything, as the successful candidates were either members of the ruling party or of other parties linked with the ruling party in one of the National Front coalitions left over from the Second World War period. As a result all politics took place within the communist party, or rather within the oligarchy that held power at the top (since periodic attempts by ordinary members to exert political influence, as in Poland in 1956 and 1980 and in Czechoslovakia in 1968, eventually came to nothing). Factional conflicts within the oligarchy were the basic stuff of politics, and they reached a height in the late 1980s, when a vital issue was at stake: how to deal with the evident crisis of communist rule. Younger or more liberal members of the oligarchy wanted to pursue various reforming strategies of defensive liberalization, while established leaders (such as Husák, Kádár, Honecker, Zhivkov) saw the only option as to hold firmly onto power and continue to use traditional methods of repression. It required a push from outside the system to bring a decision. This is one reason why Eastern Europe suffered in the immediate pre-revolutionary years from what has been called 'leadership drift'.[14]

The absence of genuine political activity was a well-nigh universal phenomenon throughout the communist world, until the Gorbachev reforms transformed the situation. The sole exception was Poland, where the 1980s saw a constant political battle, sometimes open, sometimes under cover, between the independent trade union Solidarity and the partially restored dictatorship of the communist party under General Jaruzelski. Elsewhere dissidence was either purely individual (in Romania and Bulgaria) or confined within small groups without sufficient support to worry the rulers enough to enforce a political dialogue with them. In Hungary 'the few dissidents who existed in 1987' would have 'found it hard to fill a private coffeehouse'[15] while as late as 1988 there were only two thousand dissidents in Czechoslovakia.[16] In East Germany 'opposition did not take place within a mass movement as in Poland' but was engaged in by 'tiny groups under church roofs'.[17]

East European society in the 1980s was more stratified than in previous decades. At the top sat the families of the *nomenklatura*, in the middle the technical and scientific intelligentsia and members of the free professions, at the bottom the workers and collective farmers. Tendencies to egalitarianism were a feature of the Stalin period, which saw a reduction of the gap between middle- and working-class incomes. This trend did not last beyond the 1950s in Poland, Hungary, Yugoslavia and the USSR. In Czechoslovakia, the GDR, Romania and Bulgaria, however, there continued to be a more egalitarian distribution of income than prevailed in the West, and this was still true in the 1980s. But the upward social mobility of the 1940s and 1950s was a thing of the past everywhere in Eastern Europe. Those fortunate workers and peasants who had taken advantage of the opportunities of an earlier era remained in place in their managerial positions, denying the next generation any chance of advancement. In Poland, where grievances of this kind played an important part in the decline of support for communism, the proportion of people who stayed at the same level socially in the 1960s was actually higher than the corresponding proportion for the 1930s, under Piłsudski.[18] And the coming of economic reform in the 1970s and 1980s strengthened the trend towards inequality. The more radical the economic reform, the greater the inequality.

The economies of Eastern Europe were in principle entirely state controlled (with the exception of Polish and Yugoslav agriculture), but in practice private enterprise had made definite inroads by the 1980s. The collective farmers used their private plots to good advantage (in Bulgaria more fruit was produced on private than on collective land); in some countries (notably Hungary) private trading was legal and flourishing; above all, unofficial private enterprise, or the 'second economy', played a large part in economic activity. That is why the transition to full-scale private enterprise, when it came, could take place smoothly and easily. And the need for such a transition was increasingly being recognized in the 1980s. The countries of Eastern Europe were demonstrably in economic crisis, marked by a massive increase in foreign debt, a growing tendency to stagnation, and a growing recognition that reforms which took the existing system as a framework just would not work.

In fact the reforms of the 1980s worsened the crisis of the socialist system; growth rates slowed, although growth itself continued even as late as 1988 (Central and Eastern European total GDP grew by 1.5 per cent during that year). 1989 was the first year of actual decline (by 0.7 per cent). The serious economic crisis of the late 1980s went hand in hand with a decline in popular support for the communist system, as measured in public opinion surveys. In Poland the proportion of a survey sample expressing confidence in the regime fell from 53 per cent in 1987 to 27 per cent in August 1988, rose to 72 per cent in November, and fell back to 35 per cent in July 1989. In

Hungary the proportion favouring a multi-party system rose from 50 per cent in January 1989 to 65 per cent in July 1989 and 75 per cent in October 1989.[19]

In the intellectual and cultural spheres the originally firmly anchored Marxist-Leninist world view had given place by the 1980s to a situation of 'cultural drift'.[20] The main feature of this was a turn towards new ideas that could neither be accommodated within the official Marxist framework nor convincingly denounced as purely bourgeois. These ideas might be religious (whether traditional or non-traditional, indigenous or imported from outside), political (for example feminist) or even musical (rock and punk music). What they had in common was their Western origin; the re-entry of Eastern Europe into the Western economy was preceded by its rediscovery of Western culture and Western ideas. In sum, the fortress of official ideology and the official worldview was rapidly crumbling to pieces.[21]

The overall picture at the end of the 1980s, then, was of a system cracking at every joint, a system waiting to collapse, but needing a push. But before we discuss the nature of the push that came, a comment is in order about the distinctive situation in the south-eastern part of the region, otherwise known as 'the Balkans'.

THE BALKAN COUNTRIES

It is not easy to generalize about the Balkan countries. As Tom Gallagher has pointed out, 'the region is not a monolith'.[22] The concept of 'the Balkans' has recently been dissected by Maria Todorova, who concludes that it is a 'pejorative designation' used for 'hegemonic purposes' and in order to legitimate the granting of special advantages and favours to the lands of East-Central Europe by establishing a 'constituting other'.[23] The phrase 'South-Eastern Europe' is probably less prejudicial. But it would be a mistake to abandon the attempt to generalize entirely. The region does, after all, have many historical features in common, such as: in medieval times the predominance of the Orthodox form of Christianity; in early modern times the rule of the Ottoman Turks; relative economic backwardness; and in the recent present the maintenance of a fairly unreformed Stalinist political and economic system, underpinned by close economic and political connections with the Soviet Union. There were, however, two countries of South-Eastern Europe which stood out as exceptions to this uniform pattern: Albania, because of its exceptional isolation and remoteness from outside influences, and Yugoslavia, because of its ethnic diversity and the originality of its brand of communism.

We shall look first at Albania. Despite its isolation from the rest of Europe, Albania underwent very far-reaching changes in the communist era. The country the communists took over in 1944 was hardly a homogeneous unit at all. It was riven by linguistic, social and religious divisions. In language, it was divided between the Geg dialect in the north, and the Tosk in the south. The pre-1944 literature of Albanian was written in Geg and was largely incomprehensible to the Tosks of the south. The ruler of Albania in the inter-war years, King Ahmed Zogu, was a Geg and he made very little progress in integrating the two parts of the country. Socially, there was a wide gap between the mountainous and backward north, with its patriarchal, clan-based system, where loyalty was given exclusively to the extended family and the state was regarded as hostile while the concept of the nation was non-existent, and the semi-feudal south, dominated by landowners, or *beys*, who had destroyed the power of the clans centuries before but were equally hostile to state interference. On top of this came a three-way religious division, between the Muslims, the Orthodox and the Roman Catholics.

After 1944 the Albanian communists took ruthless measures to establish national unity and homogeneity. They broke the power of the northern clans, partly by the trial and incarceration of royalist rebels in 1945, and in general by a drive towards collectivization, which was followed by the 'cultural revolution' of the 1960s. They destroyed the southern *beys* by the land reform of August 1945. They stamped out the blood feud, so that whereas in the 1920s, 20 per cent of male deaths in the north-east could be attributed to feuds[24] there were only 20 feud-based murders between 1966 and 1970.[25] They endeavoured to replace religious diversity with universal adherence to Marxism-Leninism; this implied both measures to suppress all three religions (not entirely successful, despite the proclamation of Albania as an atheist state in 1967) and an expansion of education. They established a uniform literary language in 1972, incorporating the basic common elements of both dialects.

As it approached the 1990s, then, Albania had become a nation. It was extremely homogeneous (according to the census of 1989, 98 per cent of the population were ethnic Albanians) and thus the basis for ethnic conflict was absent, except for the question of irredentism towards Kosovo to the north-east and the relatively small Greek minority (120 000 people at most) in the south. The communists had succeeded in many ways, but they had failed the most important test: they were unable to improve the people's standard of living. The country remained far poorer than any other part of Europe, so poor in fact that the dearest wish of most of its inhabitants was to leave. Ten per cent of the population succeeded in leaving between 1990 and 1993. We shall examine the fate of those who stayed in chapters 4 and 8.

YUGOSLAVIA: THE WARNING SIGNS OF DISINTEGRATION

Yugoslavia had its fair share of the problems of economic stagnation, foreign debt, decline of morale, growth of dissidence and crumbling of ideological certainties which beset other communist regimes during the 1980s, and these often occupied the foreground at that time, so that its exceptional character, so apparent in the years after the break with the Soviet Union, seemed to stand out less and less as time went on. Yugoslavia's politics, to use Joseph Rothschild's phrase, had 'turned parochial'.[26] What outside observers largely failed to notice was the return in the 1980s of the ethnic problems the communists claimed to have solved long before.

Communist Yugoslavia ('the second Yugoslavia') displayed greater ethnic diversity than any other European state. Its population was composed in 1948 of Serbs (41.5 per cent), Montenegrins (2.7 per cent), Croats (24.0 per cent), Slovenes (9.0 per cent), Macedonians (5.1 per cent), Muslims of Bosnia-Herzegovina and the Sandžak (5.1 per cent), Albanians (4.8 per cent), and Hungarians (3.1 per cent). Other assorted nationalities made up the remaining 4.7 per cent of the population.[27] The 'first Yugoslavia' of the inter-war years had been even more diverse. In what follows we shall attempt to summarize the main components of this diversity, from the point of view of their present-day significance.

First, the Serbian problem. The Serbs were the only people who inhabited parts of Yugoslavia outside their own republic in any numbers. Their presence in Croatia, and also to some extent in Bosnia-Herzegovina, was a result of the decision made in 1578 by the Habsburg ruler of the area to create a buffer zone protected by armed colonists to protect the rest of the empire from the Ottoman Turks. It was called the Military Frontier, or 'Krajina', and it was populated by Serbs (or at least people who became Serbs in the course of time)[28] from further south, who had been encouraged to settle there by tax exemption and other privileges. The Croat nobility were resentful at the arbitrary removal of a part of their state; the Croat peasants envied the privileges enjoyed by the Serbs; in reaction to this hostility the latter drew closer together to form a cohesive unit. The Krajina itself was incorporated into Croatia in 1881, but the Krajina Serbs remained there, holding on to their military traditions in a poor and backward region. They were the Cossacks of the Habsburg Empire.[29]

The diversity of the country's ethnic make-up was not necessarily a reason for ethnic conflict to develop, provided that the nations involved gave their allegiance to a higher Yugoslav identity. The trouble was very little progress had been made towards creating a sense of 'Yugoslav' nationality even though the ideological basis of the state was the idea of South Slav unity, first developed by the nationalists of the nineteenth century. The Serbs, who constituted the leading nation in terms of numbers and strength, were never in a position to enforce their will completely on the Croats, the second nation in size. The Cvetković-Maček Agreement of 1939 marked Belgrade's recognition that a separate Croat nation existed and had to be given autonomy. The experiment was, however, shortlived. It was brought to an end in 1941 by the German conquest of Yugoslavia and its subsequent partition into no less than ten fragments.[30]

Over the next few years, inter-ethnic hatred subsequently reached depths unequalled elsewhere in Eastern Europe, and serious atrocities were committed during the Second World War on all sides – by Croats against Serbs, by Serbs against Croats and Muslims, by Muslims against Serbs – which left traces in the collective consciousness of all the nations that had made up Yugoslavia. The memory of those acts of violence lay in wait, ready to resurface at the appropriate moment. An interesting argument has been put forward by Stjepan Meštrović that this was inevitable. Acts of barbaric violence, he claims, are inherent in the South Slavic character. This has roots in the remote past. The 'power-hungry, aggressive Dinaric herdsmen' arrived from the Urals in early medieval times and conquered the Balkan peninsula. Their character traits predisposed them to 'brutality, hatred and excessive violence', partly because of their highly patriarchal social organization. Croats were not immune from this, he says, but this type of character is much more widespread among Serbs, and explains the 'criminal, gratuitous and non-rational violence' with which the Yugoslav War of 1991 was conducted on the Serb side.[31] This may well be an explanation of the brutality with which the recent Yugoslav conflict has been conducted (on all sides); but it does not explain why these primitive forces were not held in check, and it certainly does not explain why Yugoslavia disintegrated. For this, there is no substitute for a historical examination, which we shall attempt here and in Chapter 5.

During the communist interregnum, between 1945 and 1991, an attempt was made to overcome past enmities. The Communist Party of Yugoslavia drew much of its strength during the war from its multinational, supra-ethnic character, and over the subsequent period it genuinely tried to resolve ethnic problems in a spirit of concord and unity. This attitude was expressed succinctly in the ubiquitous Titoist slogan 'brotherhood and unity'.

Communist Yugoslavia's sense of unity was a fragile bloom, however, and it needed nurturing. Twenty years after the end of the war the old problems began to raise their heads again, and some new ones emerged. The moves of the late 1960s towards decentralization marked the abandonment of the communists' attempt to create a unified and integrated 'Yugoslav' nation. The 1963 Constitution transferred sovereignty to the nations of the Yugoslav republics, despite the fact that only two of them approached ethnic homogeneity (Slovenia, which was 96 per cent Slovene, and Montenegro, which was 87 per cent Montenegrin). From now on, Yugoslavia would consist of at least five separate nations. Shortly afterwards, the ruling party itself was subdivided. At the Ninth Congress of the SKJ[32] (League of Communists of Yugoslavia) in 1969, it was confirmed that the League consisted of eight sections, one for each republic (Serbia, Croatia, Slovenia, Macedonia, Montenegro, Bosnia-Herzegovina) and one for each autonomous province (Vojvodina and Kosovo-Metohija); these sections increasingly represented the particular interests of the local nationality, whether Serb, Croat, Slovene, Macedonian or Montenegrin.[33] The republics and provinces of Yugoslavia became more and more autarchic, owing to increased decentralization to regional level and the decision to select the regional cadres of the SKJ according to an 'ethnic key', on the basis of proportional representation.

The situation was made more complicated in 1968 by the recognition of two further nationalities, the Bosnian Muslims and the Albanians. The Central Committee of the Bosnian branch of the League of Communists accepted the Muslims as a nation in their own right (previously they had been forced to define themselves as Serbs or Croats).[34] This decision was confirmed in 1969 by the Yugoslav leadership as a whole. When, in 1974, most powers were devolved to the republican level, this meant that in Bosnia-Herzegovina the Bosnian Muslims took over, as the majority community. For the first time since 1878 they were 'part of the in crowd', as Francine Friedman has put it.[35]

Similar, if not quite as much progress was made by the Albanians of Kosovo. By the 1974 Constitution the province of Kosovo was made autonomous within Serbia (alongside Vojvodina). The Serbian Central Committee allowed the ethnically Albanian communists of Kosovo-Metohija an autonomous position in their own province, renamed Kosovo (in Albanian: Kosova), thereby beginning a process of Albanian political and cultural emancipation which continued until 1981. Albanian became an official language alongside Serbo-Croat; the capital, Priština, acquired a university; and the Albanian ethnic character of the province was reflected in appointments to the local leadership of the ruling party.

Belgrade's concessions to the Albanian population of Kosovo were perceived by nationalistically inclined Serbs as an attack on them. The issue blew up in 1981, shortly after death removed the restraining hand of President Tito (May 1980). Kosovo, though a province of Serbia, had been inhabited from the beginning largely by Albanians. As time went on, it became more and more Albanian in composition, owing to the higher Albanian birthrate. But it also fell behind the rest of the country economically. By 1991 the ratio between GDP per capita in Kosovo and in Slovenia (to take the richest Yugoslav republic for purposes of comparison) was 1:7.5. Unemployment was far higher than in the rest of the country (by the late 1980s it was running at 50 per cent). This severe and increasing economic backwardness, combined with a sense that they would prefer to live in their own country, led members of the local Serbian minority to leave the province in droves. According to the census of 1991 Kosovo was ethnically 81.6 per cent Albanian.[36] In 1981 the Kosovo Albanians demanded that their province be upgraded to the status of a Yugoslav republic, worthy of standing beside Slovenia or Croatia or Serbia itself. The reply of the Serbian police to the Kosovan demonstrations of the early 1980s was brutal; over 3000 Albanians were arrested and 100 killed between 1981 and 1985. These measures did not change anything constitutionally, since Kosovo retained the extensive autonomy granted by the eighteenth amendment in 1968 and reaffirmed by the Constitution of 1974; but they made it clear to the Albanians that their autonomy was a paper right which could not effectively be exercised.

REFORM AND REVOLUTION IN EAST-CENTRAL EUROPE

If the word 'revolution' implies a sudden and far-reaching change from one political system to another, it can only be applied with reservations to what happened in Central and Eastern Europe in 1989. It is most applicable to East Germany, and least true of Hungary. The other countries occupy varying places on a scale between them. We shall begin by examining the case of East Germany, known at that time as the German Democratic Republic.

Here there really was a sudden and far-reaching change worthy of being called a revolution. The reason why the East German 'revolution' of 1989 was so thorough was that once the country ceased to be communist, it ceased to have a reason for separate existence. The dissidents of New Forum who made the revolution were unable to maintain themselves in the new situation, marked as it was by the tremendous weight of the larger Germany to the West. Once Erich Honecker, the last hard-line leader of the SED (Socialist Unity Party of Germany), had been forced out, his successor Hans Modrow tried to preserve some communist influence in the new era by bringing all the other political parties into his cabinet (28 January 1990), an endeavour to deal with the situation by co-opting his opponents. The resulting so-called 'government of moral responsibility' preserved political continuity until March. But the elections of 18 March 1990 were a disappointment for both the former dissidents and the former *apparatchiks*. They resulted in a landslide victory for the local CDU (Christian Democratic Union), led by Lothar de Maizière, a former professional violinist (and allegedly a former Stasi informer)[37] who had only been in charge of the party since November. The CDU gained 163 seats against the 88 of the SPD, the 88 of the PDS (the Party of Democratic Socialism, the successor of the former ruling party) and the 21 of Alliance '90 (a coalition made up of various groupings of former dissidents). On 12 April, De Maizière formed a coalition government along with four other parties, including the SPD; the coalition's policy was the rapid reunification of Germany and the establishment of a one-to-one exchange rate between the currencies of East and West. Here, then, there was to be no political or economic continuity with the communist past but a complete and abrupt break.

Elsewhere in East-Central Europe, in Poland, Czechoslovakia and Hungary, there was, despite appearances, continuity and evolution between past and present. In all three cases, 'roundtable talks' took place in 1989 and 1990 between the government and opposition sides, resulting in amicable compromises. In Poland the compromise arrived at in 1989 brought Solidarity to power alongside the communists, and under a communist president. In Czechoslovakia the readiness of the communists to surrender power, once the initial push had been given by the 'velvet revolution', meant a relatively smooth transition. The old-style communist-run parliament helped to smooth the way by co-opting 120 non-communists into its ranks on 30 January 1990. In Hungary continuity was ensured by close personal links between members of the ruling party and the leading opposition group, the Hungarian Democratic Forum (MDF).

It followed from this general picture of continuity between communism and post-communism that there was no attempt to turn the clock back all the way to pre-communist days. The pre-1947 political parties either did not reappear at all, or, if they did, failed to make any electoral headway. Lech Wałęsa's attempt to assert a symbolic continuity with the old Poland in December 1990 by solemnly receiving government insignia from the head of the exiled London Polish government had no practical consequences.[38] Similarly, successive attempts by former King Mihai of Romania to return to his country under various pretexts (for example the December 1993 celebrations of the seventy-fifth anniversary of the unification of Romania and Transylvania; the October 1994 fiftieth anniversary of his own coup against the pro-Nazi dictator General Antonescu) were foiled by the government without giving rise to any serious protest. In Bulgaria Simeon II was allowed to visit his former kingdom in May 1996, and the president received him (the socialist prime minister did not) but this did not improve the electoral fortunes of the Bulgarian monarchists, who received a mere 2 per cent of the votes in the April 1997 elections.[39]

Although monarchism has remained a minority creed in Eastern Europe, and monarchist parties have had no electoral success anywhere, former political parties of the centre and right, sometimes with monarchist leanings, did re-emerge in three countries. In Bulgaria the Bulgarian Agrarian National Union – Nikola Petkov (BZNS–NP) was founded in 1989. The addition of the name of Nikola Petkov was a reference back to the immediate post-war period when Petkov had led the struggle against the communist takeover of his country, until executed on a trumped-up charge in 1947. But the party did not do well, falling below the 4 per cent threshold in October 1991 when it ventured outside the comfortable umbrella of the Union of Democratic Forces (SDS) and splitting in half in March 1992. It recovered somewhat in April 1997 as part of the victorious centre-right coalition. In Romania the National Peasant Party (PNTCD) and the National Liberal Party (PNL) resurfaced and demanded a return to the 1923 constitution.[40] The demand was not granted, but the National Peasant Party survived to form an important component in the coalition government which came to power in 1996. In Hungary, finally, two special-interest groups of the early post-war period re-emerged after 1989: the Independent Smallholders' Party (FKGP) and the Christian Democrats (KDNP). They were unable to do more than appeal to minority constituencies (gaining respectively 11.7 per cent and 6.6 per cent of the vote at the March 1990 elections), and they played a minor role in subsequent political crises, which were dominated by relations between the four major parties: the Hungarian Democratic Forum (MDF), the Alliance of Free Democrats (SZDSZ), the Young Democrats (FIDESZ) and the (post-communist) Hungarian Socialist Party (MSZP).

We shall examine the Balkan pattern in more detail in Chapter 4. In East-Central Europe, in contrast to the Balkans, there was no attempt to hark back to the political battles of the 1940s. The pre-communist past was dead and could not be resuscitated. The new regimes were compelled to move into uncharted territory, sometimes boldly, sometimes with hesitation and not a few backward glances.

3 History Changes Gear: the Transition in East-Central Europe

THE POLITICS OF TRANSITION IN EAST-CENTRAL EUROPE

We shall now look briefly at political developments during the early stages of the transition in the countries of East-Central Europe, starting with Hungary. In Hungary it was the communist party itself which undertook a series of measures during 1989 by which it destroyed its own power position. This was a result of the victory of the liberal communists over the conservatives, or 'defenders of the castle' (Bruszt) around Károly Grósz. The liberals started by pushing through a commitment to multiparty pluralism in February 1989, followed by the renunciation of democratic centralism (April), and the abandonment of the *nomenklatura* system (May). During the summer of 1989 they engaged in a series of roundtable negotiations with the non-communist opposition, culminating in the agreement of September under which they agreed to their opponents' demand for a 'one-step transition to democracy'. At the same time the defence of the 'iron curtain' frontier with Austria was abandoned (September), a move which set off an exodus of East German holidaymakers westwards and ultimately led to the fall of the GDR. This extraordinary series of renunciations was crowned by the Fourteenth Congress of the communist party (or, to use its official title, Hungarian Socialist Workers' Party, MSZMP) held between 6 and 10 October 1989. At this congress, the party transformed itself into a Hungarian Socialist Party (MSZP) committed to 'multiparty democracy and an efficient market economy'.[1] These dramatic changes in policy could only have been achieved through the simultaneous pressure of the reformers from above and 'reform circles' organizing within the MSZMP.[2]

From the point of view of the liberal faction of the communist leadership, the purpose of these measures was to retain power in the new era which was felt to be approaching. As Elemér Hankiss has pointed out, the Hungarian *nomenklatura* temporarily abandoned its position in order to 'convert the power it had possessed in the old system into a new kind of power'.[3] The specific method used was to make sure a popularly elected communist president was in place before his legitimacy could be challenged by a popularly elected non-communist parliament. The more moderate section of the opposition, the MDF, was prepared to go along with this plan, since the proposed candidate, the liberal communist Imre Pozsgay, had shown his readiness to co-operate with the Forum from the very outset (he attended its founding meeting, and he was on friendly personal terms with József Antall, its leader).

On 18 September 1989 the majority of the opposition's round table representatives, consisting of the MDF, the Hungarian People's Party, the FKGP and the Association of the Friends of Bajcsy-Zsilinszky (Antall had started his political career as a member of this association in 1988), signed an agreement with the ruling communist party for the early holding of direct presidential elections.[4]

This compromise solution to the problem of transition from communism was challenged from two sides. On the 'left' the opponents of a communist surrender formed their own party, the Hungarian Socialist Workers' Party, which claimed to be the true successor of the former ruling party, and indeed was led by Károly Grósz, its last leader. There were also some people within the newly formed MSZP who were not happy about its commitment to an 'efficient market economy', because this implied drastic cuts in state subsidies and public expenditure. The leader of the liberal faction, Prime Minister Miklos Németh, defeated the challenge from this left-wing, welfarist group by threatening resignation. The Németh government's austerity measures were put through the National Assembly on 20 December 1989.

Another, ultimately more significant, group disliked the compromise of 1989. This was the numerically small[5] but influential minority side of the Roundtable talks of 1989, consisting of the Free Democrats, the Young Democrats, and the Liga (League of Free Trade Unions, a dissident trade union movement founded in 1988 to counter the official communist-run trade unions). The SZDSZ and its allies refused to sign the 18 September agreement, and insisted that a referendum be held on the proposal to hold direct presidential elections before parliamentary elections. Their public campaign in favour of a referendum succeeded; the former communists conceded the point. But the MDF, still inclined towards a Pozsgay presidency, called on the people to boycott the referendum, as a turnout of less than 50 per cent would make it invalid. The voters rejected this advice; 58 per cent of them went to the polls on 26 November, and they decided, admittedly by an extremely narrow margin (0.07 per cent), to hold the parliamentary elections first.

When the elections took place they showed that the MSZP had failed in its attempt to retain power in the new situation. The MDF, campaigning on a platform which combined anti-communism, conservative nationalism and economic gradualism gained support under all these headings from different parts of the country and several sections of the population. Anti-communism had a strong appeal in Budapest; while populist nods in the direction of Hungarian national minorities outside the country, namely in Romania and Slovakia, were helpful in the eastern part of the country. A determinedly moderate stance on economic issues appealed to pensioners and to people who expected to suffer from an abrupt transition to private enterprise. József Antall proclaimed his aim to be 'a reasonable and socially controlled process of privatization'. The MDF ended up as the biggest party, with 24.7 per cent of the vote and 165 seats. The second largest party was the less populist, more liberal SZDSZ, with 21.4 per cent and 91 seats. They were stronger in the west of the country and in Budapest, the wealthy and more market-oriented capital city. The Hungarian Socialist Party was only able to secure 10.9 per cent of the vote and 32 seats, having been beaten into fourth place by the right-wing Smallholders Party (FKGP). Imre Pozsgay, the great hope of the party liberals, and top of the party's list of candidates, was only able to secure third place in his own constituency. The Patriotic People's Front, which Pozsgay headed, performed so badly (1.87 per cent) that it was dissolved soon afterwards (May 1990). The small parties which had favoured Pozsgay's candidature in 1989, the Hungarian People's Party and the Friends of Bajcsy-Zsilinszky, gained less than 1 per cent of the vote. The extreme left did badly too: the Hungarian Socialist Workers' Party fell below the 4 per cent threshold for parliamentary representation, receiving only 3.68 per cent of the vote. The main communist successor party, the MSZP, drew its own conclusions from its electoral failure by replacing the party chairman, Rezsö Nyers, with Gyula Horn (26 May 1990).

The MDF, as the largest party in parliament, formed a government in May 1990, under the leadership of Antall, in coalition with the two pre-1947 parties, the Smallholders and the Christian Democrats. However, it was not strong enough to impose a president as well, and an agreement was made with the second strongest party, the SZDSZ, to put forward Árpád Göncz as candidate for president. Göncz was duly elected, on 3 August 1990.

Prime Minister Antall's government pursued a moderate course in economic policy. It did not favour rapid privatization, nor did it support the shock therapy advocated by the Free Democrats and FIDESZ. It also opposed the agricultural restitution proposals of its coalition ally the FKGP. In fact, when two Smallholder ministers, Ferenc Nagy and Jenö Gerbovics, endeavoured to force the issue of land restitution they were dismissed from the government (12 January 1991). Antall did, however, comply with the IMF's requirement that the budget deficit be reduced. He cut subsidies, and increased prices. The price of fuel was raised by 65 per cent on 25 October, causing a strike by the taxi drivers of Budapest, which led the government to moderate the increase to 35 per cent. Antall also expanded social services and welfare payments in order to head off popular discontent. Privatization moved forward very slowly. A State Privatization Agency was set up, but by 1992 it had only sold off 2 per cent of its portfolio.[6] The Hungarian economic transition was evidently going to be gradual.

Where the Antall coalition was rather more radical than its neighbours was in the sphere of anti-communist and nationalist measures. This was largely a result of the pressure exerted by the FKGP. In March 1991 a compromise was reached with that party over its demand for total restitution. There would be not restitution but compensation, in the form of vouchers for the purchase of state property to a maximum value of 200 000 forints ($2600 at the rate of exchange then current) and full compensation for land confiscated since May 1939 (law of 26 June 1991). The churches would recover their property, which had been nationalized in 1948 (law of 10 July 1991). A further compensation law was passed in May 1992. It provided that victims of 'Nazi and communist actions between 1939 and 1989' would receive shares in companies. Some acts 'in defence of Magyardom' were also undertaken: in March 1991 the Ministry of Finance limited foreign investments; in October tight border controls were imposed on Romanian immigrants, and a system of work permits was introduced whereby ethnic Hungarians would have priority for jobs.

These measures met strong opposition from many quarters. Democrats and socialists opposed them in parliament; and when the coalition went even further down the anti-communist road by passing a law to allow the prosecution of people who had committed the crimes of 'murder and treason' during the communist period, it was prevented from doing so by President Göncz, who refused to sign the bill, and by the Constitutional Court, which ruled on 3 March 1992 that such retrospective legislation was inadmissible.

Antall's reaction to this opposition was to compromise; he was a man who responded to pressure rather than having a policy of his own. Before 1989 he had been the director of a museum, 'a typical non-party intellectual and second-rank pundit of the cultural establishment of the Kádár regime'.[7] He was well qualified to hold together a fissiparous party by leading from the centre. But Antall's concessions were regarded as a surrender to communism by the radical wing of the FKGP, which gained the upper hand at a party congress held in November 1991. The leader of the FKGP, József Torgyan, favoured prosecuting communists for 'crimes against Magyardom', and he tried to whip up a hysterical campaign against the government for its readiness to compromise. He had 33 of the 45 FKGP parliamentary deputies expelled over the issue (21 February 1992) and announced that the rump faithful to him would now leave the government coalition. Torgyan's campaign took to the streets with a big demonstration in Budapest on 25 April 1992; but the size of the demonstration reflected not so much a popular determination to punish the former communists as a readiness to protest against the rise of unemployment and the fall in real wages brought about by inflation. The driving force behind the campaign was economic rather than political.[8]

The Antall government continued to pursue a moderate, centrist course in the next two years. It was subject to conflicting pressures. On the left, the Democratic Charter Movement organized a 50 000 strong demonstration against right-wing and racist trends in Hungary, at which Antall was attacked for failing to distance himself from such trends. President Göncz, a man strongly imbued with liberal values, fought a stubborn rearguard action against right-wing pressures on the media, refusing to dismiss the heads of Hungarian radio (Csaba Gombar) and television (Elemér Hankiss) who had been accused by the right of 'downplaying Hungarian national values' and 'allowing the TV to become a mouthpiece for the opposition'.[9] The pressure from the right was strong, and it reached its height in the next two years. Not only did the Smallholder Torgyan continue his agitation, but a radical rightist demagogue emerged within Antall's own party: István Csurka, the poet and novelist who was Vice-President of the MDF. Csurka combined anticommunist witch-hunting, Hungarian nationalism and anti-semitism in a heady brew which might have proved dangerous. He asserted in August 1992 that an international Zionist conspiracy by Jews, communists and liberals at home and the IMF abroad was 'smothering Hungary'. He added that 'society now has to support the strong, fit-for-life families who are prepared for work and achievement' rather than 'the cumulatively underprivileged strata' whose degeneration was 'due to genetic causes' and who 'have lived among us for too long' – an implied attack on the 500 000 Hungarian gypsies (Roma).[10] His supporters demonstrated against communists in the media (19 September 1992) and succeeded in shouting down the President himself during a public commemoration of the 1956 revolution (23 October 1992). Csurka tried to exploit these initial successes by forming a movement to promote 'Hungarianism', *Magyar Út* (November 1992). He challenged Antall for the post of party chairman of the MDF the following January, gaining 20 per cent of the vote.

The Prime Minister at first seemed to respond to rightist pressures: he forced Hankiss, a target of the right, out of his television post (he was suspended on 9 December 1992 and resigned on 6 January 1993); he moved to secure control of the media by appointing supporters of his government to head both radio and television (László Csúcs and Gábor Nahlik respectively); and he allowed members of his cabinet to attend the reburial of Admiral Horthy, the prewar dictator of Hungary, describing him as a 'committed Hungarian patriot' (September 1993). But he also had Csurka expelled from the MDF, alongside three of his parliamentary supporters (June 1993). The skinheads who had shouted down President Göncz were dealt with by a law banning the wearing of Nazi or communist symbols in public (14 April 1993). A law on minority rights, guaranteeing the use of minority mother tongues in education, was approved on 7 July 1993 by a majority of 304 to 3.

Antall's political balancing act was brought to an end by his death from cancer (12 December 1993). He was replaced by Peter Boross, a former catering company manager with no record in dissident politics. Boross was a lacklustre figure who continued Antall's policies without his style; he tried to win the May 1994 general elections by having 129 journalists sacked for criticizing his government (4 March) and by making the radio into a government propaganda institution; he played for anti-communist support by bringing forward legislation to exclude those involved in the suppression of the 1956 revolution from public life; he played for nationalist support by prohibiting foreigners from purchasing land (6 April); the MDF-controlled media engaged in a hate campaign against the Socialists, bringing up 1956 again and again. None of this worked. The MDF was heavily defeated in May, and the MSZP, now led by Gyula Horn, won an absolute majority of parliamentary seats (209 out of 386) with a 33.0 per cent share of the vote. MDF representation sank to 37. The Hungarian Justice and Life Party (MIÉP) set up by Csurka after his expulsion from the MDF secured a mere 1.6 per cent, gaining no parliamentary seats. On 15 July Horn formed a coalition government along with the Free Democrats, who had won 70 seats.

The failure of both the extreme right and the extreme left in the May 1994 elections, and the victory of the MSZP, which had by now established its social democratic credentials, were clear signs that the political transition to parliamentary democracy had taken place in Hungary; the economic transition to the free market remained problematic. We shall examine further developments and draw a provisional balance in the final chapter.

POLAND: THE RADICALS AT THE HELM

In Poland, as in Hungary, the change from communism to post-communism was marked by considerable continuity. Despite its suppression of Solidarity in 1981, the communist leadership, under General Jaruzelski, set a course towards economic reform and stabilization during the 1980s. But the economic reforms met with increasing resistance from both sides of the political spectrum: the intelligentsia and the skilled workers, supporters of Solidarity, who in theory should have favoured reform, opposed it because they opposed the government itself; while party members, pensioners and the unskilled, who generally supported the government, opposed the reforms as such because they damaged their immediate interests (for instance, the price rises of the 1980s meant that by 1988 real wages were 10 per cent below their 1981 level).

It was clear by the end of the 1980s that reform could only come about through compromise with the Solidarity opposition. Solidarity's hidden strength was such that no reform programme could be carried out effectively without the union's consent. This lesson was drawn for the first time by Prime Minister Mieczysław Rakowski, who introduced the new policy on 14 October 1988 with the words: 'Compromise is possible. Compromise is necessary'. But it took the threat of resignation by the top leaders of the communist party (Polish United Workers' Party, or PZPR) to convince the 10th Plenum of the Central Committee, meeting in January 1989, that the party must engage in round table discussions with the leaders of Solidarity. Two months of hard bargaining between the 'social side' (that is Solidarity) and the 'government coalition side' resulted in an agreement which was in effect a PZPR surrender, although it had the appearance of a compromise. There were to be free elections, Solidarity was legalized, but certain apparent safeguards for communist power such as a guaranteed bloc of 38 per cent of the seats in the Sejm, the Lower House of Parliament, were also built in.

On economic policy, the agreement provided for wage indexation and the protection of workers.

Solidarity's overwhelming victory in the June 1989 elections to the Sejm and the Senate, although apparently nullified by the undemocratic elements of the April agreement, marked in reality a decisive blow struck at the old order. There followed a hectic, unstable phase of manoeuvring by both sides. Rakowski reacted to his party's defeat by accepting the radical reform strategy summed up in the phrase 'shock therapy'; paradoxically, the first Polish shock therapy measures were carried out by the last Polish communist government. Early in August prices were freed, subsidies were abolished, rationing of commodities was abandoned. This was entirely in line with the views of the main leaders of Solidarity at the time, as they had now become convinced by the arguments in favour of economic liberalism.[11] Politically, the PZPR needed the support of its former coalition partners, the ZSL (United Peasant Party) and the SD (Democratic Party) to assemble a parliamentary majority. Their decision to end 40 years of subservience by coming out in support of Solidarity meant that the game was up for the party that had ruled Poland since 1944. But the strength of the communists in the Polish army, as well as continuing uncertainty about the Soviet attitude to a complete collapse of communism in Poland, made a compromise look necessary. Adam Michnik found the appropriate formula: 'Yours the president, ours the prime minister'. General Jaruzelski was elected President of Poland in July 1989 with the indirect help of Solidarity's deputies. Tadeusz Mazowiecki, of Solidarity, was almost unanimously elected Prime Minister on 24 August, with the support of the PZPR's deputies.

The new government continued and deepened the radical course of 'shock therapy' already begun by the communists. These measures, master-minded by the young Minister of Finance, Leszek Balcerowicz, deserve separate treatment owing to their wider significance. We shall deal with them more fully in Chapter 6. Here we shall look only at their political consequences. The initially severe fall in real incomes and industrial production, combined with continuing inflation, caused a split in the Solidarity movement, between the supporters of the Mazowiecki government, which had inherited the crisis, and arguably worsened it with its radical economic measures, and the rank and file, particularly the workers, who struck in May 1990, supported by the peasants, who blockaded the railways in protest. Somewhat surprisingly, Lech Wałęsa, the charismatic leader of the Solidarity movement, acted as spokesman for this discontent, declaring that he wanted to wage a 'war at the top' within Poland, and setting up a party for this purpose: he called it the Centre Citizens' Alliance. The Mazowiecki camp in turn set up their own party, the Citizens' Movement for Democratic Action, or ROAD. Wałęsa's challenge was made stronger by the fact that he combined his attack on the shock therapy measures with criticism of Mazowiecki's continuing co-operation with the ex-communists. In response, the Mazowiecki government had to make both economic and political concessions. In the economic sphere it softened the impact of the *popiwek*, the tremendously unpopular tax which forced employers to hold down wages, it raised state expenditure on housing and agriculture and it reduced the rate of interest to 34 per cent a year (July); politically it conceded the dismissal of three former PZPR ministers, including Czesław Kiszczak, the Minister of the Interior (July). It also agreed in September 1990 to hold direct elections to the Polish presidency, a move which would favour Wałęsa's chances, given his great popular standing.

The presidential elections of 25 November 1990 brought two predictable results and one surprise. Mazowiecki was predictably defeated (he received 18 per cent); Wałęsa predictably came top of the poll (with 40 per cent); but a completely unknown Pole from Canada called Stanisław Tymiński gained 23 per cent of the vote on the first round. Both the vote for Tymiński and the failure of Mazowiecki were political consequences of popular disillusionment with the reform programme. Wałęsa easily won the second round on 9 December (with 74 per cent). He thereupon resigned as chair of Solidarity, and proceeded to justify his reputation as a maverick by immediately shifting back to the reform course he had attacked so strongly a few months before. He nominated Jan Krzysztof Bielecki of the Liberal-Democratic Congress (KLD) to replace Mazowiecki as Prime Minister, and Bielecki retained Leszek Balcerowicz at the Ministry of Finance (January 1991). The new government was as economically liberal as the old one had been. It raised the rate of interest to 72 per cent, it raised prices, it continued the *popiwek*, and it locked the peasants out of access to cheap credit, setting off a further episode of railway blockading (March).

The international reward came quickly, in the shape of a 50 per cent reduction in Poland's foreign debt by the Paris Club (15 March 1991), and a series of loans from the IMF (18 April), the EBRD (25 June) and the World Bank (14 August). But free market policies could only be continued at the cost of waging a war on two fronts, against Solidarity as a trade union and against the Polish parliament, which still had a theoretically communist, and therefore uncontrollable, majority. In February

1991 the trade union Solidarity decided to withdraw the 'protective umbrella' it had held over Solidarity-based governments and to establish its own political party.[12] The Bielecki government also began to have problems with the President; Wałęsa shifted his position yet again, now coming out against the prime minister he had nominated seven months before. On 30 August Bielecki clashed with the Sejm over cuts of 14.5 per cent in public spending intended to bring Poland's budget deficit within the limits approved by the IMF; this time the former communists, with one eye on the forthcoming elections, took the lead in opposing him. Bielecki was outvoted, and on 27 September a budget which overshot IMF spending targets by 1.5 billion złoty was approved. This resulted in the immediate suspension of IMF aid to Poland.

Shortly afterwards (27 October) the Polish electorate delivered a mixed verdict on Solidarity's two years in power. At 43 per cent the turnout was extremely low, which could be interpreted as a sign of disillusionment. The results showed a political spectrum marked by extreme fragmentation. Twenty-nine parties were able to secure seats, including a Party of Beer Lovers; and the major political camps were in approximate equilibrium. There were no outright winners, and very few losers. The parties which stemmed from the Solidarity movement did best, though given the internecine fighting between them this fact was of little significance. Mazowiecki's Democratic Union (UD) received 12.3 per cent of the vote; Bielecki's Liberal Democratic Congress (KLD) 7.5 per cent; Solidarity, the trade union, now a political party as well, 5.1 per cent; the Centre Citizens' Alliance, 8.7 per cent; the Peasant Alliance, Solidarity's peasant offshoot, gained 5.5 per cent.

The most surprising result was achieved by the former communists and their supporters. Since the débâcle of 1989, when the PZPR had been unable to secure a single seat except those already reserved for it by law, there had been a complete transformation on the left. At its 11th Congress (26–9 January 1990) the former communist party had turned itself into the Social Democracy of the Republic of Poland (SDRP), a party committed to parliamentary democracy, and led by a young (36 years old) and fairly untainted journalist, Aleksandr Kwaśniewski, who claimed to represent 'the social democratic majority' in Poland.[13] He formed an electoral alliance with various smaller left-wing parties, calling the resulting combination the Alliance of the Democratic Left (SLD), and he began to agitate (rather demagogically in view of his failure to offer an alternative) against the social consequences of the Solidarity governments' reform measures. The SLD did well in October 1991, with 12.0 per cent of the vote, as did the communists' former rural partner the Polish Peasant Party (PSL, formerly ZSL) with 8.7 per cent. The success of the SLD was partly due to the existence of a large as yet unmobilized social democratic constituency, which Solidarity had alienated over the previous two years.[14]

The 1991 elections marked the start of a period of extreme parliamentary instability. President Wałęsa proposed to solve Poland's problems in the following characteristically eccentric manner: he would take over as Prime Minister, while retaining the Presidency. Naturally enough, none of the politicians favoured this solution, and in November a heterogeneous centre-right coalition of five parties was set up under Jan Olszewski of the Centre Citizens' Alliance, which was originally the presidential party, but broke with Wałęsa shortly after the elections. Olszewski's political line was a curious combination of anti-communist zeal and support for state interventionism. He claimed to be making a fresh start, but his proposals for active anti-recession measures were never actually implemented. The Sejm rejected his economic programme (5 March 1992), because the pro-market right (the UD and the KLD) refused to swallow its relaxation of tight monetary controls. Olszewski was equally unlucky with the other half of his programme. A 'Lustration Law' was passed in May 1992, but the main result of this was a tremendous political crisis, because prominent present-day leaders such as Leszek Moczulski and Wałęsa himself were allegedly implicated in collaboration with the previous regime's secret police.[15] The crisis was only resolved with the resignation of the Olszewski government and the election of Hanna Suchocka of the UD as Prime Minister, leading a coalition of the seven Solidarity-based parties (11 July).

Suchocka's coalition was as fragile as previous governments had been. A fissure ran through its centre, between the three liberal, 'Westernizing' parties led by the UD and the four Catholic, traditionalist parties led by the Christian National Union. The abortion issue[16] was likely to drive a wedge between these two ideological camps; moreover, the government was constantly on the horns of a dilemma in its economic policy. Either it refused concessions to strikers who were protesting against the consequences of austerity measures, in which case Solidarity (the trade union) threatened a general strike against Solidarity (the government); or it made the concessions, in which case inflation would return and Western financial institutions would refuse any further reductions in Poland's foreign debt. The divisions on this issue were such that even at the outset the government programme was only accepted by 166 votes to 163 (17 October 1992).

The Suchocka government chose the course of confrontation with Solidarity and the striking workers, and with success, but there was a political cost: the alienation of its own supporters. In December 1992 it faced down a miners' strike, but now its measures could only be passed through parliament with the support of the former communist party's SLD alliance. Thus, on 18 March 1993 the Sejm rejected a mass privatization bill covering six hundred enterprises; the government resubmitted it on 30 April (with some concessions to Solidarity) and it was only passed thanks to SLD support. In April, Rural Solidarity (the Porozumienie Ludowe, Peasant Alliance, or PL) withdrew from the government in protest against its decision to abolish subsidized prices for wheat and rye. Finally, on 28 May 1993, the Solidarity group of deputies brought down their own government, because it had rejected demands from teachers and health care workers to increase expenditure on education and welfare.

President Wałęsa thereupon dissolved parliament, setting fresh elections for September 1993, under new rules intended to reduce the fragmentation of the political scene by setting a 5 per cent threshold, which parties had to pass before being qualified to elect deputies to the Sejm. The Right, more fragmented than the Left, was thereby placed at a disadvantage. This was worsened by the addition of an 8 per cent threshold for alliances of parties, which would strike at the right-wing parties' favourite technique for overcoming their divisions. In the Sejm elected on 19 September 1993 the number of parties fell from 29 to 6; 35.1 per cent of the electorate found themselves unrepresented in parliament, although this hardly changed popular perceptions, given that in June 1992, when there were still 29 parties to choose from, a mere 3 per cent of those polled felt they were represented by a political party.

The apparent paradox of the elections of 1993 was that the voters delivered a stinging protest against the politicians' handling of the economy just at the point when Poland was emerging from the crisis of transition. GDP grew by 2.6 per cent in 1992 and 3.8 per cent in 1993. Inflation had been falling since 1990: it was down from 585.8 per cent a year to 36.9 per cent. There were various signs that people were becoming increasingly wealthy. Private car ownership rose from 1.2 million in 1990 to 6.4 million in 1992. The private enterprise sector was expanding fast: by 1993 there were 63 500 private firms and 59 per cent of all employees were employed in the private sector. But the beneficiaries of these achievements were a minority of Poles. By August 1993 unemployment was at 15 per cent; real wages fell during the year by 4 per cent. In June, 80 per cent of the respondents in a public opinion survey pronounced their material situation 'bad'. Both Left and Right exploited the situation shamelessly, criticizing all the post-1990 economic reforms. The elections resulted in a victory for the SLD and the PSL, its agrarian ally, which had managed to reunite the farming constituency by absorbing most of Rural Solidarity. The SLD received 20.6 per cent of the vote and 173 seats; the PSL 15.5 per cent and 128 seats. An extra factor favouring the SLD was its rejection of clerical interference, especially on the abortion issue. This gained it the support of many young Poles. The right-wing parties did badly, partly because they were simply not believed by the electors (they promised everything to everyone and advocated a strongly state interventionist policy against the social crisis), partly because of their fragmentation, which kept them below the 5 per cent and 8 per cent thresholds. The extreme right KPN just crept above the threshold, with 5.8 per cent. Solidarity itself, with 4.9 per cent, failed to get any seats at all. This was the voters' verdict on the ambiguous position the union found itself in, torn between its role as a party of government and its commitment to defending its members' material interests. The Union of Labour (UP), which was essentially the left wing of the Solidarity movement in combination with Tadeusz Fiszbach's Social Democratic Union (USRP), an ex-communist splinter group which had originally entered the SLD but later decided to withdraw from it, did well, capitalizing on the workers' discontent with the results of economic reform: it gained 7.3 per cent of the vote and received 42 seats.[17] Finally, the UD, the consistent supporters of free market reform, whose constituency was the minority of Poles who had done well (or hoped to do well) out of the changes, held on to 10.4 per cent of the vote and 74 seats in the Sejm. Results for the Upper House of parliament, the Senate, were not very different, but ironically gave an absolute majority to the SLD and PSL. Both parties had campaigned for the Upper House's abolition.

It soon became clear that what looked like an electoral 'shift to the left', or, as Adam Michnik put it, a 'velvet restoration', was nothing of the sort. The only genuinely left-wing party, the UP, withdrew from talks with the PSL and the SLD on forming a government when it became clear that they intended to go ahead with the process of privatization, and to continue the austerity measures they had denounced during the election campaign. The one change the new government made to existing economic policies was the abolition of the *popiwek* (December 1993), which was a concession to the urban workers who had voted for the SLD.[18] Despite this, the coalition government that emerged in October 1993 was deeply divided on other issues. The SLD, with its 37 per cent of the seats, needed the PSL's 29 per cent to form a stable parliamentary majority. The head of the PSL, Waldemar Pawlak, became prime minister, and his party received eight cabinet posts against the SLD's five. The PSL was an agrarian pressure group under strong clerical influence; the views of the dominant group within the SLD were indistinguishable from those of the neo-liberal Freedom Union: they favoured privatization, the free market, macroeconomic stabilization and fiscal discipline and opposed concessions to special interests, whether these were the Roman Catholic Church or the farmers. The SLD controlled the key economic ministries, although it was in a minority in the Pawlak cabinet, and did not possess the presidency until November 1995. This would result in repeated crises in subsequent years, especially in combination with the eccentric political interventions of President Wałęsa.

We shall take up the discussion of the mid-1990s era of unstable SLD rule in Poland in Chapter 8.

CZECHOSLOVAKIA: A VELVET REVOLUTION AND A VELVET DIVORCE

The revolution in Czechoslovakia was non-violent (it was dubbed the 'velvet revolution'), but even so it was thoroughgoing. This reflected the high degree of popular support, at least among Czechs, for radical change: 85 per cent of those polled in January 1990 wanted fundamental political and economic changes. The communists would naturally have liked the maximum of continuity, and it looked at first as if they would achieve this, with the appointment of a Government of National Reconciliation led by the communist Marián Čalfa. He put together a cabinet with 10 communist and 11 non-communist members (10 December 1989). At the final session of the Round Table which accepted Čalfa's cabinet Václav Havel gave the justification that 'the November revolt was not against the communists as such but against the totalitarian order' and therefore 'it was better to have a communist' in the cabinet than 'a non-communist adhering to the old ways'.[19] This was not the real reason. The Civic Forum (OF) negotiators allowed the communists to dominate the new government because they were not aware at this stage of just how weak the old regime actually was. They also underestimated the willingness of the Soviet Union to let key ministries, such as Defence, pass out of communist hands. So the communists could well believe after 10 December that they had limited the changes to a minimum, and hope to play a major part in future political life.

There were two reasons why this did not happen. The first was that the Communist Party itself was not ready to change; the reform communists had tried and failed in 1968 (through no fault of their own) and most of the original reformers were removed from the party in the course of the 'normalization' campaign of the early 1970s. Hence the liberal faction was in a minority position. The resignation from the party of all those communists who remained in the government after December 1989 was a clear recognition by the party reformers of their own failure to transform Czechoslovak communism. Čalfa left the party in January 1990, along with the economists Valtr Komárek and Vladimír Dlouhý; Milan Čič, the communist who was Slovak prime minister, left in March. Alone among communist parties in Eastern Europe, the Communist Party of Czechoslovakia (KSČ) decided to retain the word 'communist' in its party title, although making adjustments to the requirements of federalism by splitting into a Communist Party of Bohemia and Moravia and a Communist Party of Slovakia – Party of the Democratic Left (November 1990); this symbolized its determination to retain what it saw as the positive elements of the old system.

The second reason for the lack of political continuity in Czechoslovakia after 1989 was the wish of ordinary Czechs (and, to a lesser extent, Slovaks) to draw a line under the old era. A mere 6 per cent of the public opinion sample quoted above favoured a society on the 1968 model. The election of Alexander Dubček as President of the Federal Assembly on 29 December 1989 was an act of sentiment rather than a political statement. He was seen as a figure from the past; the party he formed failed to get any seats in the elections of June 1992. The important decision was the election of Václav Havel, a man with a record of uncompromising opposition to the communist order, as President of the republic on the same day. The few reform communists (such as Čalfa) who managed to creep back to power under the umbrella of the OF (in the Czech lands) and Public Against Violence (in Slovakia) were to lose their positions within two years, when both movements split, and in subsequent elections the Civic Movement (OH) in the Czech lands and the Christian Democratic Union in Slovakia both failed to gain any seats.

The first democratic elections held in Czechoslovakia since 1946 were essentially a plebiscite against the communist party (8–9 June 1990). People voted for Civic Forum (OF) and Public Against Violence (VPN) as a way of ensuring that the communists lost their majority.[20] In this they were successful. Although the communists were the largest political party (13.6 per cent of the voters in the Czech lands supported the Communist Party of Bohemia and Moravia [KSČM], 13.7 per cent in Slovakia its sister party the SDL') they were dwarfed by the two big popular movements (46.6 per cent voted for Civic Forum in the Czech lands, 45.9 per cent for Public Against Violence in Slovakia).[21] The other parties represented after June 1990 were the Czech and Slovak Christian Democrats (the Czech Christian Democrats did far worse, with 9 per cent, than their Slovak counterparts, on 17 per cent, because the former were damaged by charges that their leader, Josef Bartončík, had collaborated with the secret police),[22] the Slovak nationalists (SNS), and two local parties, the Moravian regionalists (HSD-MS) and the eccentrically named Hungarian minority party 'Coexistence' (ESWM) which was in coalition with the Hungarian Christian Democratic Movement (MKDH). The Social Democrats (with 3.8 per cent) failed to cross the threshold of parliamentary representation; their day had not yet come.

This was an apparently clear-cut result. The opponents of communism and supporters of radical change had won. But in fact divisions immediately emerged within the victorious camp; the coalition character of Civic Forum and Public Against Violence became apparent. The main disputes were over economic policy and the future constitutional shape of Czechoslovakia.

On economic policy there was a long tug of war between Valtr Komárek, the ex-communist Deputy Prime Minister, who favoured a 'Social Democratic' approach involving a very gradual transition to the market, with full safeguards for the maintenance of standards of living, and Václav Klaus, Minister of Finance, who was a neo-liberal free marketeer. After June 1990 Komárek was no longer in the government, but a conflict then developed between Klaus and President Havel, who was re-elected president by the Federal Assembly in July. Havel wanted slow-paced market reforms. He opposed Klaus's Polish-style 'big bang' approach to the economy. These disputes delayed the implementation of reform. Not until 13 October 1990, when Klaus was elected head of Civic Forum, was it possible for a start to be made. Then the reforms followed thick and fast.

The currency was devalued by 54.5 per cent; moves were made towards internal convertibility; the privatization of small-scale enterprise began; and a law provided for the restitution of property to former owners. Large-scale privatization was a more difficult question, but extensive discussions led eventually to a Law of General Privatization (26 February 1991), which envisaged the quasi-free distribution of shares to citizens. On 1 January 1991 controls were lifted on 85 per cent of all prices, with the result that they doubled during the month, and a tax on wage growth, analogous to the Polish *popiwek*, was imposed to make sure that wages did not rise too fast.[23] The trade unions complained, though they did not go so far as to strike. Political opposition to these measures was led by the communist party, which proclaimed 'the end of national reconciliation and the beginning of a period of hard struggle'. At its 18th Congress, held in November 1990, the party condemned the economic reforms; the government replied by seizing its assets, on the ground that 'they were acquired illegally'.[24]

Klaus did not allow himself to be deflected by opposition, either from the trade unions or the communist party. Large-scale privatization went ahead on 8 August 1991. Fifty enterprises were sold. A further 2800 were expected to be privatized over the next year. It was envisaged that 30 per cent of the labour force in privatized enterprises would be made redundant. Restitution would also go ahead: land would be restored to its pre-1948 owners (law of 21 May 1991). Financial orthodoxy was amply demonstrated by the 1992 budget, which balanced state income and expenditure. The impact of 'shock therapy' on Czechoslovakia was severe: production fell, real wages fell, and the situation was worsened during 1991 by the decline in foreign trade which resulted from the collapse of Comecon. The political impact of the measures was to split Civic Forum. The main body of the movement joined Klaus's Civic Democratic Party (ODS), which was 20 000 strong; his rival Jiří Dienstbier formed the OH, which was joined by eight out of ten Civic Forum cabinet members, but did not gain a corresponding degree of support from ordinary people. The OH turned out to be half the size of the ODS, and opinion surveys put support for it at a mere 5 per cent, compared with the 20 per cent who supported the latter party.

Conflict with Slovakia was the other major result of 'shock therapy' in Czechoslovakia. Within four months of the harmony and euphoria of November 1989, when Civic Forum and Public Against Violence had marched in step, a violent quarrel blew up over the future name of the republic (it was absolutely necessary to change it, if only to get rid of the word 'socialist'). The Czechs wanted to call it the 'Czechoslovak Federal Republic', the Slovaks the 'Czecho-Slovak Federal Republic'. The hyphen was unacceptable to the Czechs because of the echoes of March 1939 it aroused; they finally compromised on 'Czech and Slovak Federal Republic'. Behind the name there lay the issue of the respective powers of the federal and republican governments. A provisional agreement was reached in November 1990, but it was only pushed through parliament by Havel after very strenuous efforts (12 December 1990). The federal government retained power over defence, foreign policy, the currency and nationalities.[25] The negotiators were able to compromise on the control of nationality policy, but Slovak nationalists protested that the federal language law favoured the Hungarian minority by allowing the use of a minority language where over 20 per cent of a given population belonged to the minority; they demanded that Slovak be the sole official language in Slovakia. Soon afterwards, Vladimír Mečiar formed a minority faction within VPN, accusing the current VPN leaders, such as Marián Čalfa, of 'failing to defend Slovak interests' (March 1991). Mečiar and his allies were dismissed from the Slovak government (23 April 1991), but soon had their revenge. They split VPN and set up a new party, the Platform for a Democratic Slovakia, which later renamed itself the Movement for a Democratic Slovakia (HZDS) and elected Mečiar as chairman (22 June 1991). The success of the HZDS, which openly appealed to Slovak nationalist sentiments, was a direct result of the greater burden laid on Slovakia by the central government's policies of financial orthodoxy and rapid transition to the free market.

By September 1991 unemployment in Slovakia was more than twice as high as it was in the Czech lands (10 per cent against 4 per cent). The structure of industry in Slovakia made it particularly vulnerable to the decline and collapse of the Warsaw Pact. Slovak industry was heavily dependent on the export of goods, particularly armaments, to the Soviet Union. Now this market had practically disappeared. It was easy for Slovak politicians to blame Slovakia's relatively inferior performance after 1989 on the reforms themselves and the Czech connection rather than the international environment.[26] While Czechs generally favoured a continuation of the Klaus reforms, despite the attendant suffering, Slovaks swung against them (in January 1991, 52 per cent of Czechs and 39 per cent of Slovaks favoured the free market; by November 1991 the proportions were 52 per cent of Czechs and 33 per cent of Slovaks). In the Czech lands the ODS's combination of liberal economics with militant anti-communism was popular. A 'lustration law', put forward by the government in June, by which former communists and informers were to be excluded from employment, was made more severe by the Czech parliament in October 1991. In Slovakia, in contrast, the ruling Christian Democrats, led by the veteran dissident Jan Čarnogurský, lost ground continuously to Mečiar; they also suffered an internal defection, when a nationalist wing of the party set up a rival organization, the Slovak Christian Democratic Movement.

These divisions over economic policy and constitutional reconstruction set the stage for the elections of June 1992. The hottest issues in the Czech lands were economic policy and de-communization; in Slovakia the issues were also partly economic, but the constitutional question dwarfed everything else. Only one political party – the right-wing Republicans – stood in both halves of the country as an undivided entity, and they failed to gain any seats in Slovakia. All the Slovak parties except the remnant of VPN (renamed the Civic Democratic Union, or ODU, in March 1992) called for a change of economic and social policies in the direction of greater government intervention to improve social welfare; but they all equally stressed that greater autonomy, leading to independence, was a prerequisite for effective action.

The result of the elections was a defeat for the makers of the 1989 revolution, from Václav Havel downwards, and a victory for people who had had very little to do with it. In the Czech lands, Klaus's ODS–KDS coalition won 29.7 per cent of the vote and 76 seats, and in Slovakia Mečiar's HZDS won 37.3 per cent and 74 seats. Civic Forum's successors in the two halves of the country, Dienstbier's OH and Čalfa's ODU, both failed to surmount the 5 per cent hurdle, as did Dubček's Slovak Social Democratic Party. The communists did relatively well (14.1 per cent voted for the communist-led Left Bloc in the Czech lands, 14.7 per cent for the SDL' in Slovakia). In the Czech lands the balance was made up by the Republicans (6.0 per cent), the Czech Social Democrats (6.5 per cent), the Civic Democrats (6.5 per cent), the Liberal Social Union (6.5 per cent), the regionalist HSD-MS (5.9 per cent), and the Christian Democrats (6.3 per cent). The other parties represented in Slovakia were the Slovak Christian Democratic Movement (8.9 per cent), the Slovak nationalists (7.9 per cent) and the coalition of Hungarian minority parties (7.4 per cent).[27] Neither Klaus nor Mečiar had sufficient support to allow them to rule alone. They could, however, easily form coalitions with like-minded associates: Mečiar's partner was the nationalist SNS, Klaus's partners were several small centrist groups (the Civic Democratic Alliance, or ODA, the Christian Democratic Party, or KDS, and the Christian Democratic Union – Czech People's Party, or KDU–ČSL).

On 17 July 1992 the newly elected Slovak National Council approved a declaration of sovereignty, rather than independence, by 113 votes to 24. Mečiar's programme did not explicitly demand independence, but what was important for him, and entirely unacceptable to Klaus, was absolute economic autonomy. If granted, this would allow the Slovak government to return to greater state intervention in the market. It would be able to subsidize state industry, and slow down the privatization process. No compromise was possible between the two sides on this issue. In the latter half of 1992, somewhat ironically, Klaus was pressing more strongly than Mečiar for the separation of Slovakia, because this would give him a free hand to pursue his radical economic reforms. In the meantime, popular attitudes hardened in both countries. The Slovaks accused the Czechs of arrogance and centralizing tendencies; the Czechs condemned the Slovaks for excessive nationalism and inflexibility. Even so, there was never a popular majority for the break-up. In June 1992, 30 per cent of those polled in Slovakia, 16 per cent in the Czech lands, supported separation; as late as September the figures were still below 50 per cent: 41 per cent in Slovakia, 46 per cent in the Czech lands.[28]

On 23 July, after ten separate meetings, Klaus and Mečiar reached agreement on how to dissolve Czechoslovakia. A deadline of 1 January 1993 was set. There were many detailed questions to consider, but they were all settled amicably. The biggest difficulty was experienced in overcoming the harsh requirement of a majority of three-fifths for constitutional change, built in to the first post-communist constitution. This was intended to protect the Slovaks against the weight of the Czech majority, but it was now used by opponents of separation. On 1 October 1992 the Federal Assembly passed the Klaus-Mečiar bill dissolving the Federation by a large majority. But the vote in favour was not quite large enough to be constitutionally valid. The opposing votes came from the former communists and Jan Čarnogurský's Christian Democrats. This was clearly an absurd situation. When the bill next came before the assembly, on 25 November, fifty-five opponents agreed to abstain. Now it could go through with the necessary majority.

After the dissolution of the country, the two new national states set out along separate paths, which were at least temporarily divergent: the Czech Republic was marked by political stability, Slovakia by considerable instability; the Czech Republic continued to pursue the strategy of market-oriented reform, and a closer and closer approach to the West, Slovakia slowed its reforms and started to look to the East for solutions; the Czech Republic settled down to a political diet of economic discussions and financial scandals, Slovakia's politics were dominated by ethnic issues and the authoritarianism of its Prime Minister. But the severe pains of separation between the two halves of Czechoslovakia that had been predicted in 1992 did not materialize, as the following brief analysis will show.

Let us take the Czech Republic first. The situation here was marked by continuing political stability and economic progress. With the disappearance of the Slovak question from the political scene, the government was able to override the wishes of the Moravian and Silesian regionalists and adopt a centralist constitution (16 December 1992). Havel was elected president of the new republic for a five-year term (26 January 1993). Klaus continued as prime minister. There was a slight rise in unemployment (from 2.6 per cent to 3.5 per cent); GDP was practically static during 1993, falling 0.5 per cent, which was a great improvement on 1992's fall of 6.4 per cent; exports rose by 14 per cent; annual average inflation rose from 11.1 per cent to 20.6 per cent. This did not stop real wages from rising by 3 per cent during 1993. As is apparent, these economic results were not unsatisfactory. Politically, Klaus remained firmly in control. The opposition was weak and divided; an attempt was made to overcome this division by the formation of a 'realistic bloc' comprising the Czech Social Democrats (ČSSD), the Moravian and Silesian regionalists, the Liberal Social Union and the Christian Democrats (29 June 1993). There could be no co-operation with the communists (KSČM), who rejected the reforming course of their previous leader Jiří Svoboda in June 1993, electing instead a conservative, Miroslav Grebeniček, as the head of the party . A dissident minority set up a Party of the Democratic Left (16 July). Miloš Zeman, the leader of the ČSSD, rejected any fusion with these dissident communists, as he was concerned to preserve his public image from the taint of communist associations. But in any case, many reform-oriented communists found a new home in his party as individuals. The ČSSD had a promising future. But for the present Klaus was riding high. A survey conducted in September 1993 showed that his party was the most popular in the country, and Klaus himself, on 61 per cent, was the second most popular politician (President Havel came top of the poll). The politics of the Czech Republic continued to revolve quietly around issues of 'lustrace', restitution and the annual budget.

Things were different in Slovakia. Here the separation produced problems, or rather it exacerbated existing ones. Unemployment, already high, rose still higher, from 11.4 per cent to 12.2 per cent. GDP fell by 4.1 per cent; industrial production fell by 14 per cent; real wages fell by 6.4 per cent. As the sequel was to show, these consequences of the split, if they were such, were strictly temporary. Political instability could also be seen as temporary (although subsequent stability was achieved at the cost of a semi-authoritarian regime). The basic reason for the instability of the immediate post-separation years was that

Mečiar's movement was a heterogeneous coalition. It had been held together by the common goal of independence. Once Slovakia was independent, divisions came to the surface.

Mečiar's Foreign Minister, Milan Knazko, challenged him over the choice of Michal Kováč as presidential candidate (February 1993) and tried to take the party chairmanship from him (at the HZDS congress of 27–8 March 1993). He was defeated by 183 votes to 41, but confidence in Mečiar's government was now low: it fell from 75 per cent in August 1992 to 46 per cent in March 1993. Mečiar's own personal popularity plummeted. By September 1993 the HZDS was only slightly in the lead (at 15 per cent) over other parties. Seven HZDS deputies defected to Knazko, who had in the meantime set up his own party, the Alliance of Democrats of the Slovak Republic. The SNS, whose support was necessary for a parliamentary majority, opposed Mečiar over his appointment of a former communist as Minister of Defence. He was thus placed in a minority in parliament, with 66 out of 150 votes (6 April 1993). However, no alternative coalition could be put together, so Mečiar continued in office until the SNS relented and rejoined the government (November 1993). This was not the end of the instability. Turmoil within the HZDS reached its height in February 1994 with the establishment of a faction within the party, under the title Alternative of Political Realism, the aim of which was to replace Mečiar's government with a cabinet of 'non-political experts'. A month later Mečiar lost a vote of no confidence, under the combined pressure of allegations of corrupt privatization deals and a speech by President Kováč expressing 'serious reservations about the style and ethics of Mečiar's policies' (11 March 1994).

He was replaced by a coalition government, itself too broad to be stable, which was put together by Jozef Moravčik, a former Czechoslovak foreign minister, and leader of the anti-Mečiar faction with the HZDS, which had now changed its name from Alternative of Political Realism to Democratic Union of Slovakia. Moravčik's cabinet was a cabinet of defectors. It included, apart from his own party, Christian Democrats, National Democrats (defectors from the SNS), Milan Knazko's Alliance of Democrats of the Slovak Republic (defectors from the HZDS) and the post-communist and emphatically left wing SDĽ. This government could only agree on negatives: it sacked 8 out of 9 privatization officials (6 April); it removed 26 district officials for their role under the previous government (19 April); it removed the chief of police (16 March). Its political complexion ruled out a consistent economic policy: it returned to the privatization law delayed by

Mečiar, but Peter Weiss, the head of the biggest coalition party, the SDĽ, called at the same time for 'a less painful transition' and 'government support for the Slovak arms industry' (27 May 1994). The Moravčik government did not last: it was deprived of its majority by the elections of 30 September–1 October 1994. The HZDS secured 35.0 per cent of the vote, the SNS 8.6 per cent, and the newly formed extreme left Association of Workers of Slovakia (ZRS) 7.3 per cent. This only left 38.9 per cent for the government side (which translated into 50 out of the 150 seats); even with the support of the Hungarian Coalition's 17 members they remained in a minority. The newly elected National Council made its attitude clear enough when it cancelled all 38 privatization contracts concluded by the outgoing government (3 November). After two months of political manoeuvring Mečiar was able to return to power, heading a 'red-brown coalition' consisting of the HZDS, the nationalists (SNS) and the ZRS (13 December). Despite a very uneasy relationship between the president and the prime minister, and a series of authoritarian measures directed against the opposition media, this solution to Slovakia's problems lasted remarkably well until 1998. In Chapter 8 we shall try to explain why.

A NOTE ON THE BALTIC STATES

The three Baltic countries of Estonia, Latvia and Lithuania sit uneasily between the categories indicated in the introduction to this book. They were directly incorporated into the Soviet Empire rather than being attached as satellites; in that sense they belong with the other newly independent countries and deserve separate treatment along with them. But they were not within the Soviet Union for very long; and unlike the rest they had a generation of inter-war independence to look back on. They also shared in the standard post-1989 Eastern European experience of free elections, genuinely functioning democracy, a rapid transition to the market, privatization and an increasing orientation to the West, both economically and culturally. This allowed them to make a clean break with Russia after 1991, refusing to join the Commonwealth of Independent States, for instance, although every other former Soviet republic did so eventually.

Despite similarities in their position it is not entirely accurate to lump the Baltic countries together. Estonia stood out from the other two for various reasons. It had a number of advantages which have made it a candidate for early entry into the EU alongside the countries of East-Central Europe. It was the most prosperous of all the Soviet republics, with a per capita GDP in 1989 which placed it third in Eastern Europe; the subsequent decline has not altered its relative position. Its linguistic closeness to Finland made it easy to form connections with the Nordic countries. Hence it was able to 'play the Nordic card with the greatest conviction'.[29] Its geographical situation made it a bridge between the Soviet Union and the West; the strength of the reform current among the local communist elite before 1991 made it a test-bed for *perestroika*; and finally the victory of the strongly market-oriented and pro-independence forces in the elections of September 1992 was a guarantee that the transition process would be rapidly and consistently put in hand. The new post-1991 Estonia faced resolutely westwards, making sure that its dependence on Russia for energy supplies was reduced as much as possible by establishing a connection with Finland; it established a fully convertible currency; it freed prices and abolished subsidies, initially causing a rapid inflation (1992) but in the longer term squeezing it out of the economic system; it established a Privatization Agency to privatize industry and agriculture, often selling enterprises to foreign investors; it abolished restrictions on foreign landownership. By 1994 everything was going right: GDP started to grow at 4 per cent to 6 per cent a year; real wages began to rise; unemployment stayed very low; imports from Russia had fallen to 17 per cent of the total by 1993, with Finland now the largest trading partner. Politically, the outstanding problem was the very large Russian minority, but even this was important for international rather than domestic reasons, since Russian residents in Estonia have largely accepted their exclusion from political power.

Latvia and Lithuania, in contrast, started with fewer advantages. Both countries had an industrial structure closely integrated with the rest of the Soviet Union; the process of dismantling these connections was painful, and caused tremendous economic dislocation. Post-independence policies were less consistent than those of Estonia. In the Lithuanian case this was due to the harsh nationalism of the party that took the country on the road to independence; Vytautas Landsbergis, its leader, was more concerned with symbolic gestures and standing up to the Russians than with bringing the country into the Western orbit. He deterred foreign investors by refusing them the right to buy land; no proper agrarian policy was developed, so that the collective farms simply dissolved and much land went out of cultivation; privatization was seen in terms of restitution to the heirs of former owners (including grandchildren, by the law of 14 January 1992). These policies, plus

Lithuania's strong links with declining post-Soviet industries in Russia, had a severe impact on its development. Hyperinflation persisted through 1993; much of the population fell into poverty (with the average monthly salary in 1993 less than half that in Estonia). Partly as a result of these problems, male life expectancy fell by 4.9 years between 1988 and 1994, and female life expectancy by 1.7 years.

The victory, in the elections of November 1992, of the post-communist Lithuanian Democratic Labour Party (LDDP) led by Algirdas Brazauskas, confirmed by the latter's election as president in February 1993, brought to power a government which pledged the continuation of economic reforms, but without the nationalist extremes of the previous regime. Foreign investment was now encouraged; a more conciliatory attitude was taken to Russia. Privatization continued: by January 1995, 78 per cent of all state enterprises scheduled for privatization had been sold, in some cases to citizens in possession of privatization vouchers. In quantitative terms at least the economic situation was now more favourable: inflation fell to a manageable level of 25 per cent in 1996; real wages started to rise in 1994; GDP registered increases in every year from 1994 onwards. When the conservative Homeland Union (TSLK) came to power in December 1996, after a decisive election victory,[30] it was able to build on its predecessor's achievements. Political stability was promoted by a new spirit of toleration: President Brazauskas accepted his party's defeat with a good grace and agreed not to stand for a further term of office. The conservative cabinet was remodelled in March 1998 to include a leading member of the left-wing opposition, Mindaugas Stankevičius. Economically, however, there was still a long way to go by 1998. Lithuania was further away from its 1989 economic level than any other Eastern European country, and the despair of some parts of the population led to a continuous rise in the suicide rate, which by 1996 was higher than anywhere else in the world (46.4 per 100 000 people).

The Latvian picture is similarly mixed. The main difference from Lithuania is the tremendous weight and significance of the Russian-speaking population. The proportion of Russians in Latvia in 1989 was 34 per cent, to which must be added the 8 per cent of Belorussians and Ukrainians. The industrial development of Latvia after 1945 was also a process of Russianization, and the industries located in Latvia were simply branches of Soviet-wide industrial concerns, so that the end of the Soviet connection was a severe blow. Moreover, Latvia has found it very hard to re-orient its exports westwards, given that in 1991 less than 10 per cent of Latvia's production was competitive on world markets.[31]

Import dependence on Russia has been reduced (from 30 per cent in 1992 to 16 per cent in 1997) but the proportion of exports that goes to Russia has risen (from 19 per cent in 1992 to 22 per cent in 1997). Ethnic Russians, now largely excluded from political life and state administration, still play a dominant part in economic life.

The first post-independence elections (June 1993) brought to power a heterogeneous coalition party called Latvia's Way, whose only common features were, first, that its members were ethnically Latvian, and second, that they were committed to introducing a free market economy. On the Russian issue Latvia's Way was moderate (in Latvian terms), which is to say that although rejecting any idea of equal rights for the Russians it opposed the radical nationalist policy of expropriating them. But it allowed the radical nationalists to set the agenda, having refused to form a coalition with Jānis Jurkāns' party Harmony for Latvia, an anti-nationalist grouping which strongly advocated giving the Russians equal rights. A very stringent naturalization law was passed in 22 July 1994. This required five years' residence and command of the Latvian language, which was an insuperable barrier for many Russians.[32] Retired Soviet military officers are excluded permanently from civil rights. However, Russians already resident in 1940, and their descendants, have automatic citizenship. This means that a sizeable proportion of the electorate (21.2 per cent) is ethnically non-Latvian.[33] Protests by local Russians about discrimination, including demonstrations, are a permanent feature of the country's political life, and the impact of this on relations with Russia is bound to be of concern. But in practice the Russian president, Boris Yeltsin, has so far preferred conciliation to confrontation.

Successive Latvian governments have done their best to implement the transition to a market economy. Like other former Soviet countries, Latvia inherited a very high inflation (951 per cent in 1992). After independence, economic liberalization was pushed ahead rapidly.[34] For both these reasons, real personal incomes dropped by 40 per cent in 1992–3. Subsequently, the tight monetary policy pursued by the head of the State Bank, Einars Repše, led to a progressive fall in inflation, which by 1996 was, at 17 per cent, lower than in the two other Baltic states. Real wages and GDP began to increase after 1994, but so far they have not recovered very far (GDP in 1997 was only just over half its 1989 level). What Latvian governments of the first half of the 1990s did not do was privatize the economy to any significant degree. In 1994, 70 per cent of industrial capacity was still in state ownership. A start was made with voucher privatization in 1995. Andris Skele, the young businessman who became Prime Minister in December 1995 after an inconclusive general election,[35] was a supporter of land reform, but his Minister of Agriculture, Alberts Kauls, leader of the Unity Party (LVP), was not. In fact Kauls told a farming audience 'this government is doing everything to destroy you'. This led to his dismissal in May 1996 and the withdrawal of the Unity Party from the government coalition. But problems with privatization continued, and the next prime minister, Guntars Krasts, leader of the coalition of the right-wing nationalist party Fatherland and Freedom and the more moderate LNNK, dismissed his Minister of the Economy for his 'unsatisfactory approach to privatization' (3 April 1998). So the structure of the economy has not yet taken shape definitively. What is clear, though, is the increasingly Latvian character of the country (with continuing Russian emigration), and its commitment to political pluralism and democratic government.

SETTLING ACCOUNTS WITH THE PAST

Once the new regimes had come to power, whether quietly through compromise with the old order or more noisily through street demonstrations, they wanted to settle accounts with the past. There were three ways of doing this: by judicial process, by excluding communists from power and office in the future and by exposing their misdeeds through the broadest possible publicity and historical investigation. Let us take the harshest option first.

People were at first very enthusiastic about the possibility of punishing the former communist rulers by putting them on trial. But since the new regimes wanted to observe the rule of law they could not simply assume guilt; they had to face the burden of proof. The trials which resulted often turned out to be annoyingly inconclusive, and they were very slow in getting off the ground. It was difficult to bring General Jaruzelski of Poland to trial, because the courts refused to proceed on the ground that they had no jurisdiction. He was not put on trial until June 1996, on a charge of ordering the slaughter of 44 people at Gdańsk in 1970. He was not convicted, unlike lesser figures, such as the 13 members of the Security Office (UB) who were sent to prison in March 1996 for torturing detainees in 1946. Twenty-two police officers accused of shooting nine coalminers in December 1981 were luckier than this a year later: a court cleared them of all charges (21 November 1997). The trial of Erich Honecker in Germany also failed to produce a conviction. An Office for the Investigation of Communist Crimes was not set up in the Czech Republic until January 1995. In August 1995 it charged the Czech communists Miloš Jakeš, Jozef Lenárt, Karel Hoffmann and eight others with treason for signing the letter of invitation which had served as a diplomatic fig-leaf for the Soviet invasion of Czechoslovakia in August 1968.[36] But the only former communist leader actually imprisoned in Czechoslovakia after 1989 was Miroslav Štěpán. By 1997 forgetfulness, and perhaps even forgiveness, had set in. J.F. Brown, veteran Western expert on Bulgaria and top man at Radio Free Europe, summed up the new atmosphere by proclaiming: 'Goodbye (and Good Riddance!) to De-Communization'.[37]

The second way of settling accounts was to exclude former communists from office and power. This form of de-communization, potentially far more effective than political trials, was also very hard to implement, given that there was considerable continuity in personnel between old and new governments, and above all between the former communist parties and their post-communist heirs. In Romania, for instance, the prime minister from 1992 to 1996 was a veteran of the Ceauşescu-era State Planning Committee, Nicolae Văcăroiu. That meant that he brought his friends with him: in June 1996 he appointed the former Ceauşescu propagandist Dumitriu Avram as head of the Romanian News Agency, despite opposition protests.[38]

In Poland, the anti-communist Right were strongly in favour of what they called either 'dekomunizacja' (de-communization) or 'lustracja' (scrutiny, inspection), and the Olszewski government of December 1991 to June 1992 staked its political survival on the issue. This gamble on the strength of popular resentment failed, after the following extremely curious episode: Olszewski's Minister of the Interior, Antoni Macierowicz, sent out sealed envelopes containing the names of political figures who had compromised themselves by having connections with the communists in the 1980s. The list included the name of the leader of the extreme right KPN, Leszek Moczulski, a member of the government coalition, and, still worse, the name of the President himself. Lech Wałęsa was understandably furious. A presidential spokesman described the list as 'fabricated', and the Olszewski government was thrown out of office after a parliamentary vote of no confidence (5 June 1992).[39] Macierowicz himself was later charged with revealing state secrets (8 September 1993).

After this, de-communization rather went out of fashion in Poland, and when the post-communist SLD won the elections of 1993 it was in a position to block any further attempts on the ground that 'people who had collaborated with the legal organs of power' before 1989 'could not be treated as criminals' (statement of 7 July 1994). Instead of excluding former communists from office, the Minister of the Interior, Andrzej Milczanowski, tried to appoint a former member of the communist-era security services, Marian Zacharski, as head of Polish intelligence (15 August 1994). In this case he was forced to rescind the appointment after a storm of popular protest.

In the Czech Republic the process of 'lustration' (or 'screening': the Czech word is 'lustrace') was pushed forward more successfully, despite the opposition of President Havel, who condemned what he called a 'smear campaign'.[40] There was a continuous purge of the army until September 1994, when the Minister of Defence announced that enough had been done.[41] The Czech Chamber of Deputies overrode Havel's veto and acted to ban former police agents and higher level communist officials from holding public office until the year 2000.[42] Banning communist parties was another move favoured by the de-communizers. This too met with opposition. There was a dispute between the Minister of the Interior, the former dissident Jan Ruml, and Prime Minister Václav Klaus over the issue in 1996. Ruml wanted to ban the hard-line Party of Czechoslovak Communists set up by Štěpán; Klaus vetoed the idea.[43]

The lack of any really serious purge of former communists in the countries of Eastern Europe (the Czechs perhaps came nearest to succeeding) is sometimes regretted as a 'missed opportunity' which allowed representatives of the former regime to sabotage the reforms.[44] It could, however, be argued that the whole issue was actually something of an irrelevance, and that the campaign for de-communization was a harmful diversion from the struggle for genuine economic reform. The record of the Dimitrov government of 1991–2 in Bulgaria is one example of this diversionary effect; another is the slogan of Wałęsa's Centre Citizens' Alliance in Poland, 'acceleration', which was intended to refer, not, as one might think, to faster reform, but to quicker action against the former *nomenklatura*.

The third method of dealing with the communist past was publicity and historical investigation. There were many 'blank spaces' in the historiography of communist regimes, sensitive areas into which the party felt it was unwise to probe too deeply. After 1989 an immediate effort was made, often building on the work of exiled dissidents, to fill in these gaps, with the intention of revealing to the outside world the full horror of the communists' misdeeds. On 16 July 1992 President Havel publicly read out the 'letter of invitation' sent by communist hard-liners to Brezhnev in 1968 asking him to intervene in Czechoslovakia.[45] In October 1992 the Russian President Boris Yeltsin handed to President Wałęsa of Poland documents proving that the Katyn massacre of Polish officers during the Second World War had been carried out by the Narodnyi Komissariat Vnutrennikh Del (People's Commissariat for Internal Affairs) (NKVD), not the Gestapo, as had been claimed consistently throughout the Soviet period. In the early 1990s historians set to work busily in the archives to establish the true facts as they saw them and re-evaluate the communist epoch. But the initial trend towards investigating the recent past was followed quickly by a reversal of attitudes: soon everything that had happened under communism was simply consigned to the dustbin of history. By 1997 few people were interested in examining the crimes of Stalin and his Eastern European epigones. The subject disappeared from the more popular journals; and among historians there was an increasing tendency to look back before 1945, to the pre-communist past, as a more appropriate subject of investigation.

THE UNCERTAIN ROAD TO PARLIAMENTARY DEMOCRACY

Like 1848, 1989 was not only a 'springtime of nations' but a season of democratic constitutions. There were already written constitutions in existence in Eastern Europe, survivors of the previous epoch; but it was now generally felt that these should be replaced by a new model more appropriate to a multi-party democratic system subject to the rule of law. Long lists of negative and positive rights could be drawn up with little difficulty. Technical matters, such as the choice between one chamber and two, the role of referenda and the balance between proportional representation and majority voting, were settled quickly. But some aspects of constitution-making turned out to be more problematic than first imagined. In the previous era constitutions had been merely pieces of paper; now a great deal turned on their formulation and interpretation. The respective powers of parliaments and presidents needed to be defined; and some constitutions were more presidential than others.[46] Whatever the provisions of the constitution, presidents and parliaments rapidly came into conflict, sometimes for personal reasons, sometimes because conflict was inherent in the duality of power, most often because presidents and parliaments represented rival sections of society or different ideological camps.

In Poland President Wałęsa was constantly at odds with his parliament, whether it was dominated by his own party, Solidarity, which was the case until 1993, or by the post-communist SLD, after 1993. In

Czechoslovakia President Havel, though generally very concerned to be an impartial umpire rather than an interventionist arbiter, was so irritated by the Federal Assembly's behaviour in November 1991 that he proposed a period of presidential rule. We have seen that in 1995 he vetoed the Czech parliament's extension of the lustration law to the year 2000, though the parliament immediately overrode this (18 October 1995). In Hungary President Árpád Göncz was in conflict with the parliament and with Prime Minister Antall for much of his period in office (1990–4). Further east and south the conflicts were still more severe. In Slovakia President Michal Kováč was constantly at loggerheads with Prime Minister Vladimír Mečiar, even though they came from the same political party; in Bulgaria President Zhelyu Zhelev was constantly in dispute both with members of his own party the SDS and with the Bulgarian socialists who ran the government in the mid-1990s; in Albania President Berisha repeatedly rode roughshod over the constitution.

Post-communist constitution-makers often kept one eye on the threat of a communist 'restoration'; they thought they could guard against this by inserting provisions into the constitution to make it very difficult to change. In pre-1993 Czechoslovakia a three-fifths majority was required for any change to be made. This apparently sensible precaution simply increased the likelihood of a constitutional deadlock and did not contribute to the smooth functioning of parliamentary institutions.

Another problem in constructing an effective democracy was the proliferation of parties, which was a natural result of the new freedom of political choice granted to the electorate after the long years of single-party rule. This sometimes contributed to indecisive election results. In Romania in 1990, 18 parties were represented in the National Assembly; in Poland in 1991, 29 parties were able to secure seats. One answer was sought in the introduction of a 4 per cent or 5 per cent hurdle which any party had to pass in order to secure representation; if it fell below this its votes would be distributed among the other parties. This reduced, but did not always eliminate, political fragmentation, which after all had deeper causes, such as the fact that many of these societies were fractured along confessional, ethnic and geographical lines. As a result many parties represented minority sections of the population which were actually too large to be filtered out by such methods.

In any case, an effective parliamentary democracy needs more than a formal set of rules governing elections and representation; it needs to be underpinned by a network of informal organizations, through which citizens can participate in, and influence, the running of their country. In the 1970s and 1980s the East European dissidents were well aware of this, which is one reason why they developed a concept of 'civil society'. The institutions of civil society were a way of overcoming the fragmentation of modern individuals, who are only linked via the market. They would also, it was hoped, bridge the gap between the individual and the state. But in the post-communist era a curious reversal came about: civil society, which had flourished in opposition to communism because it provided a refuge against the potentially all-powerful state, now withered and died. Attempts to resuscitate it, such as the Democratic Charter Movement in Hungary, were shortlived and unsuccessful.[47] Even in Poland, where civil society had been at its strongest in opposition to communism, the Solidarity movement went into decline after 1989, and has only recovered some of its standing by turning itself into a political party, and entering into alliances with more conventional political organizations.

Another essential feature of a functioning democracy is a system of constitutional courts. They are a check on those in power; but their decisions reflect their composition. This has often meant that they have felt able to stretch their interpretation of the constitution to include matters that would be regarded as extraneous in the West. The Hungarian Constitutional Court, for instance, took up the defence of the existing welfare provision against the March 1995 austerity measures of the Minister of Finance, Lajos Bokros, by ruling them unconstitutional.[48] In some countries constitutional courts have helped the cause of democracy by standing up courageously against authoritarian rulers. In Albania Judge Zef Brozi, despite being a former ally of President Berisha, ordered the release of Fatos Nano, the Socialist leader, whom Berisha had detained unconstitutionally; in Bulgaria the Constitutional Court was such a thorn in Zhan Videnov's flesh that he tried to throw it out of its offices.[49] One way of dealing with stubborn constitutional courts was to pack them with the ruler's cronies. In Romania Ion Iliescu made sure of the obedience of the court in this way. Another method used has been to get rid of the court altogether or just ignore its decisions. This has been seen more often in the CIS (for example Kazakhstan, Russia, Belarus). But there is one Eastern European example: Slovakia. Here the National Council, dominated by supporters of Prime Minister Mečiar, defied the Constitutional Court's ruling that František Gaulieder, a member of the HZDS who had quarrelled with Mečiar, should not have been expelled, and must be readmitted to the National Council (30 September 1997).

History Changes Gear

The democratic safeguards represented by the institutions of civil society cannot function effectively without the support of a free press, radio and television. Here, as in other cases, there is a distinction between the countries of East-Central Europe which are in the front line of applications to join the European Union and the rest. Authoritarian rulers in other parts of Eastern Europe, from Mečiar's Slovakia to Milošević's Serbia, have made sure they controlled at least the important parts of the media. Mečiar removed all unreliable officials from the controlling authorities of Slovak television and radio in November 1994 and replaced them with his own people.[50] He was described in May 1996 as 'one of the worst enemies of the press in Eastern Europe'.[51] In Bulgaria in June 1996 the BSP government dismissed the head of state television, Ivan Granitski, for not reporting favourably on its activities. In Romania the government controlled the major television station in 1996, although it did not control the press. In Albania, under the rule of Berisha, the government controlled all electronic media. In Croatia, under Tuđman, two liberal radio stations were closed down in 1996, although Radio 101 was saved by a big public campaign. Control of the media plays an important part in keeping Milošević in power in Serbia. The fall from power of authoritarian rulers and former *nomenklaturists* in the last two years in Bulgaria and Romania has brought some improvement in the situation in those countries at least.

CULTURAL CROSS-CURRENTS

During the communist period three competing cultures could be identified: the communist culture imposed from above, the indigenous cultural traditions, and the culture of the West. Western culture was present in communist Eastern Europe from the beginning because the cultural connections of the pre-1948 epoch could not be cut off completely, whatever Stalin ordered. Later, during the final communist decades, the modernization process itself inevitably brought Western influence as a by-product,[52] and the media revolution made it ever easier to smuggle in the products of Western culture, which progressively increased in attractiveness as the culture of communism withered and decayed. Culturally speaking, then, Eastern Europe was a very lively place in the final communist years. Side by side with the increasingly diverse cultural forms tolerated by the state ran an enthusiastically propagated culture of dissidence, which governments found it impossible to eradicate. In Poland the government simply gave up: the Minister of Culture admitted this in 1987: 'As for the so-called second circuit (that is dissident publications) we do not particularly support it, but we do not go out of our way to persecute it.'[53] Even so, communist parties always tried to exert as much control as possible over the cultural scene. It was therefore marked by a very high degree of state involvement and patronage. The state, in András Török's phrase, 'was Santa Claus for artists'.[54] In this sphere, as in all others, subsequent governments reacted by withdrawing from direct intervention. This meant both a steep fall in state expenditure on cultural production (for example in Poland spending on culture fell from 2 per cent of the total budget in 1989 to 0.7 per cent in 1993[55]) and a tendency to inactivity on the part of Ministers of Culture.[56] In Romania the main trend of the early 1990s was described as being one of cultural collapse, within the context of a decentralization carried through by Andrei Plesu, the philosopher who was Minister of Culture from December 1989 to September 1991. But economic factors have played an equally important part in the post-communist cultural decline. The tremendous price rises, and the universal fall in personal incomes, have resulted in a collapse in cinema, theatre and museum attendance, and a steep plunge in newspaper circulation.[57] There has admittedly been one very definite counter-trend: the spread of television, which opens the possibility of a different mode of cultural input.[58]

The initial impact of the fall of communism was to impose commercial pressures on artists and writers. These actually had a more adverse effect on cultural production than the fairly loose restrictions imposed during the late communist era; in addition, exposure to a superficially more attractive Western culture made many East Europeans into translators and imitators of readymade Western models instead of independent creators. Opponents of this trend, former dissidents rather than nostalgic communists, reacted with a bitterness made more acute by disappointment. This is how the modern Czech writer Jáchym Topol put his grievances about Western cultural imports in 1993:

> Nothing sleazy about money, the sleazeballs said, and they parcelled up the streets and squares to fit the size of their stands... Every lunatic with a couple of crowns, a world view and a vision set down in this city and founded organizations or movements or newspapers creating CULTURE or at least some cute little sect for the local suckers or some limited liability company, it's nothin' but paper, right?... and when the money ran out they vanished.[59]

The imitative nature of much modern Eastern European culture also reflects a growing trend towards Western ownership of the institutions that promote culture or provide resources to cultural producers. There have been very few attempts to obstruct the creeping Westernization of cultural institutions, because such a policy would run counter to the main aim of encouraging foreign investment. In Hungary in 1995 the institution in charge of the privatization process (the Hungarian State Privatization and Holding Company, or ÁPV Rt.) accepted a bid by a consortium of Hungarian musicians for the recording company Hungaroton, even though its value was less than half that offered by the international investor Polygram.[60] But this was a highly unusual step; the general rule is to sell to the highest bidder.

The first of the three competing cultures identified at the beginning of this section, communist culture imposed from above, disappeared almost without trace (the obvious symbol of this disappearance has been the systematic removal of monuments erected by the previous regime). The second culture, in contrast, the indigenous cultural tradition, has some chance of surviving into the new era, and either resisting Western influence or making a fruitful symbiosis with it. One aspect of the return to the roots of Eastern European culture is a strong religious revival, much encouraged by post-communist governments, which have been ready to spend money on reconstructing churches, mosques and synagogues.

In the case of religion, the cultural question shades into social psychology. The religious revival is an expression of a fear of the unknown and a need to believe. The same psychological mechanism has also worked to the advantage of financial swindlers. The Albanian pyramid schemes which collapsed in 1997 are the most notorious example,[61] but the same thing happened in Romania three years earlier. On 25 August 1994 Ion Stoica, the owner of Caritas Investments, was arrested for running a fraudulent pyramid scheme, in which two million Romanians had invested a total of $1 billion during the previous two years (he eventually received a six-year prison sentence).[62] 'Caritas' was a fraud with millenarian overtones; people invested in it partly because of a 'need for economic security' and a 'dream of making a financial killing', but mainly because they had 'faith' in the scheme.[63]

Another kind of credulity is belief in the blandishments of commercial advertisers. Advertising (except the political kind) was absent from communist Eastern Europe. Westernization has made it ubiquitous. Sometimes this is harmless, but not always. In the case of smoking, advertising campaigns, combined with the sophisticated image that the cigarette still possesses in the East, led to an increase in the proportion of adult males who smoke from 35 per cent to 37.5 per cent in the Czech Republic between 1989 and 1993, and from 40 per cent to 42 per cent in Poland between 1990 and 1992. Alan Lopez, of the World Health Organization, reported in 1994 that 'Eastern Europe has the highest lung-cancer rate in the world'. Needless to say, current lung-cancer rates can hardly be blamed on the most recent increases in tobacco consumption, but the warnings for future health have not been heeded. What changed with the fall of communism was not the habit of smoking, but the quality of the available cigarettes and the prestige of the brand smoked. The chairman of the well-known tobacco conglomerate BAT Industries, Patrick Sheehy, has commented, in reference to Eastern Europe, 'These are the most exciting times I have seen in the tobacco industry for the last forty years.'[64]

Cigarettes enter the post-communist world both legally and illegally. Their high size to value ratio means that they can be smuggled across borders very profitably. The smuggling of cigarettes has been particularly prevalent in areas where normal customs checks are made difficult by local wars. A piquant example comes from Montenegro. Smuggling across the border with Bosnia-Herzegovina was organized until 1995 by the Montenegrin leader Goran Rakočević; once a Bosnian Serb entity was in place (after the Dayton Agreement) Rakočević was pushed out of the trade by Momčilo Krajišnik, the Bosnian Serb leader. It is alleged that the fall of the pro-Milošević faction in the Montenegrin ruling party, the DPSCG, was Rakočević's revenge for this.

4 Hesitant Beginnings in South-Eastern Europe: a 'Balkan Lag'?

The countries of South-Eastern Europe (referred to traditionally as the Balkans, although Maria Todorova's strictures on the use of the term are well founded)[1] have tended to lag behind East-Central Europe in emancipating themselves from their communist past. This is partly (but only partly) a result of ethnic conflict, which is far more important here than further north. The one exception to this rule – former Czechoslovakia – in fact proves it, because the ethnic conflict is largely concentrated in Slovakia, which in several ways fits the Balkan pattern of the retention of communist-era structures.

Jean-Yves Potel refers in this connection to a 'special Balkan exit route from communism'.[2] In taking this route, he says, the groups which came to power after 1989 took their policies from the arsenal of local nationalism, using such powerful slogans as Greater Serbia, Greater Croatia, or Great Bulgaria. Potel's stress on the use of nationalist programmes by former members of the communist elite to retain control is somewhat one sided, however; there are several other distinct reasons why the Balkan transition was different.

First, South-Eastern Europe was relatively poor. We examined the historical reasons for this poverty earlier. Serbia was a partial exception, enjoying a relatively high GDP per capita ($2752) before the recent wars (although this had fallen by 1993 to $1710). The rest were all below $1700 per capita. The figure for Albania was a mere $562.[3] Second, there has since 1989 been a substantial flight of capital. Where there are any new rich, their money has tended to leave the homeland for securer pastures in the West. It has not been reinvested. This has reinforced the backwardness that was already historically determined. Third, a political culture of authoritarianism has been inherited from the Ottoman and Orthodox past, along with a tendency to define individuals collectively, through the community they belong to. It was this political culture that the communists made use of after 1945 as a means of securing their power.

Finally, there was practically no culture of opposition or dissidence in the Balkans. Linz and Stepan's quantitative study is eloquent on this point: Albania (0), Romania (2) and Bulgaria (13) bring up the rear in an index of dissidence dominated by East-Central Europe – Poland above all.[4] This lack of open resistance had the result that even where communist dictatorships were overthrown their successors behaved in the same way. Sali Berisha in Albania is an example of an anti-communist who came to power but continued to use the methods of the former communist regime. In Bulgaria the short-lived Dimitrov government was highly confrontational, while its successful opponents, the Bulgarian socialists, were far closer in their approach to their communist predecessors than their Polish or Hungarian counterparts. In Romania the head of the FSN, Ion Iliescu, was also dictatorial but in a more subtle way, dismissing ministers as scapegoats when his own policies met with opposition, setting up a Council of National Unity and ignoring it, and above all bringing in mobs of supporters to destroy resistance in the streets.

These points can most easily be demonstrated by a case-by-case examination of the Balkan countries, although we shall postpone discussion of the fate of the Yugoslav successor states to Chapter 5, because of the paramount role of ethnic conflict there. We begin with Bulgaria.

BULGARIA: POLITICAL CONFRONTATION AND POLARIZATION

Post-communist Bulgarian politics were marked by the following features: extremism, polarization, intra-party factionalism and an unstable equilibrium of forces. The instability had several causes, the main ones being the position of the Turkish minority and its party, which had its own agenda somewhat different from that of the rival Bulgarian factions, the existence of three rival trade union confederations, and the lack of any real opposition party (the chief opposition grouping, the Union of Democratic Forces, or SDS, was a federation of different groups and movements, not a unified party, and it fell prey to repeated splits, or the 'peeling off' of rival factions[5]). Faced with this situation, the highly respected President of Bulgaria, Zhelyu Zhelev, a philosopher and dissident under the communist regime, struggled to combine a commitment to constitutionalism and fair play with a sense of what was practicable at the given moment.

An extra feature, unique to Bulgaria, which is part of the explanation for the delay in the transition from communism there, was the country's psychological closeness to Russia. Bulgaria had been the Soviet Union's most faithful satellite for forty years; indeed, if we contemplate Tito's independent Yugoslavia, Ceauşescu's maverick Romania, and Hoxha's isolated Albania, it was its sole Balkan satellite. Even after 1989 it continued to be the case that what happened in Moscow was meaningful in Sofia in a sense in which it was not anywhere else in Eastern Europe. The August 1991 coup by Soviet hard-liners, which was seen elsewhere as a purely external event, was a vital matter for Bulgarian internal politics. The Bulgarian Socialist Party (BSP) was obliged to take an official position. When it issued an equivocal public statement, failing to condemn the coup, its leader Andrei Lukanov, who had been trying to push it in a more liberal direction, felt compelled to resign from the Party Presidium (19 August 1991). For the BSP's opponents in the Union of Democratic Forces (SDS) it was a matter of great importance that the Bulgarian ex-communists had wavered in August 1991 and that some of them seemed to favour the hard-line plotters who had moved against Gorbachev. In Bulgaria, then, the August 1991 coup was a political touchstone. For Bulgaria's neighbour Romania the events of August 1991 were naturally cause for concern, but nothing more, even though Romania was closer geographically to the Soviet Union.

The initial phase of Bulgarian post-communist politics was marked by three main features: the failure of the reform communist, or social democratic, faction to take over the Bulgarian Communist, now Socialist Party;[6] the continuing use by the Bulgarian communists and socialists of various unsavoury techniques to retain as much power as possible; and the ultimately successful counter-action of the democratic and anti-communist forces in Bulgarian society to these methods, using weapons of mass protest, such as strikes, demonstrations and sit-ins.

For Bulgaria, the starting point of the post-communist era was the fall of Todor Zhivkov, who had ruled the country for 35 years (10 November 1989). This was really a palace revolution by a more flexible faction of the communist party, led by Petur Mladenov, which wanted to retain as much power as possible in the new era but recognized that the old way of ruling the country would no longer work. Mladenov's strategy necessitated a move towards democracy. The road therefore lay open for the transformation of the various semi-legal pressure groups that had grown up in the final years of Zhivkov's authoritarian rule into legal and open political parties. The process was rapid. It was complete by the beginning of January 1990. Most of the former pressure groups combined together on 7 December 1989 to form the Union of Democratic Forces (SDS). This contained 17 groups altogether, but only 5 were of real importance: the Bulgarian Social Democratic Party, the environmental group Ekoglasnost, the Green Party, the independent labour confederation *Podkrepa*, and the Bulgarian Agrarian National Union – Nikola Petkov (BZNS–NP).[7] From the moment of its formation, the SDS pushed strongly for genuine change. At round table talks held on 3–4 January 1990 the SDS representatives demanded: the repeal of Article 1 of the constitution (which guaranteed the leading role of the communist party); a multiparty system; the dissolution of communist cells in the factories, the army and the police; and the postponement of general elections from June to November to give the opposition time to organize properly. All these points were granted except the postponement of elections. Despite this the Bulgarian Communist Party remained in control, though making certain necessary adjustments to the new era. The communists tried to have it both ways, pursuing a 'third road' between communism and capitalism. On 21 February 1990 they endorsed a manifesto which was both reformist and Marxist. According to the new Manifesto the Bulgarian Communist Party was 'a new type of modern Marxist party committed to democratic and humane socialism' and a 'socially oriented market economy'. In April the party changed its name to 'Bulgarian Socialist Party', after a referendum of party members had voted overwhelmingly in favour of this.

In the initial phase of the Bulgarian transition, then, the former ruling party directed the changes and dominated the political scene. This first phase ended with the resignation of Mladenov, who had been communist/socialist President of Bulgaria since November 1989. His removal was a result of the application by the SDS and their student allies of extra-parliamentary protest tactics, backed up by the pressure of more liberal elements within the BSP. The latter abandoned Mladenov on 6 July because the SDS managed to procure and show a videotape on which he was heard urging that tanks be brought in to crush an anti-communist demonstration held the previous December.

The fall of Mladenov was somewhat surprising in that it occurred shortly after his party had won Bulgaria's first post-communist elections (10 June 1990). Although marred by some violence, they were described as 'fair' by international observers, and resulted in a clear victory for the socialists (with 46.25 per cent of the vote and 211 out of 400 seats, giving them an absolute majority in the Assembly) over the SDS (38 per cent and 144 seats). The BSP won because it was supported by country people and pensioners who feared change; the strength of the SDS in the major cities was not enough to counterbalance these forces.[8] The SDS leaders, however, could not believe their defeat was a genuine result; they denied the validity of the June 1990 vote, and they spent the next year in an ultimately successful attempt to 'correct' it through popular pressure. Wolfgang Höpken has caught the implicit paradox well: in Bulgaria the political transition took place in reverse. Only after the end of communism did the country begin 'to catch up on the phase of extra-parliamentary confrontation which in the countries of East-Central Europe had preceded the fall of the communist party and free elections'.[9] The videotape campaign against President Mladenov was the first step. It was followed by the election as President of SDS member Zhelyu Zhelev under the continuing pressure of a student encampment in the centre of the capital of Bulgaria, Sofia. The students called this camp 'the city of truth'. The opposition demonstrations of the summer of 1990 were, however, marred by an act of vandalism: the BSP headquarters building was set on fire (26 August 1990), allegedly at the instigation of Konstantin Trenchev, leader of the non-communist trade union federation *Podkrepa*.

The executive branch of the government was still in the hands of the BSP at this stage. The Prime Minister was Andrei Lukanov, leader of a more liberal faction of the party, who since first being appointed (February 1990) had repeatedly tried to get the SDS to enter a coalition but always met with a refusal. The SDS leaders Petur Beron (until December 1990) and Filip Dimitrov (after December) were playing for high stakes throughout; in this they were unusual, as practically everywhere else in Eastern Europe liberal and democratic forces initially ruled in coalition with their communist rivals, only pushing them out later. Here a complete and immediate surrender of power was demanded, despite the minority position of the SDS in the Bulgarian parliament. It was in line with this policy of negativity and boycott that the SDS opposed Lukanov's radical economic reform programme of 10 October, which was largely in line with IMF recommendations, covering as it did small-scale privatization, land reform, price liberalization and measures to encourage foreign investment. The reform, Lukanov said, would 'increase inflation and unemployment', but it 'had to be carried through'. He would prefer an all-party coalition to do this. The SDS response was to renew its extra-parliamentary pressure, starting with a boycott of parliament by all democratic deputies after it had lost a no-confidence motion (23 November), followed by a general strike call from *Podkrepa*, student sit-ins and the erection of barricades on the streets of the capital (28 November).

At this point the old-style socialist-run trade union, now renamed the Confederation of the Independent Trade Unions of Bulgaria (CITUB), a giant organization which dwarfed the anti-communist *Podkrepa* federation (and which *Podkrepa* refused to join in March 1990 precisely because it was viewed as a survival of the communist era) began to free itself from the tutelage of the BSP, rather as the OPZZ had done in Poland when it joined the 1988 strike movement. In the general strike of November 1990 the CITUB stood shoulder to shoulder with *Podkrepa*. Its revolt was more on economic than political grounds, and the union was careful to make this distinction by staying out on strike until 6 December, although the strictly political issue had already been settled on 30 November with the resignation of the Lukanov government.

Lukanov's resignation was the first of a series of BSP surrenders to extra-parliamentary pressure. He did not feel strong enough to resist. Admittedly, he had in his favour an absolute majority of parliamentary seats gained in an internationally recognized election held a few months earlier! He did not, however, have the capital city on his side (the division between the 'blue' cities and the 'red' countryside was clearly marked in this and subsequent elections). Nor did he have the support of the organized working class: the two biggest trade union federations stood in opposition. Students, and young people in general, were against him as well. It was agreed that fresh elections would be held within a year; in the meantime a transitional cabinet was set up under Dimitur Popov, a judge without party affiliations (20 December 1990). Popov presided over a cabinet containing the two polar opposites of Bulgarian politics, the SDS and the BSP, with a sprinkling of Agrarian Party (BZNS–NP) and non-party ministers sitting beside them. In practice the Popov cabinet was dominated by the SDS.[10] The period of political transition in Bulgaria had come to an end. It looked as if Bulgaria had made up the ground lost in the previous year. But fresh surprises were to follow. We shall deal with the sequel in Chapter 8.

ROMANIA: THE MANIPULATIVE POLITICS OF ION ILIESCU

Divergent views have been held as to whether Romania is one of the Balkan countries. Uncertainty on this point is reflected in an even division of geographical opinion. Hall and Danta report that out of 13 geographies of the Balkans surveyed by them 6 included Romania, 6 excluded it, and 1 included the east but not the west of the country.[11] Romania's Balkan character may be in doubt, but it certainly suffered after 1989 from what we have described as the 'Balkan lag'. At the end of that year a 'revolution' removed one small sector of the communist elite (the Ceauşescus and their circle) to the advantage of the major part of it, which immediately organized itself as the National Salvation Front (FSN). We cannot be certain of the precise composition of the Front, as this was kept secret, but the consensus is that it was dominated by former communists. Moreover, it was similar in structure to the communist party. The main decisions were made, not by the 145-strong Council of the Front, but by an Executive Office of 11 people, 10 of whom were members of the former *nomenklatura*, headed by Ion Iliescu. There was just one outsider, Ion Caramitru.[12]

This situation was a disappointment to many of those who participated in the revolution of December 1989; they had risked their lives in the expectation that the ensuing changes would go further than the mere overthrow of the tyrant. This applied particularly to the students, whose protests against the new regime grew from January 1990 onwards when the true character of the FSN started to be apparent. It also became clear at this time that the Front was not proposing to step gracefully off the stage having accomplished the removal of the Ceauşescus, but intended rather to take part in the forthcoming elections as a political party.[13] The student protesters were backed up by some former dissidents who had initially joined the FSN with high hopes of political change and now left it (Doina Cornea, veteran dissident and leader of the protests of the 1980s against Ceauşescu's 'systematization' plans[14] resigned on 23 January; Dumitriu Mazilu, first vice-president, resigned on 26 January after complaining of 'Stalinist campaigning' by the Front; the poetess Ana Blandiana left on 31 January).

The political battle-lines had already been drawn up, and appropriate methods of struggle established, by the end of January. The anti-FSN faction relied on its strong presence in the capital, Bucharest, and mounted a series of demonstrations which culminated on 18 February in a mass invasion of the FSN's headquarters by 20 000 demonstrators demanding that it relinquish power; but the FSN had plenty of physical support too, and it could call on some compact groups of men closely connected to the former regime. Industrial workers, for instance, were given time off to demonstrate in favour of the FSN; they broke into the offices of two recently re-founded opposition political parties, the National Liberals (PNL) and the Christian Democratic National Peasants' Party (PNTCD) on 29 January. The liberal leader, Radu Campeanu, had to escape from his office through a side window.[15] The miners of the Jiu Valley and Maramureş were especially dangerous to the opposition, and the new regime exploited them from the very beginning. They were encouraged to come to Bucharest to smash up opposition meetings; they arrived *en masse* on 19 February (allegedly to take revenge for the sacking of the FSN offices by anti-communist protesters the day before). Iliescu's other method of staying in power, also highly effective, was to manipulate the new institutions from within. A Provisional Council of National Unity was set up as a power-sharing mini-parliament on 1 February. This looked like a concession to the opposition, but the predominance of the FSN was ensured by guaranteeing 90 seats on the Council to a hand-picked group of 'people who were active in the revolution of 1989', and by adding members of various ethnic minority organizations which were simply FSN satellites. The composition of the Provisional Council's Executive Bureau reflected this built-in FSN majority; it was headed by Ion Iliescu, and the two vice-presidents were also members of the FSN. The impression of continuity was strengthened by the re-emergence of the secret police, the supposedly disbanded *Securitate* (April 1990). This former instrument of Ceauşescu's dictatorship was now called the Romanian Intelligence Service, but its methods did not change and it was run by a former *Securitate* colonel, Virgil Magureanu.[16]

Despite the ultimate control exercised by the FSN, a lively spectrum of political opinion and activity quickly developed in Romania. We have already noted the re-emergence of two of the pre-1947 parties, the National Liberals and the PNTCD; and new parties were formed to represent various pressure groups, such as the environmentalists. The latter formed two rival groups, the Romanian Ecological Movement and the Romanian Ecological Party. The Hungarian ethnic minority lined up behind the Hungarian Democratic Union of Romania (UDMR), under the honorary presidency of Bishop László Tökés, who was in a sense the founding father of the 1989 Revolution, and the advocate of friendship and democratic co-operation between the two major nations living in Transylvania. To the forces of Romanian nationalism this was a threatening development, and they reacted quickly. Romanian Cradle (VR) was formed in February 1990 to 'defend Romanian unity' and fight against the 'dilution of national culture'.[17] From it emerged the Party of Romanian National Unity (PUNR), which was set up in May 1990. The Greater Romania Party (PRM) started off as a group of journalists writing for a nationalist journal, *România Mare*, which began to appear in June 1990, and claimed a circulation of 600 000. The PRM developed into a political party in May 1991.

The activities of the Romanian nationalists soured the atmosphere of concord between Hungarians and Romanians which had prevailed in the early days of the revolution, when members of both ethnic groups had fought jointly against the Ceauşescu regime. In March 1990, in Tîrgu Mureş, a town which was a centre of the Hungarian minority community, members of Romanian Cradle attacked a peaceful Hungarian demonstration; the FSN government was not directly responsible for this act of violence, but it tried to turn the events to its own electoral advantage by blaming the clashes on Hungarians from across the border (21 March). Nevertheless, it had no wish to exacerbate the situation on the ground, and it facilitated talks between the rival groups which ended in a call for mutual respect by both sides (24 March). This defused the situation.

Elections had been set for May 1990. The FSN was in a good position to win them. The electoral law of 14 March required that political activity be based on respect for national independence, sovereignty, integrity and dignity; the FSN made effective use of this anti-democratic provision. It claimed that opposition groups had links outside the country, that many were returned exiles, and that they would sell Romania to foreigners. Using its control of the mass media, the FSN also appealed to the conservative sentiments of people outside Bucharest, pointing out that the privatization and restitution policies advocated by the opposition would harm most ordinary people, bringing unemployment and a fall in the standard of living. The tactic worked. The FSN won the elections of 20 May 1990 very easily, gaining 66.3 per cent of the vote; Iliescu won a simultaneous presidential election with 86 per cent. Participation was high (at 86 per cent of the electorate). International observers pronounced the election fair, and indeed a poll of voting intentions taken in April had indicated that 57 per cent of those polled would vote for the FSN. So this was a genuine victory of country over town, of the provinces over the capital city, of fear of the unknown over hope for the future.

The opposition was also weakened by its extreme fragmentation: 72 parties took part in the elections, and 18 of them gained seats in the National Assembly. It was typical of this situation that the second-largest party was not even ethnically Romanian: this was Tökés's Hungarian Democratic Union (UDMR), which gained 7.2 per cent of the vote. Even the most successful ethnically Romanian opposition parties garnered tiny percentages of the vote: the National Liberals got 6.4 per cent, the PNTCD and the Romanian Ecological Movement were both on 2.6 per cent.

An attempt by the opposition to protest against this unwelcome electoral verdict by launching mass demonstrations in the centre of

Bucharest (11 June) was met with extreme measures by Iliescu. He accused the protesters of trying to overthrow the elected government by 'legionary methods' (this was a historical reference to the activities of the Romanian Fascists of the 1930s, the Legion of the Archangel Michael, or Iron Guard), and he called on his friends the miners of the Jiu Valley again. They too used 'legionary methods'! Between 13 and 15 June 7000 miners rampaged through the streets of Bucharest killing and maiming, leaving behind 6 people dead and 502 injured. The combination of rhetoric and brute force by which the FSN retained power in 1990 had an uncanny resemblance to communist tactics back in 1945, when the 'National Democratic' (in fact communist) Front fought street battles to gain power. The difference (an important one) was that Soviet pressure was no longer a factor in the situation.[18]

So the FSN was able to fight off the first challenge to its authority. It was helped in this by the disunity of the opposition. In fact half of the anti-FSN coalition – the Romanian nationalist camp – was not really an opposition at all, more a pressure group aimed at encouraging the FSN to take a harder line against the Hungarian minority. The Romanian nationalists could be bought off by Iliescu without difficulty.

Having fixed itself firmly in power, the FSN government, under its prime minister Petre Roman, now faced the task of dealing with the economic situation inherited from Ceauşescu. It shared the commitment to a market economy that was common ground throughout Eastern Europe, but it was held back by its gradualist approach, and a readiness to give way to pressure from the streets (provided it was non-political). An attempt made in November 1990 to cut subsidies and to de-control the prices of consumer goods (they were set to rise by 120 per cent) gave rise to two months of demonstrations, which forced the postponement of the planned price increases. The demonstrations were co-ordinated by the newly formed Civic Alliance, an umbrella group of opposition parties under Nicolae Manulescu, which, although in favour of a free market economy, did not want it to be introduced by the FSN government. There were simultaneous anti-government protests in Timişoara, the town where the 1989 revolution had started. Bishop Tökés, hero of 1989, called for a 'second revolution'. This time, he said, it must be 'a peaceful, Christian one'.

As a result of Roman's surrender to pressure from the Civic Alliance, Romania experienced a 5.4 per cent increase in real wages in 1990, while GDP was declining by 5.6 per cent, and industrial production by 20 per cent. Inflation was low, at 6 per cent, and unemployment was very low, at 1 per cent. These figures, favourable as they sounded in some respects, were typical of an economy that had not yet entered the period of transition. Privatization, too, was practically nonexistent. A few months later, however, the prime minister again tried to move forward.

His programme, which envisaged a 'social democratic party committed to the market economy', was adopted overwhelmingly in March 1991 at the FSN Congress,[19] and he felt able to begin again with price liberalization (1 April). The government said that people would be 30 per cent worse off in real terms, but that there would be compensatory wage increases and a ceiling of 125 per cent on increases in food prices. In fact in August the National Statistical Commission reported that the increase over October 1990 was 144 per cent. Unemployment rose to 3 per cent. Real wages fell by 18 per cent. By the end of the year inflation was running at 170 per cent. The reaction of the two main trade unions, CNSLR-Frăţia and Cartelul Alfa, was to demand Roman's resignation (June 1991); in September the Jiu Valley miners went on strike, returning to Bucharest, where this time, in an astounding reversal of alliances, they fought violent street battles with the police side by side with the student protesters they had beaten up the year before. Roman took the fall for his economic reforms, being replaced by Theodor Stolojan on 1 October. Stolojan persuaded the miners to go home, and moderated Roman's policies, though he did not reverse them. The currency was made convertible, but continued state control of the prices of basic necessities until May 1992 was promised. Talks between the government and the trade unions over the demand for the establishment of a minimum wage ended in deadlock (February 1992). The Stolojan government began at last to move ahead with privatization, partly for the usual reasons (in order to secure a loan from the IMF). On 1 June 1992 a voucher privatization scheme was introduced, although safeguards were built in to make sure that the state retained control of the larger enterprises. Seventy per cent of the capital in the 6000 enterprises to be sold off was vested in 'a state ownership fund'. The other 30 per cent was distributed to the public in the form of vouchers. The first ever Romanian privatization took place in August, when Vranco Textiles was sold to the Italian firm Incom.

The FSN was now split down the middle over the future pace of reform. Roman stayed in control formally at a national convention held in March 1992, receiving the support of 63 per cent of the delegates, but the opponents of radical reform formed their own party in April 1992, the 'FSN – 22 December' (which was soon renamed the Democratic National Salvation Front, or FDSN).[20] This was essentially President

Iliescu's faction. A fierce four-cornered political battle raged throughout the summer between the two successors to the FSN, the opposition's newly formed Democratic Convention (CDR),[21] and the various Romanian nationalist groupings. It culminated in the elections of September 1992, which were a victory for Iliescu and his party, the FDSN. In the voting for the Lower House of the Romanian parliament, the Chamber of Deputies, the FDSN secured 27.7 per cent against the CDR's 20.0 per cent and the 10.2 per cent of the 'official' FSN under Roman; in the simultaneous presidential election Iliescu won the first round with a relative majority of 47 per cent against the 31 per cent of the CDR candidate, Emil Constantinescu. He was deprived of an absolute majority by the intervention of the nationalist Gheorghe Funar, who received 11 per cent.[22] But he won the second round with a majority of 61 per cent against Constantinescu's 39 per cent.

The Democratic Convention, an alliance of 18 parties of the centre and right which should have overcome the fragmentation of opposition forces, was defeated for two reasons: it engaged in too much negative campaigning, stressing the need to settle accounts with communism, the danger from a renewed *Securitate* and the neo-communist character of the FDSN; and, more important, it gave the impression of wanting to turn the clock back to 1944. Its candidates were often old men, veteran exiles belonging to the National Peasant Party (one of the historic Romanian parties trying to make a comeback);[23] it was too close to the monarchy, an institution most Romanians rejected; its programme of restitution looked likely to return power to the big landowners.[24] In addition, the victory of Iliescu in the second round (11 October 1992) owed much to the support of the extreme right, once their candidate Gheorghe Funar had been eliminated.

Despite its electoral success, the FDSN did not have enough parliamentary seats to rule by itself. The survival of the resulting minority cabinet depended on the toleration of the extreme left Socialist Party of Labour (with 13 seats), and the two extreme right parties, Funar's PUNR (30 seats) and Tudor's *România Mare* (16 seats). The new prime minister was Nicolae Văcăroiu, an economist whose *nomenklatura* background was sufficiently indicated by his long service on the State Planning Commission under Ceaușescu. Moreover, he had been removed from Roman's government in 1990 for opposing price liberalization. Văcăroiu announced that while reforms would continue 'the government would assume special responsibility for the social costs of that process'. Moreover, the state, he asserted, 'must intensify its control over the enterprises'. In other words, any reforms would be subject to the veto of two important pressure groups, the trade unions and the industrial managers.

For over a year the Văcăroiu government drifted. It was caught between the requirements of the IMF, which demanded 'progress in restructuring state enterprises and curbing inflation', and the pressure of the trade unions, which, although they were sharply divided politically between supporters and opponents of communist-era structures, were able to combine in defence of the workers' standard of living and guaranteed employment. And in Romania the workers certainly needed defending, as the following stark figures demonstrate. Wage rises consistently failed to match the rocketing inflation of these years. The real wage figures for 1991, 1992 and 1993 showed falls of 53.2 per cent, 40.9 per cent, and 54.0 per cent; there was nothing worse than this in the whole of Eastern Europe at any time during the period of transition.[25] Unemployment also rose, from 3 per cent in 1991 to 10.2 per cent in 1993.

On 12 April 1993 strikes against price rises took place, organized by CNSLR-Frăţia, the largest trade union, which normally supported the government; four smaller anti-government trade unions joined it later in the month in calling for a general strike. Agreement on cancellation of the strike was obtained by an increase in the minimum wage and wage increases based on the rising cost of living (7 May). This in turn brought a severe rebuke from the IMF (23 July) and of course no more loans were forthcoming. On 2 August the Jiu Valley miners struck work, demanding an immediate doubling of their wages; almost as much was granted to them on 11 August. Mass demonstrations were organized on 18 and 19 November by the trade unions in support of an Eleven Point Programme, which combined various contradictory demands. They wanted further wage increases, but they also wanted more rapid economic reform, quicker privatization and the restructuring of the state sector.[26] Further demonstrations were called on 21 December 1993 to demand the resignation of the prime minister. Finally, on 28 January 1994 one million workers took part in a 'warning strike' organized by the CNSLR-Frăţia, the Alfa-Cartel and the National Trade Union Bloc (BNS). The same contradictory demands were put forward: improved wages and social security payments side-by-side with rapid economic reform.

President Iliescu was prepared to concede the latter but not the former. On 9 February 1994 he instructed his government to prepare a package of economic reforms combining austerity and privatization, which would satisfy the IMF and thereby gain the much needed loan and with it the seal of international approval. To survive, the government would need to face down the internal opposition. It successfully rode out a militant miners' strike (on 16 February the miners stormed the head office of the lignite company in the Jiu Valley) and a general strike (28 February–1 March) called by the miners, the Alfa-Cartel and CNSLR-Frăţia. Once again, the weak point of the trade union opposition was its programmatic inconsistency. Demands for 'protection of workers' rights', 'social security' and 'collective labour contracts' sat uneasily alongside calls for 'privatization' and 'passing the 1994 budget'. Opposition also came from the Agrarian Democratic Party, which represented a new class of small private farmers. They were up in arms about a land tax that was part of the IMF package. The Văcăroiu government made the same reply to all protesters: it was implementing necessary reforms, and temporary sacrifices would have to be made by some people. It could also point to the confidence now displayed by the international financial institutions: the IMF approved a credit of $454 million on 11 May, to be followed by smaller sums from the European Community and the World Bank.

The other half of President Iliescu's strategy was to bring the extreme left and extreme right on board, thereby weakening the opposition. The Văcăroiu government survived a vote of no confidence on 30 June with extreme right backing; in return two members of Funar's party, Valeriu Tabaru and Adrian Turica, were appointed ministers (18 August). The protests fizzled out and political stability returned; President Iliescu and his post-communist faction of the FSN had, it seemed, conducted an about-face on economic policy without losing power. It took several years before the opposition was able to combine and defeat him; we shall examine how this happened in Chapter 8.

ALBANIA: THE IMPOSSIBILITY OF ESCAPE

On the eve of the transition from communism Albania was in many ways unique in Europe. It was completely isolated internationally, having quarrelled first with Yugoslavia, then with the Soviet Union and then with China. Its people were so poor, despite the policy of economic growth its communist rulers claimed to have pursued for 45 years, that their per capita GDP in the 1990s placed them firmly in the Asian or African category of low-income countries. There was also very little dissent within the country, and no inclination on the part of the ruling communist party to follow the example of the Gorbachev reforms in the Soviet Union.

The revolutions of 1989 appeared to pass Albania by, but the year 1990 saw the beginnings of a hesitant movement towards economic liberalization. President Ramiz Alia (who had succeeded Enver Hoxha, the first leader of Albanian communism, in 1985) decided that the only way to survive into the new era which appeared to be dawning was to start reforms. In February 1990 a plenum of the Central Committee of the ruling party (the Party of Labour of Albania, or PPSH) gave local authorities and enterprises greater economic autonomy, and allowed the collective farmers to sell their surplus product freely.[27] Political liberalization followed. In November 1990 Alia said that the PPSH would give up its monopoly of power, hitherto anchored in the constitution; this concession was made against the background of the first manifestation of public unrest since 1945. There were continuous anti-government demonstrations by student dissidents in Tirana and other major towns from December onwards; there were divisions on the communist party's Central Committee about the appropriate reaction to such activities, especially when demonstrators vandalized the Enver Hoxha officers' club (February 1991). Some party leaders favoured repression. Alia's solution was different. He maintained order by imposing presidential rule, but he conceded all the demonstrators' demands.[28] Thenceforward, opposition parties were allowed to function openly, and at the end of December a new, democratic constitution was issued. This set up a combined parliamentary and presidential system. The leading role of the Party of Labour was no longer mentioned. Elections held under the new constitution took place on 31 March 1991, with second and third rounds on 7 and 14 April. They resulted in a victory for the ruling party. The communists gained 56.2 per cent of the vote, against the 38.7 per cent who supported the Democratic Party (PDSH), the opposition movement recently founded by Professor Gramoz Pashko and Dr Sali Berisha.

This result was not fraudulent, despite claims made at the time by the Democrats. The explanation for their failure lay in the lack of any parliamentary tradition and the very short interval between the end of Stalinist rule and the elections.[29] As the most famous Albanian writer Ismail Kadaré put it: 'It is not the same thing to emerge from post-Stalinism as from Stalinism. Stalin died in 1953 for the rest of Eastern Europe, but for Albania he died very recently.' A further factor was the fear of change felt by the rural population in particular. The verdict of the urban population was decisively in favour of the PDSH: but its 65 per cent of the urban vote was outweighed by the strong support the former communists received in the country districts.

What followed, as in Bulgaria and Romania, was a sustained attempt by the Democrats of the cities to 'correct' by street pressure the verdict delivered at the ballot box by the countryside. On 2 April anti-communist rioters stormed the Party of Labour's headquarters in the northern city of Shkodër; they also beat up peasants who had come into town to sell their produce![30] The initial reaction of President Alia (who had been elected to this post by the new People's Assembly, which the opposition was boycotting) was to denounce the protests and demonstrations and resist the call to resign. But the prime minister he had appointed, a young economist called Fatos Nano, did not last long: a general strike forced his removal (4 June 1991). A coalition of all the parties was set up under Ylli Bufi. There were 12 PPSH members in the cabinet (including the prime minister), 7 Democrats and 5 from smaller parties. Bufi's policy was to 'continue the democratization' and 'restore stability'. He did not really succeed in either aim. Strikes and protests continued, many desperate people simply fled the country. More would have left, but there was nowhere for them to go. In September a package of economic and financial reforms was announced, including privatization and the distribution of some collective farm land to peasant families (which resulted in a disorganized land-grab during the autumn of 1991). The measures did not go far enough; Sali Berisha, who had in the meantime been elected head of the Democratic Party, called for the withdrawal of his party's ministers from the government, charging the Socialists[31] with deliberate obstruction of the reform process. Bufi, who had been described as a 'dictator' by Berisha, was compelled to resign (6 December). His replacement was Vilson Ahmeti, a former top PPSH official and Minister of Food, but now a non-party man.

Finally Alia conceded fresh elections. When these were held (22 and 29 March 1992) they resulted in a tremendous victory for the Democratic Party. It won 62 per cent of the vote and 92 out of the 140 seats in the People's Assembly; the Socialist Party won only 25 per cent and 38 seats. The PDSH's improved organization was one reason for the victory; another reason was the clear preference expressed by United States diplomats. The US Ambassador, William Ryerson, appeared on Democratic Party platforms, and promised American aid for the new Albania. But the poll itself was accepted as valid by international observers.[32] The change to Democratic Party rule was completed a few days later by the election of Dr Sali Berisha, a heart surgeon and former communist, who originated from Tropoja in the far north of the country, as president in succession to Alia. He appointed as prime minister

Alexander Meksi, a structural engineer and expert on Byzantine architecture, who had no political background.

Meksi set up a coalition cabinet dominated by the Democrats (13 April). His programme was to catch up on the reforms that had already been proceeding for two years in the rest of Eastern Europe. Privatization was to be pursued energetically, food prices were to be freed of controls, unemployment benefits were to be reduced below the existing level of 80 per cent of the previous wage. These measures were rewarded by an immediate IMF loan of $35 million, followed by a promise of a further $60 million secured by Berisha on a trip to the United States (June 1992). For the population, however, they brought little relief. A 500 per cent rise in the price of bread on 1 July, followed by the discontinuation of the unemployment benefit paid to laid off workers in the state sector, sparked off another wave of attempted emigrations. The Democrats' reaction was to treat these acts of desperation as a public order problem, and to blame the former communists for stirring up the people. Harsh measures were taken to break up strikes and protests; in December a strike and mine occupation by chrome miners at Bulquize, near the Yugoslav border, was ended by the threat to dynamite the mineshaft.[33] The communist-era secret police, the *Sigurimi*, was replaced by a new organization, Shërbimi Informativ Kombëtar (National Information Service) (SHIK), with many of the same personnel, and inspiring similar terror. Berisha was launched on an authoritarian course which belied the title of his party; this met with criticism from some Democrats, including Gramoz Pashko, who was expelled by Berisha for 'trying to impose his ideas on the whole party'. In November 1992 Pashko set up a rival party, the Democratic Alliance. Berisha, however, remained in control of Albania. He built a network of support which had, it is claimed, all the characteristics of a clan, except that it was based on political and mafia connections, rather than old-fashioned blood relationships.[34] The methods he used to stay in power gave increasing cause for concern both within the country and internationally.

5 National Minorities and Ethnic Conflict

Significant national minorities have long been present almost everywhere in Eastern Europe.[1] Leaving aside former Yugoslavia for the moment, the main examples are: Hungarians in Slovakia and Romania, Turks in Bulgaria, Russians in the three Baltic states,[2] Jews in Hungary,[3] and communities of Roma scattered over most of the region.[4] The existence of minorities has not given rise to ethnic conflict necessarily and ineluctably, although everywhere there have been extremist groups which have endeavoured to stir it up by advancing absurdly exaggerated national demands. The re-emergence of such groups was one of the by-products of the free market in political ideas opened up by the revolutions of 1989. The national minorities and the competing nationalist parties and movements in Eastern Europe in the early 1990s have been examined in great detail, and very comprehensively, by Janusz Bugajski.[5] Rather than replicate this work here, I shall instead indicate the possible areas of conflict, the most significant national minorities, and the degree of political and social instability they produced, or suffered.

TOUCHSTONES OF ETHNICITY AND SYMBOLS UNDER DISPUTE

Almost immediately after the collapse of communism, ethnic issues began to come to the surface, or, where they were already visible, to become more significant. These issues fall under six headings.

First, the immigration of ethnic groups and protests against it. This could occur both between countries and within them. Migration between countries (international migration) has generally been on a small scale. Examples are the movement of Roma from one country to another, and the gradual exodus of ethnic Russians from the Baltic States. The largest population movements have taken place in South-Eastern Europe. Ethnic Turks have left Bulgaria, Greeks and Albanians have left Albania and the many victims of 'ethnic cleansing' have been forced across borders in former Yugoslavia. Domestic migration is occasionally an issue, as in Romania, where the continuing flow of ethnic Romanians to Transylvania is seen as threatening by some members of the local Hungarian minority.

Second, censuses. Where questions of ethnicity are involved these often cease to be exercises in scientific demography and become instead emotionally charged attempts to count up potential supporters of the national cause. In Romania, the Hungarian minority complained that the January 1992 census was unfair because it subdivided them into five ethnic groups, thus denying their status as a single nation.[6] In Bosnia and Herzegovina, the census of 1991 was regarded as an election, and the election of 1996 turned into a census: each time, the three major ethnic groups lined up their supporters.

Third, the public use of national languages. Road and railway signs were a typical source of discord as early as the nineteenth century, and the issue has resurfaced with a vengeance since 1989. In Croatia the conflict was between the Roman alphabet (used by Croats) and the Cyrillic alphabet (used by Serbs); in Romania the first thing the newly elected Romanian nationalist mayor of Cluj-Napoca, Gheorghe Funar, did was to order the removal of Hungarian language road signs from his city (March 1992); in Slovakia there has been continuous conflict over the local use of Hungarian road and railway signs.

Fourth, the protection or destruction of public monuments. Here is another Romanian example: 'archaeological excavations' ordered by Funar threatened to undermine a local statue of King Matthias of Hungary; in this case they were halted (8 July 1994) then resumed (2 August) after a promise that the statue would not be damaged.

Fifth, flying the national flag. In Romania the Chamber of Deputies voted on 9 November 1994 to impose a three year prison sentence on anyone flying the national flag of other states. This was clearly directed against the Hungarian minority. They were also prohibited from singing the Hungarian national anthem.

Sixth, the recovery and reinterpretation of the national past. In some cases this process involved whitewashing past regimes which had acted brutally against local ethnic minorities; their sensitivities were naturally offended by these measures. In Slovakia, for example, there was a campaign to rehabilitate the wartime regime of Monsignor Josef Tiso, which was a cause for concern among both Hungarians and Jews; in Croatia the same was done for Ante Pavelić and the Croat state set up during the Second World War as a Nazi satellite. This was very disturbing for Serbs, and not just them, since Pavelić, apart from butchering Serbs, also collaborated in the holocaust of the Jews. A decision to rename a Zagreb street in honour of Mile Budek,

Minister of Culture under Pavelić, was abandoned under strong US pressure.[7]

REASONS FOR CONFLICT

We now need to explain why these ethnic issues and activities have often given rise to conflict rather than being treated in a spirit of co-operation and tolerance. The first reason is the legacy of the past. This has in many cases taken the very physical and concrete form of what A.J. Motyl calls 'abandoned brethren, former imperial populations stranded on the periphery'.[8] For former Yugoslavia, this means Serbs; for the former Soviet Union, Russians. We shall examine the Yugoslav situation in detail later on, but here the contrast needs to be underlined between the decision of the Serbian government under Slobodan Milošević to identify itself completely with the defence of its co-nationals in the newly independent states of Croatia and Bosnia, and the attitude of the Russian government under Boris Yeltsin, which was far more ambiguous.

One of the distinctive elements of Yeltsin's approach, which contrasted with Gorbachev's in 1991, was to support the aspirations of almost all the non-Russians for independence, even where this might damage the interests of local ethnically Russian groups. This was his great historical contribution to the relatively peaceful unravelling of the Soviet Empire; only one of the conflicts of the closing days of the Empire – the war in Moldova – involved Russians as principals. That is not to say that post-imperial Russia has entirely dissociated itself from the ethnic Russians in other states. In fact the 1990s saw an increasing tendency on the part of Russian policy-makers to concern themselves with the fate of Russians in the 'near abroad'. But so far this has stayed within the bounds of peaceful pressure, except in Chechnia, which the Russian government regards as part of Russia.

There are many other examples of 'abandoned brethren' left over from former empires, but in most cases the relevant nation was too small, or too weak, or simply did not have the political will, to make strong claims on their behalf. The exception here was Croatia, where the Croats did make claims on behalf of co-nationals in Bosnia-Herzegovina, and with success. In general, though, this did not happen. Albania has carefully avoided laying claim to Kosovo; Hungary has never associated itself with calls for Hungarian autonomy within Romania, let alone separatism; Bulgaria has left Macedonia alone.

The second source of ethnic conflict that should be mentioned is rival claims to the same territory, based on history, real or imagined, or on the existence of ethnically mixed populations. These points only become relevant when the decision is made to set up a nation-state where none existed before; without this decision the conflict remains merely latent. The only new nation-states set up in Eastern Europe have arisen out of former Yugoslavia (the one exception here, Slovakia, is not subject to rival claims, since the verdict of history has gone against Hungary and only a lunatic fringe there thinks this can be reversed).

Ethnic conflict has led to extremely violent clashes in many parts of the former Soviet Union; but in Eastern Europe this has been much rarer. Leaving aside racist attacks, generally against Roma but in Romania in 1990 against the Hungarian minority – these attacks, though unpleasant, are not likely to lead to full-scale civil war – the only cases of extreme violence have occurred in former Yugoslavia, and most of this chapter will inevitably revolve around that unhappy country.

THE COLLAPSE OF YUGOSLAVIA AND THE YUGOSLAV CIVIL WARS

There were plenty of voices raised after the event to suggest that the disintegration of Yugoslavia was an inevitable process, resulting from the artificiality of the state. This is certainly a seductive point of view. We saw earlier that there were ethnic conflicts in Yugoslavia's past as well as its present and that the communists swept the issue under the carpet by suppressing any open attempt to separate the ethnic groups that made up the country. It was very easy after the event to dismiss the idea of Yugoslavia as a 'fantasy' or an 'illusion' on the basis that there was no such thing as a Yugoslav nation,[9] or, putting it even more strongly, to say that Yugoslavia had to break up because it bestrode 'historic fault lines between three civilizations' (Western Catholic, Eastern Orthodox and Muslim).[10] This view has also been taken by some historically inclined local leaders. Franjo Tudman, for instance, told a reporter in 1991 that 'Croats belong to a different culture, a different civilization from the Serbs. Croats are part of Western Europe, part of the Mediterranean tradition. The Serbs belong to the East. They are Eastern peoples, like the Turks and the Albanians.'[11]

But if we take a close look at the processes at work in the break-up of Yugoslavia we see a number of contingent factors as well, relating to the immediate past and the current situation. Writers generally favourable to 'Yugoslavism', for example Susan Woodward[12] and Catherine Samary,[13] stress these contingent factors. In fact they come close to denying the role of historic ethnic conflicts and hatreds altogether. We do not need to follow them all the way in this view to admit that certain decisions taken during the period of communist rule were as important as the more long-range factors. Local communist elites were faced in the late 1980s with the problem of preserving their power in the new situation created by first the decline and then the collapse of communism. They found an easy answer in mobilizing ethnic nationalism. This was possible because of the extreme decentralization of the Yugoslav federation, introduced in the late 1960s as a way of introducing an element of local autonomy without dismantling the communist structure.[14] The result of those reforms was to hand power, not to the people, but to provincial elites. Tito's purges of 1971–2, directed mainly against Croat communists who were flirting with nationalism, created the misleading impression that he had stepped in against federalism. It was not so. Tito's actions on this occasion were directed against liberalism, and in defence of the single-party dictatorship. This became clear when the Constitution of 1974 was issued. Now each Yugoslav republic and province had a power of veto and a degree of autonomy limited only by the reserved areas of the armed forces and foreign policy.

Yet a state called 'Yugoslavia' continued to exist, and to be seen as a political and economic entity by the outside world. Hence the economic reforms pressed for by the IMF in the 1980s were implemented at federal level. But they created explosive social conditions within the country, such as large-scale unemployment, particularly of former soldiers and security police, and a decline in social welfare, which could be blamed by unscrupulous members of local elites on the central government. By the end of 1990, the federal prime minister, Ante Marković, having struggled for over a year to reform the country, was close to despair. He accused republican leaders of undermining his reforms. No-one wanted to make sacrifices for the good of Yugoslavia as a whole; they were all thinking of their own local advantage. This also applied to the Serbs. In fact Marković reserved his sharpest criticism for the Serbian prime minister Stanko Radmilović, who had erected a tariff barrier against Slovene and Croat exports to his republic (1 November), thereby disrupting the Yugoslav common market.

Financial and economic questions were undoubtedly important. But we must not ignore the background of ethnic conflict. In the late 1980s the federal government abandoned the method of promotion according to the 'ethnic key', because instead of taking the sting out of national antagonisms it seemed to exacerbate them. The government started trying to appoint cadres on the basis of merit and competence alone. Republican leaderships countered by using the rhetoric of ethnic nationalism against the federal authorities; so the situation became worse still.[15] The late 1980s also saw the rise of nationalist sentiments among the intelligentsia. The Croats started to raise the question of the national language again. In the freer atmosphere that now prevailed, they were emboldened to repeat the Declaration of 1966 on the Name and Status of the Croatian Language, signed at that time by 140 Croatian intellectuals, but suppressed by the authorities a year later on the ground that it was nationalistic. The 1966 Declaration had denounced the 1954 Novi Sad agreement that established a common Croatian and Serbian literary language, claiming instead that the Croat language was entirely separate from Serbian, and that there was no such thing as a 'Serbo-Croatian' or 'Croato-Serb' language.[16] The revival in the 1980s of the demand for linguistic separation was part of a general revival of Croat national culture; whether this could be accommodated within a common Yugoslav framework was more than doubtful.

But it was the Serbs, and one Serb in particular, Slobodan Milošević, the ambitious politician who was determined to become the leader of the Serbian League of Communists, who sparked off the process that led to the disintegration of the country. Milošević probably did not intend to destroy Yugoslavia, but the leaders of the other republics saw his attempt to remodel the country as a serious threat; this in turn led them to move towards full-scale national separatism.

Milošević's aims were, first, to establish himself in a dominant position in Serbia, then to re-integrate the formerly autonomous provinces into Serbia and thirdly, and finally, to 'make Yugoslavia function again' by altering the 1974 Constitution, in particular by turning the country into 'a unified economic area' where the federal government could take 'decisive action'.[17] The first aim was achieved at one stroke, at the Eighth Session of the Central Committee of the Serbian League of Communists (Savez Komunista Jugoslavije; League of Communists of Yugoslavia; SKJ), when liberals, especially those 'soft' on Kosovo, including Milošević's predecessor and former mentor Ivan Stambolić, were purged (September 1987). This cleared the way for him to take over the leadership of the Serbian SKJ on a programme of Serbian nationalism masquerading as a 'popular anti-bureaucratic revolution'. He was thus able to manipulate the 'increasingly pronounced social despair' in Yugoslavia as a means of securing a mere 'change in the *nomenklatura*'.[18]

The second aim was achieved in stages. First, the Vojvodinan, Kosovan and Montenegrin provincial and republican leaderships were forced out of office (in October 1988, November 1988 and January 1989 respectively) by 'anti-bureaucratic revolutions' of a Serbian nationalist character, in an atmosphere of hysteria whipped up by the state-controlled media. Then the Serbian Assembly in Belgrade voted for a number of 'constitutional amendments' which in practice abolished Kosovan and Vojvodinan autonomy (28 March 1989).

These events cannot be explained without reference to the rise of Serbian national feeling, promoted strongly by the Belgrade media in the late 1980s. In 1986 some Serbian intellectuals started to promote the idea that the Serbs, as a nation, had sacrificed themselves to the idea of Yugoslavia during the war and afterwards, and that it was time to restore the balance. According to the notorious 'Memorandum of the Serbian Academy', produced in that year, Tito and his colleagues were to blame for allowing the 'physical, political, legal and cultural genocide of Serbs in Kosovo and Metohija'. 'After four decades in the new Yugoslavia', the Memorandum continued, 'the Serbian nation alone does not have her own state'. The solution was to establish 'the complete national and cultural integrity of the Serbian nation, regardless of which republic or province it is in'.[19] Although the Memorandum was too critical of the existing order to be issued publicly, it set the subsequent agenda of Serbian nationalism, which was implemented by Milošević in the early 1990s. The Serbian musical scene of the late 1980s also reflected and encouraged the rise of nationalism among young people, with the appearance of the phenomenon of 'turbo-folk rock'. The lyrics to this music recalled the injustices suffered by Serbs at the hands of various enemies, particularly Albanians, through the ages, and praised the current Serbian leader for his decision to support the national cause. Here is a sample: 'The outcry against us, your brothers and sisters, does not cease. Help us, Slobo, you are our father and our mother.'[20]

Milošević's third aim, the restoration of a united Yugoslavia, was never achieved, because the achievement of the first two aims pushed both the Slovene and the Croat party leaderships down the path of separatism, out of fear that their autonomy would now come under attack as well. There was a further motive for Croat resistance to Milošević: the presence of a large Serbian minority within Croatia, which could be expected to respond to his Serbian nationalist line. In fact in 1989 radio transmitters in Vojvodina began to beam propaganda broadcasts towards Serbian minorities in both Croatia and Bosnia-Herzegovina.[21]

The usual conflicts over the degree of admissible reform, and the best way to conduct the transition from communism, had been building up in Yugoslavia since the mid-1980s; but once the issue of Yugoslavia's existence as a state was raised, as it was in 1989, these conflicts entirely changed their nature. The issues of the dismantling of communist rule, and the establishment of the free market and multi-party democracy, posed on a state level in the rest of Eastern Europe, immediately took on a regional, 'republican' colouring in Yugoslavia. The reforming all-Yugoslav government headed after 1989 by Ante Marković found itself caught in this contradiction. Marković wanted to create an integrated economic system for the whole country, but on a market rather than a socialist basis. He planned to get rid of 'socially owned property' (the equivalent of state-owned property in other Eastern European countries) and replace it with private property, hoping to secure Western aid and an influx of foreign capital.[22] But the more effectively Yugoslavia reformed, the stronger Serbia would be. The resistance to Marković was led at this stage by Slovenia. It was not that the Slovene party leaders wanted to oppose reform as such, but they wanted the country to be transformed first into a confederation of separate states, with complete control over their own affairs. Moreover, no republican government, whether located in Ljubljana, Zagreb or Belgrade, was prepared to offer its people the diet of austerity, unemployment and cuts in public spending that was also a part of the Marković plan.

So the Yugoslav government's programme of 'shock therapy', which was as radical as the Polish one, and was introduced at roughly the same time (1 January 1990), was ignored by local republican governments, including those in Slovenia and Croatia, which granted wage-increases and subsidies in the hope of gaining popular support in the impending democratic elections.[23] Inflation, which fell in the earlier part of 1990 under the impact of Marković's stabilization measures, later returned to the high levels of the previous year (the annual rate for 1990 was 122 per cent).[24]

It was, however, ethnic rather than economic or financial issues that were the cynosure of Yugoslav eyes in 1989 and subsequently. In 1989 the Kosovo question was raised by Serbia's reintegration of that province, and its treatment of those who protested against this. The miners of Trepča, ethnic Albanians, went on strike and occupied their mine, demanding the dismissal of the Kosovo police chief and the retention of the 1974 constitutional position. Their movement was defused by promises of reform (which were not kept) and mass arrests. Further demonstrations by the general population in March and April were suppressed by riot police at the cost of many deaths, possibly one hundred.[25] A further 27 Kosovo Albanians were killed when the Yugoslav People's Army (JNA) sent in tanks to suppress renewed protests (February 1990). But what was really significant for the future of Yugoslavia was the reaction of the Slovene communist leader Milan Kučan, who took the side of the Albanian miners and addressed a solidarity demonstration in their favour; for the Slovenes, Serbian measures in Kosovo were a sign that no compromise was possible on Slovene independence, since Belgrade was clearly launched on a Serbian nationalist path.

There were tactical considerations involved as well. The Slovene communists adopted the same tactic as many communists in peripheral parts of the Soviet Union, who were in a similar situation: they themselves took charge of the national movement to avoid being swept from office by a flood of national feeling. Kučan's opportunity came at the Fourteenth Congress of the SKJ, held in January 1990. Milošević hoped that this congress would create a new, more tightly centralized Yugoslav party under his control. The Slovene party delegation, in contrast, came to Belgrade with a programme of decentralization: they wanted to set up a new federal party structure, which would have dissolved the League of Communists into eight separate units 'free to reform at their own pace'. Milošević rejected this proposal outright and used the support he commanded among the other delegations to inflict a crushing defeat on the Slovenes. The 126 Slovene delegates thereupon walked out. But the Croat delegation, the second largest, refused to continue participating without them. The president of the Central Committee (a Macedonian) had no option but to adjourn the Congress indefinitely (23 January 1990). 'When we left', remarked the Slovene communist leader Milan Kučan, 'the party ceased to exist'.[26] One could well add: Yugoslavia also ceased to exist. The disintegration of the SKJ was underlined on 30 March 1990 when its Central Committee failed to muster a quorum owing to boycotts by the Slovenes, Croats and Macedonians and a walkout by the Bosnian delegation.

The main objective of the non-Serb branches of the SKJ was to position themselves favourably to take advantage of the new situation created by the fall of single-party rule; they did not want the non-communist parties already emerging locally to be able to outbid them in the forthcoming elections, which would for the first time be held under free conditions and offer a political choice to the electorate. In the upshot, the communists did not do as well as they had expected. In Slovenia, although Kučan gained the presidency after the second round of elections (with 58.3 per cent against Jože Pučnik's 41.7 per cent) this was a personal rather than a party victory. He immediately resigned from the League, which had secured only 17 per cent of the vote in elections for the Socio-Political Chamber (22 April 1990). The Demos coalition (an alliance of six non-communist parties) took 55 per cent and an absolute majority of the seats (47 out of 80).

As a result of these elections, the first non-communist government of Slovenia took office (May 1990). The new prime minister was Lojže Peterle, leader of the Christian Democratic Party. A declaration of Slovene sovereignty followed soon afterwards (2 July). This did not necessarily imply 'secession straight away', said Peterle,[27] but he made his view of the future clear a month later when he proclaimed: 'The federation is dead de facto, but it is still operating de jure. What has been taking place recently in Yugoslavia implies the gradual disintegration of the federal state.'[28]

In Croatia, meanwhile, similar developments were taking place. Elections held on 22–3 April and 6–7 May were won by the Croatian Democratic Union (HDZ), a party founded by Franjo Tuđman in January 1990 as a broad movement for all nationalist Croats. Tuđman was also elected president. The League of Communists (now renamed League of Communists – Party of Democratic Change) did rather better than it had in Slovenia, securing 37 per cent of the vote, but under the single-constituency, first-past-the-post system in operation in Croatia, the HDZ's 41.5 per cent translated into an absolute majority of seats (205 out of 356, or 57.6 per cent) while the League was reduced to 75 (21 per cent of the total). The situation here, however, was more complex and more difficult than in Slovenia, in that there was a substantial Serbian minority within the republic (12.2 per cent of the population, according to the 1991 census).[29] Many of these Serbs, especially those dwelling in the relatively compact and largely rural settlement area of the Krajina, where they made up 69 per cent of the population, were strongly affected by the negative propaganda coming from Belgrade. The victorious HDZ made no effort to counter this by acting in a conciliatory manner towards the Serbian minority. Instead, Franjo Tuđman formed an alliance with 'the most conservative forces inside the republic and abroad; people who harked back to the ultranationalist post-World War II Croatian emigration'.[30]

The newly formed Croatian government now took a number of steps which were likely to provoke the Serbian side to violent resistance, understandable though they were in the context of nation-building: the wartime 'Independent State of Croatia' (NDH), which was associated with genocidal crimes carried out by the Ustaše against local Serbian and Jewish minorities, was historically rehabilitated;[31] pictures of the Ustaša leader Ante Pavelić were hung in the police stations; the name of the new currency unit, the *kuna*, was the same as the name of the wartime Ustaša currency; three-quarters of the statues erected in memory of anti-Fascist fighters after the war were destroyed;[32] the Croatian white and red checked flag, the *šahovnica*, used during the war by the Ustaše, was re-established; large numbers of Serbian public officials were dismissed and the government made sure that no more would be appointed by introducing an official document (the *domovnica*) which made proof of Croatian origin a requirement for most public acts, such as starting a business or getting a passport; the Latin alphabet was declared official in Croatia, thus excluding use of the Cyrillic script, favoured by Serbs.[33]

All these actions worsened the atmosphere, and made it easier for the local Serbian nationalist leader Jovan Rašković to start moving towards separatism (though he might have done this anyway). On 25 July 1990 Rašković held a rally attended by 100 000 people at which he proclaimed that the Serbs in Croatia 'had a right to determine who they will live with'; on 31 July the Serbian National Council in Croatia called for a referendum on 'immediate cultural autonomy' for the Croatian Serbs. Croatia was unable to stop this referendum happening because of the intervention of the Yugoslav authorities in Belgrade: the Yugoslav air force intercepted Croatian helicopters in the region and forced them to turn back (17 August). Serbian extremists in the Knin area (called the Martićevci, after the name of their leader Milan Martić, the local police chief) seized weapons from local police stations, and set up log barricades on all roads into Knin. This 'log revolution' set an example which was later imitated by the Serbs in other parts of Croatia and in Bosnia-Herzegovina. The referendum went ahead as planned (18 August). It was limited to Serb residents of the area, and it naturally resulted in a unanimous vote for Serbian sovereignty and autonomy. On 1 October 1990 an 'Autonomous Serbian Region of Krajina' was set up under the control of Rašković and his Serbian Democratic Party (SDS). On 3 October the federal authorities instructed Croatia to withdraw its police from the Krajina; the Croats were forced to comply. From that time onwards, the Croatian government's writ no longer ran there. Croatia's move towards independence was therefore likely to be resisted by a substantial minority of its inhabitants; and the media battle between Belgrade and Zagreb in the next few months made a violent outcome more likely.[34]

In the closing months of 1990 and the early part of 1991 the situation rapidly degenerated towards armed conflict. It was clear that Yugoslavia would be unable to dissolve peacefully into its component parts, in contrast to the Soviet Union.[35] The reasons for this violent denouement can be summarized as follows. First, the determination of the Slovenes and Croats to secede from Yugoslavia. This required the use of force, or at least the threat of it; hence both republics used these months to build up parallel militias, on the basis of the territorial defence units that already existed there. Second, the equal determination of the remnants of the Yugoslav authorities to prevent Slovenia and Croatia from seceding. Very little was left of 'federal socialist Yugoslavia' by late 1990, but what there was was very dangerous: above all, the JNA still existed, headed by General Veljko Kadijević, who had been Minister of Defence since 1988.[36] Serbia's action in May 1991 in blocking the candidature of the Croat Stipe Mesić to the post of president of Yugoslavia (it was the Croats' turn, under the system of rotation) was aimed at making sure no-one could prevent the JNA from acting against Slovene and Croat 'separatists'.

The third reason for the conflict was the attitude of Slobodan Milošević. President of Serbia since December 1989, he was also able to exert a decisive influence on the federal army.[37] Milošević was determined to make sure that even if Slovenia and Croatia could not be kept within Yugoslavia, Serbian national interests would still be protected. Whether this was a deep-seated conviction on his part is doubtful; he was concerned to keep power and had already decided as early as 1987 that the way to do this was to exploit the latent strength of Serbian nationalism. Given that the Serbian minority in Slovenia was a scattered group of negligible significance (2.4 per cent of the population in 1991) that republic could be allowed to leave without too much trouble. During the short war which followed the Slovene declaration of independence (25 June–3 July 1991) only a tenth of the twenty thousand JNA troops stationed in Slovenia were in action; this reflected Milošević's lack of interest in the conflict.[38] The situation was different in Croatia. Here Milošević insisted that the substantial Serbian minority must not be included in the new state. The same would later apply in the case of Bosnia-Herzegovina.

The fourth factor was the attitude of the local minority community itself. The forces which came to the top in Krajina were entirely hostile to the new Croat state, and they rapidly formed an alliance with both the Serb leaders in Belgrade and the Yugoslav army. The Krajina Serbs replied to the Croat constitution of 22 December 1990, which declared Croatia to be 'the national state of the Croatian people', by adopting a resolution in favour of the separation of Krajina from Croatia (28

February 1991). On 1 April 1991 the Krajina Executive Council decided to apply to become part of Serbia proper; the Serbian Assembly did not endorse this, but practical co-operation with the army was brought closer when the Yugoslav Presidency voted to give it 'wider powers in Croatia' in response to Croat–Serb clashes in Krajina (9 May 1991).

When civil war finally broke out, in the summer, the JNA intervened on the Serbian side, causing the Prime Minister of Yugoslavia, Ante Marković, to complain that the Yugoslav Minister of Defence (Kadijević) and his deputy (General Blagoje Adžić) had 'taken one side in the civil war', a fact which 'one would have to be blind not to notice'.[39]

The interaction of these four factors pushed Yugoslavia towards war as the year 1991 went by; the stark logic of the situation was not particularly affected by extraneous events mentioned by some authors, such as decisions by Germany or the European Union or the United States to recognize independence declarations. What might have genuinely affected the course of events, in contrast, was a propensity to compromise. But this was absent at every step of the way. There were forces favouring compromise, but Yugoslavia's tragedy was that owing to the media war and the overheated atmosphere of national recrimination and mutual fear these forces remained weak. They also made mistakes. Yugoslav Prime Minister Ante Marković formed his Alliance of Reform Forces on 29 July 1990. This was three months too late; the decisive elections had already taken place in Slovenia and Croatia. When the elections took place in the other republics, in November and December 1990, the Alliance of Reform Forces received very little support: it won 13 out of 240 seats in Bosnia-Herzegovina, 11 out of 120 seats in Macedonia, 17 out of 83 seats in Montenegro and 2 out of 250 seats in Serbia.

The League of Communists, which, like the Alliance, was a force for ethnic compromise in Bosnia-Herzegovina and Macedonia, also failed. In Bosnia-Herzegovina, where the elections took place in three rounds on 18 November, 2 December and 9 December, it only took 19 out of 240 seats. In Macedonia it secured 25.8 per cent of the votes and 31 seats out of 120, a less disastrous defeat.

The winners in every case were populist, ethnically based parties. In Bosnia-Herzegovina most of the seats fell to the three nationalist parties: the Muslim SDA (86), the Serbian SDS (72) and the Croat HDZ (44). In Macedonia the Macedonian nationalist party elegantly entitled VMRO–DPMNE (Internal Macedonian Revolutionary Organization – Democratic Party of Macedonian National Unity) did best with 31.7 per cent of the vote and 38 seats, while the Albanian minority parties together secured 25 seats. Another general feature which stood out in these results was this: the winners of the 1990 Yugoslav elections were not dissident opponents of communism, as was the case elsewhere in Eastern Europe. The leaders of the new, victorious, anti-communist parties were almost all either current or previous officials of the SKJ, who had decided the time was ripe to swap horses.

And what of Serbia and Montenegro? Post-communist 'socialist' parties committed to the defence of 'Yugoslavia' won elections in both republics in 1990. In Montenegro the League of Communists had 83 seats out of 125; in Serbia the former League of Communists, now Socialist Party of Serbia (SPS) took 194 seats out of 250. But the defence of the state itself now became an ethnic question, as the other nations were moving inexorably towards independence. In fact the questions of political democracy and economic reform that were so central in the rest of Eastern Europe were pushed to the sidelines over most of Yugoslavia by the ethnic conflict. In the long run they would reassert themselves, and they always threatened to do so when ethnic issues temporarily receded into the background, but for most of the 1990s it was ethnic conflict, either potentially or actually, that dominated the situation.

The brief and only partly serious military conflict in Slovenia was followed by a serious shooting war in Croatia between June and December 1991. During these months the JNA, now entirely under Serbian control, assisted local Serb militias, and paramilitary formations from Serbia proper, to seize a third of Croatian territory. Croats who found themselves on the wrong side of the lines were forced across the new borders by Serb paramilitaries. (The same was true in reverse for Serbs in Croat territory.) The Croat town of Vukovar, in Eastern Slavonia, underwent a long siege (from August to November). When it finally fell many of the defenders were murdered.[40] Shortly afterwards (23 November) a cease-fire was arranged between Croatia and the Krajina Serbs. It did not address the political status of the area. But the *de facto* position was that Croatia's size had been reduced by a third, and there was an independent Serb state of Krajina. Losses on both sides had been heavy: an estimated 20 000 dead and 30 000 wounded.

As the sequel was to show, this division of Croatia into two parts was an unstable situation. Croatia never recognized the independence of Krajina. The mini-state only survived thanks to Belgrade's protection; once Milošević decided it was time to turn into a peacemaker Krajina's days were numbered. During the summer of 1995 impending NATO intervention in Bosnia against the Serbs created a favourable diplomatic environment for the Croat leader Franjo Tuđman; under cover of preparations for the relief of the Bosnian town of Bihać, which was at that time under attack from both Bosnian and Krajina Serbs, a large military force was built up. 'Operation Storm', an attack by 200 000 Croat soldiers on the 40 000–strong Krajina Serb army, began on 4 August 1995 and ended with complete victory four days later. The capital, Knin, and the surrounding region were overrun. Hundreds of thousands of Serbs fled or were driven out. Some went to Banja Luka in Serb-controlled Bosnia; some to Serbia itself. For the first time, the *šahovnica* was hoisted over the castle of Knin. With the signing of the agreement to re-integrate Eastern Slavonia into Croatia shortly afterwards (12 November 1995) all the territory cut off in 1991 from the independent Croatian state had finally been recovered. A nation 'forged in war'[41] could now devote itself to the arts of peace. But there were still some obstacles to pass on the road to normality.

TUĐMAN'S STRANGLEHOLD ON CROATIA

Croatia's misfortune was that it was as ready as any other East European state to make the transition to the market economy and multiparty democracy but it was prevented from doing so by the need first of all to achieve independence and then recover a third of its national territory from Serbian separatists. In communist times, Croatia was less export-oriented than Slovenia (in 1990, 70 per cent of Croatia's material product was produced for domestic, that is Yugoslav, use), and the cutting of trade links with Serbia – which of course counted as part of the domestic market until 1992 – was a severe blow to the economy. In 1993 Croatia exported nothing to any state of Former Yugoslavia except Slovenia. It was compelled to break through to the Western market, and it succeeded remarkably well, with 58 per cent of its exports going to Western economies in 1993 plus a further 15 per cent to Slovenia; by then only 9.5 per cent of its exports went to the former CMEA (Comecon) countries.[42]

The result of the wars waged by Croatia after 1991 against both Serbs and Bosnian Muslims was to create a contrast with more fortunate Slovenia that had not existed before. Traditional structures were retained under President Tuđman instead of being modernized; foreign investment failed to come in.[43] But he continued to enjoy a paramount position, partly as the standard bearer of the Croat national revival, partly through authoritarian means. The secret police (SZUP, or Service for the Protection of Constitutional Order) possessed wide powers and was not subject to parliamentary control. Ninety per cent of judgeships were in the hands of the HDZ. Domestic opponents were treated as potentially disloyal to the state. They were therefore constantly hamstrung by the need to stress their *državotvornost* (state-upholding character). This search by the opposition for national respectability naturally ruled out strikes, demonstrations or acts of civil disobedience. Electoral districts were drawn to favour the ruling party, the HDZ. The television was completely under its control; the press were under constant pressure from high taxation and from court cases brought by the authorities (the libel law of 1995 made it an offence to libel any of the five top representatives of the Croatian state).[44]

These methods by themselves were insufficient to stop the rise of opposition. In elections held in February 1993 the Croat Socio-Liberal Party (HSLS), which was supported by the younger generation in the towns and cities, increased its vote from 19 per cent to 27 per cent on a programme of separation of church and state, respect for human rights, reductions in military spending, pluralism in the media and opposition to the war in Bosnia.[45] But Tuđman had an extra trick up his sleeve: the conquest of Krajina. The October 1995 elections were timed to take advantage of the military victory won in August. The election slogan of the HDZ was 'Vote for Tuđman, the man who wins'. It was effective. There were some irregularities in the conduct of the elections, but Western observers recognized them as 'fair'. Tuđman's party, the HDZ, secured 43.6 per cent of the vote and a majority of the seats. The HSLS share of the vote fell to 11.6 per cent; as so often in South-Eastern Europe, the opposition, though it was defeated in the countryside and smaller towns, made a strong showing in the capital. Left and centre opponents of the HDZ were able to win 14 out of 17 seats in Zagreb. Elsewhere the preponderance of clerical, conservative, middle-aged, rural and small-town voters ensured an HDZ victory. Having won the 1995 elections, Tuđman went on to retain his position in presidential elections with 61.4 per cent of the vote (15 June 1997), using his control of the press and the state's funds. At least, this is what his opponents claimed. Moreover, Tuđman's opponent in the presidential elections, Vlado Gotovac, was beaten up on the day of the election, allegedly by members of the president's bodyguard.[46]

There are nevertheless several reasons for optimism about Croatia. Some of the phenomena noted above can be explained as distortions arising from the situation of permanent conflict between 1990 and 1995. Economically, too, the picture is becoming brighter. Since 1995 there has been a moderate economic upturn, based on the activities of small, newly founded firms. There has also been a gradual decline in nationalist extremism and a growth in toleration for non-Croat ethnic groups; opinion is strongly in favour of democracy (more strongly than anywhere else in Eastern Europe, to judge by the opinion polls) and there is 80 per cent support for a future entry into the EU. The HDZ issued a new slogan in April 1997: 'Tuđman and not the Balkans'; ironically it is Tuđman himself, with his ethnic prejudices and his authoritarianism, who is the main obstacle to Croatia's move away from the Balkans and towards the European Union.

SLOVENIA: THE ONE THAT GOT AWAY

Even in its days as a part of Federal Yugoslavia, Slovenia was always oriented towards the West rather than the South or the East. It was also much more outward-looking than the rest of the country. In 1990 the value of its exports amounted to 51 per cent of GNP, and with only 8 per cent of the population it accounted for 25 per cent of Yugoslavia's total exports. Originally it exported equally to the West and the communist bloc; but after the collapse of Comecon trade, it was able to compensate for this by expanding exports to Western Europe. In 1993, 64 per cent of its exports went to the EU and the European Free Trade Association (EFTA) countries; in 1995, 67 per cent of its exports went to the EU. After suffering the usual initial post-communist economic decline, its GDP began to grow again in 1994. It was an excellent candidate for membership in the EU for both economic, structural and political reasons. Economically it was clearly successful, with a per capita income of $9000 in 1995; structurally its agricultural sector was minute, at only 4.7 per cent of GDP, which would mean there would be no 'drain on EU finances'.[47] Politically, it was characterized by free electoral competition, with no restrictions on the media and no damaging conflicts between president and prime minister, and an absence of ethnic strife, partly because of its relative homogeneity (Slovenes made up 87.8 per cent of the population in 1991), partly because of its generous attitude to some minorities (the 8500 Hungarians and the 3000 Italians received parliamentary representation entirely out of proportion to their share of the electorate).

The only perceptible problems in Slovenia are 'a tendency to indulge in the national pastime of complaining'[48] and the inability of the electorate to produce a clear decision, with the result that government is a perpetual coalition. Elections in 1992 and 1996 both produced deadlock.

In each case a coalition was constructed by Janez Drnovšek, the Liberal Democratic prime minister. In 1993 he was in alliance with the Christian Democrats, the ex-communists (renamed United List of Social Democrats), the Social Democrats and the Greens. In 1996 it was harder for him to stay in power, as the Christian Democrats went into opposition. Finally, on 9 January 1997, he managed by 46 to 44 votes to get confirmed for a second term, having constructed a multi-coloured parliamentary coalition with the ex-communists, the Slovene National Party and the Hungarian and Italian ethnic minority deputies.

BOSNIA-HERZEGOVINA: THROUGH HELL TO INDEPENDENCE

> The path that you are taking is the path that led Croatia to a hell, except the hell in Bosnia-Herzegovina will be a hundred times worse and will lead to the disappearance of the Muslim nation. (Radovan Karadžić)[49]

Bosnia-Herzegovina[50] had the most difficult ethnic problems of all, since it was divided three ways, between Bosnian Muslims, Serbs and Croats. It was, in a way, a miniature Yugoslavia (or, alternatively, Yugoslavia was a big Bosnia). As with Yugoslavia as a whole, there are serious differences of opinion over whether the legacy of past history was hatred and division between the three major ethnic components of the population or a growing feeling of a common destiny and a softening of ethnic conflict. There was certainly a record of ethno-religious violence in war-time Bosnia, in which all three groups were involved, including the Muslims.[51] But does this justify the view that the murderers of 1992 were simply 'settling the accounts of centuries of hatred'?[52] Noel Malcolm comments, right at the end of his careful study of the Bosnian question, that to view things in this way 'is to read from the script prepared by Karadžić and Milošević'. He prefers to lay the blame on 'young urban gangsters in expensive sunglasses from Serbia, members of the paramilitary forces raised by Arkan[53] and others'.[54]

There is now a large accumulation of literature on the conflict in Bosnia.[55] Most of it deals with the historical background. In what follows, in contrast, I shall summarize the main events of the 1990s. In November and December 1990 elections were held, which constituted in effect a census of the three ethnic communities, Bosnian Muslims, Croats and Serbs. A few months later there was a real census; as far as

Bosnia was concerned it confirmed the results of the elections. The majority group, in both the census and the elections, were the Bosnian Muslims (election result: 35.8 per cent of seats for the main Muslim party, the SDA; census result: 43.6 per cent declared themselves to be Muslims). The leader of the SDA, Alija Izetbegović, was elected president. The SDA had only a relative majority in the Bosnian Assembly, however. On 20 December 1991 it formed a coalition government with the other two nationalist parties, the Serbian Democratic Party (SDS) representing the Bosnian Serbs, and the Croat Democratic Union (HDZ), representing the Croats.

The aim of the leaders of the SDA was to take a single, united Bosnia-Herzegovina out of Yugoslavia and to do this peacefully, with the agreement of all the national communities. They could not achieve this goal because they faced four obstacles: the manoeuvres of Slobodan Milošević, who considered it to his advantage to identify himself with Serb national demands; the attitude of the Croat leader Franjo Tuđman, who wanted to include the 'Croat' area of Bosnia – known as Western Herzegovina – in his new state, and in March 1991 engaged in covert negotiations with Milošević for this purpose; the strong nationalist traditions of the local Croats, which led them to support this goal; and the resistance of the local Serb population, which voted overwhelmingly in favour of remaining in Yugoslavia at the plebiscite of 9–10 November 1991. In February 1992 Serb nationalist deputies withdrew from the Bosnian Assembly, declaring an independent 'Serbian Republic' (*Republika Srpska*) a month later.

In view of the level of hostility to the idea of retaining a unified Bosnian state, President Izetbegović was tempted for a while by the idea of surrendering to his opponents. On 23 February 1992 he met the Bosnian Serb and Bosnian Croat leaders at Lisbon and agreed to 'devolve power to the ethnic entities within Bosnia-Herzegovina'. But he could not carry his party with him. When he returned to Sarajevo he had to fall back on a simple declaration of independence. As he admitted a year later 'We decided for independence. Of course we could have chosen the other option.'[56] This decision has been criticized. Warren Zimmermann, the US ambassador in Belgrade, called it 'disastrous', because 'it gave the Serbs the pretext they were looking for'.[57] L.J. Cohen considers that in view of Izetbegović's rejection of the Lisbon Agreement 'it is not surprising that many Bosnian Serbs had serious reservations about their status in a state led by him'.[58] There is no way of knowing whether these speculations about the Bosnian Serb attitude are well founded. In any case, the failure of the Lisbon Agreement marked the collapse of the attempt to avoid war. There now began a three-way conflict between Bosnian Serbs, Bosnian Muslims[59] and Bosnian Croats.

This nationally coloured way of describing the contending parties was not initially accepted by Izetbegović and his colleagues in the SDA. They preferred to be called 'the Bosnian government', a description that was certainly factually correct though slightly misleading. They also stressed their support for a multi-ethnic state and society in Bosnia, which would continue the long tradition of tolerance between ethnic groups. But the forces of nationalist hatred were too much for them. The entirely false and malicious claim that the SDA was likely to set up a fundamentalist Islamic state was given an apparent justification by Izetbegović's background as a veteran Islamic activist: he had twice received prison sentences in former Yugoslavia for counter-revolutionary activities (in 1946 and 1983).

The armed conflict between Serbs and Muslims began in March 1992. The first shot was, paradoxically, fired by those with most to lose: gunmen, presumably Muslims, fired on a Serbian wedding party which was 'provocatively' carrying Serbian flags in a Muslim-inhabited section of Sarajevo. The Serbs' reaction was to set up barricades around 'their' sector – another 'log revolution' – and the fighting escalated from that point.

This is not the place to recount subsequent events in their full and amply documented frightfulness; let it simply be said that the overwhelming consensus of observers and of the evidence is that the war was accompanied by many atrocities, usually committed by the Serbian side, the first being the massacre of three thousand Muslims in the town of Brčko in the summer of 1992, photographed from the air by the American Central Intelligence Agency, which refused to reveal the pictures to the public.[60] The peculiar savagery of the war in Bosnia was no doubt in part a result of the settling of old scores. Massacres tended to occur in places where they had happened during the Second World War (Prijedor, Kozara).[61] To some extent they reflected the peculiar personality of Radovan Karadžić, Bosnian Serb leader, psychiatrist and bloodthirsty poet, who wrote the lines 'Take no pity let's go/kill that scum down in the city' in the 1970s, uncannily anticipating the murders he was to encourage in the 1990s.[62] But the events also had a grim practical significance: they arose from the fact that there were very few ethnically unmixed districts in Bosnia. Only 10 of the 110 communes in the republic had populations which were over 90 per cent Muslim, Serb or Croat; all the rest were in varying degrees mixed.[63]

Moreover, ethnic mixture was increasing. A quarter of all marriages involved people of different nationalities. To create ethnically based states much population movement was required; the exiled Yugoslav historian Steven Pavlowitch has put the point well: 'because of the way they were intermixed... those who want them separated irreparably must commit irreparable crimes'.[64] The phrase 'ethnic cleansing' came into currency internationally in 1992 to cover this process, although the activity itself was neither unique to Yugoslavia nor particularly modern.

At first the conflict was between Serbs on one side, Muslims and Croats on the other. Soon, however, tensions also developed between the Muslims and the Croats. In July 1992 the 'Croatian Community of Herceg-Bosna' was proclaimed as a separate state; the Bosnian government declared this illegal. In October 1992 Croatian forces seized various towns in Herzegovina, including Mostar, which was made capital of the mini-state of Herceg-Bosna. Finally, in April 1993, a definitive breach occurred when Croatian irregulars owing allegiance to the extreme nationalist Party of Rights (HSP – 1861) massacred Muslims in the village of Ahmici, near Vitez. This set off a full-scale war between Croats and Muslims in Bosnia.[65] The three-way conflict that raged during 1993 was reduced to a two-way conflict between the Bosnian Serbs and the rest in February 1994 with the signing of a Muslim–Croat cease-fire. This was followed by the establishment of a Muslim–Croat Federation a month later, and the setting up of a joint government of both the Muslim–Croat Federation and the Republic of Bosnia-Herzegovina in July 1994.

It took several years before the international community, led by the USA, was finally induced to take forceful (and eventually forcible) action to end the conflict. In the meantime, international negotiators struggled to work out a peace settlement that would suit all sides; this was an attempt to square the circle. First there was the Vance–Owen Plan of 1993, fathered jointly by Cyrus Vance and Lord David Owen. Under this proposal Bosnia-Herzegovina was to be divided into ten provinces, with each of the three major ethnic groups recognized as 'constituent units' of the future state. But the plan conceded the complexity of the ethnic situation on the ground by drawing the boundaries of each of these ten provinces in such a way as to ensure that they were populated by a mixture of ethnic groups. The Croats alone were prepared to accept the Vance–Owen Plan in its entirety; both the Bosnian Serbs and the Bosnian Muslims objected to it. The United States also had reservations. The US Secretary of State, Warren Christopher, rejected the Vance–Owen Plan because it allegedly 'rewarded ethnic cleansing', and because 'any peace plan would have to be accepted by all parties' (10 February 1993). Washington's refusal to support the Vance–Owen Plan destroyed any chance that the other warring parties would accept it.[66] On 26 April the Bosnian Serb Assembly rejected the plan, thereby forcing its abandonment, despite strong support delivered in person by Milošević, who was hoping that acceptance would encourage the UN to lift the sanctions on Yugoslavia.

On 16 June a new proposal was put forward, known as the Owen–Stoltenberg Plan after the names of its two sponsors. This was much closer to the solution eventually arrived at. It divided Bosnia into three parts, and it implied further large-scale population movement to create three ethnically homogeneous states: *Republika Srpska* (for the Serbs), Herceg-Bosna (for the Croats) and Bosna (for the Muslims). Radovan Karadžić of the SDS naturally welcomed it; Izetbegović was opposed. This plan also rapidly became of purely archival significance. Without the United States any European initiative lacked credibility. Moreover, no peace plan could succeed unless backed by the threat of overwhelming force. Bosnia had to wait until 1994 before the United States was ready to seize the nettle of actual military involvement.

The reason for the change in the US attitude was simple: the Bosnian Serbs committed one horrifying atrocity too many. The mainly Muslim inhabitants of the capital of Bosnia, Sarajevo, had become accustomed to risking their lives when they went out onto the street. But now the Bosnian Serbs besieging Sarajevo fired a mortar bomb at the people shopping at a peaceful market place in the city. It found its target and killed 68, wounding many more (5 February 1994). Karadžić claimed that the incident was a Bosnian government 'fake', adding that the Bosnian forces themselves had deliberately committed this atrocity to make propaganda for their own side. The claim was surely false, in fact it was an obscene attempt at obfuscation, but the idea behind it was valid, in the sense that the Sarajevo market place massacre was the first of several bizarre 'own goals' achieved by the Bosnian Serb forces. Though it paled into insignificance before previous secret atrocities, it was committed very publicly, and the pictures were shown round the world. There could be no doubt that it had happened. As David Rieff has said, 'It was the television cameras that saved Sarajevo'.[67]

The reaction of world, and most relevantly United States, public opinion was strong, and President Clinton responded to that. The way to NATO involvement was now open. On 9 February NATO ambassadors agreed, almost unanimously, to implement a request for air strikes if one came; and an ultimatum was issued to the Bosnian Serbs calling for withdrawal from a 20-kilometre exclusion zone round the city by 20 February. Failure to comply would be punished by air strikes. As it turned out, this was to be merely a dry run for what happened a year later. Boris Yeltsin, the Russian President, who had again taken up the traditional nineteenth-century Russian policy of protecting the Serbs, found a way of stopping the air strikes. He launched his own diplomatic initiative. If the Bosnian Serbs would kindly comply with NATO's demands, Russia would deploy her own troops, under UN auspices, between Serb and Muslim forces in Bosnia. This plan was accepted by the Serbs, and the UN special envoy in Bosnia, Yasushi Akashi, reported on 20 February that 'sufficient progress' had been made in withdrawals, so that the air strikes were not needed.

The war itself continued, despite the occasional negotiated ceasefire, always violated soon afterwards. Finally, in the summer of 1995, two decisive events brought the conflict to an end: the fall of Srebrenica (11 July 1995) to Bosnian Serb troops and the Markale market place massacre (28 August 1995). Srebrenica should have been safe, as it was one of six 'protected areas' designated by the UN under Resolution 836 of 4 June 1993, but the Bosnian Serbs swept the UN peacekeeping forces aside.[68] News of Srebrenica's fall was followed quickly by evidence of the massacre of an estimated seven thousand local Muslims.[69] But even this was not quite enough to enforce international involvement. In fact, the United Nations High Commission on Refugees (UNHCR) representative in Bosnia, the former prime minister of Poland Tadeusz Mazowiecki, resigned his post in protest against what he called 'the international community's hypocrisy and inaction' (27 July). This was a little hasty, though understandable. On 28 August the second decisive event followed: 37 people were slaughtered by a Bosnian Serb shell in another Sarajevo market place atrocity – this was the Markale massacre. NATO responded with 'Operation Deliberate Force', a series of air strikes on Bosnian Serb artillery emplacements which was not suspended until 14 September. The Russian president, Boris Yeltsin, condemned the NATO air strikes as a 'cruel bombardment'. But the Serbian leader Slobodan Milošević took the hint: he started to negotiate with the American envoy Richard Holbrooke. He had decided in effect that it was time to end the war; not exactly to 'betray' the Bosnian Serbs as some of them claimed, but to force them to consolidate their military victory. He calculated correctly that the Serbs could gain nothing further by military action.

The peace agreement, initialled on 21 November at Dayton, Ohio, and finally signed in Paris on 14 December 1995, was a compromise, certainly, but it gave the Bosnian Serbs most of what they had been fighting for. They kept Srebrenica and Žepa, the towns they had conquered in July 1995, though they lost their part of Sarajevo. Some of their leaders were being pursued for war crimes; but given the *de facto* independence of *Republika Srpska* it would be very difficult to bring anyone to justice. The other side, the Muslim–Croat Federation, also had some reason to be satisfied with the outcome. Bosnia-Hercegovina continued to exist, theoretically, but it had been divided into two parts; or even three parts, if one takes into account the separate status of the Croat area of Bosnia, known as 'Herceg-Bosna'. NATO involvement, which had brought the war to an end, was to continue, in the shape of a 60 000-strong Implementation Force (IFOR). We shall examine the sequel in Chapter 8.

MACEDONIA

The small Yugoslav republic of Macedonia was an island of peace in the surrounding storms, although it too held tremendous potential for ethnic conflict.[70] As elsewhere, the new political parties which emerged in the wake of the collapse of the communist monopoly of power were committed to ethnic goals. The main Macedonian nationalist party was the VMRO-DPMNE. It used the name, and claimed to represent the traditions, of a renowned terrorist grouping of the 1920s, the Internal Macedonian Revolutionary Organization, which had been active both in Macedonia and Bulgaria. The main Albanian party was the PDP (Party for Democratic Prosperity), which defended the interests of the rather large Albanian minority (22.9 per cent in 1991), but did not advance separatist aims.

The first free elections in Macedonia, held in November and December 1990[71] produced an unclear result, with anti-communist nationalists (VMRO-DPMNE) and national communists (now calling themselves the League of Communists of Macedonia – Party of Democratic Transformation)[72] in a roughly even balance.[73] The resultant parliamentary arithmetic necessitated a constant search for coalition partners among the other three parties: the Albanians of the PDP and the NDP, and the federalist reformers of the Macedonian branch of Marković's Alliance of Reform Forces. The Macedonian nationalists were the strongest party, but the Assembly elected the communist Kiro Gligorov as president of the republic.

On 8 September 1991 a referendum on Macedonian independence was held. The overwhelming majority (99 per cent) of those who voted supported the idea in a 74 per cent turnout (the Albanian minority boycotted the referendum). Gligorov was able to negotiate a peaceful withdrawal from Macedonia by Yugoslavia's armed forces early in 1992, and on 20 November 1992 the country declared its independence. The main opposition to Macedonia's recognition as an independent country came not from Serbia (although Milošević did make the cynical suggestion to his Bulgarian and Greek counterparts that they could join him in partitioning the republic) but from Greece. The Greek government, with strong support from Greek public opinion, insisted that the name 'Macedonia' was part of the Greek heritage and could not be taken over by another nation. The United Nations eventually accepted Macedonia as a member under a different name: 'FYROM', or Former Yugoslav Republic of Macedonia (8 April 1993). This compromise was not accepted by the Macedonian nationalists of VMRO–DPMNE, who introduced a vote of no-confidence into the Assembly, which they lost (13 April).[74] The nationalists' subsequent agitation was not successful: VMRO–DPMNE's candidate Ljupco Georgievski was heavily defeated in the October 1994 presidential elections (he gained 14 per cent of the vote) and the party boycotted the Assembly elections, with the result that it was unrepresented there for the next four years.

The secret of Macedonia's success in avoiding the violent ethnic conflicts in the rest of former Yugoslavia has been the spirit of tolerance promoted by its president, and the practical recognition of the Albanian minority's cultural autonomy. This does not mean that relations between the two ethnic groups are particularly good, but rather that the government tries to avoid raising tensions by operating 'a quasi-apartheid system, with separate newspapers, and separate primary and secondary schools'. In February 1996 five ministers from the ethnic Albanian party were included in the cabinet. The only area where the Albanians' cultural demands were not granted was in higher education. The prime minister, Branko Crvenkovski, denounced the proposal to establish a separate Albanian university as liable to lead to the 'ghettoisation and disintegration of Macedonia'.[75]

So far Macedonia, or FYROM, has been able to continue its uneasy balancing act: it has balanced successfully for five years between names, between ethnic groups and between the maintenance of communist-era structures and the gradual entry of the forces of democracy and the free market. The victory of VMRO–DPMNE in the October–November 1998 elections has led to a change of government, but no change in policy.

THE 'THIRD YUGOSLAVIA'

With Slovenia and Croatia independent, and Bosnia-Herzegovina and Macedonia firmly on course in the same direction, Milošević's Serbia had only one possible partner left: Montenegro. At a referendum held in March 1992, 96 per cent of Montenegro's voters (though only 66 per cent of the electorate, owing to an Albanian and Muslim boycott) supported remaining in Yugoslavia. On 27 April 1992 the leaders of Serbia and Montenegro together proclaimed the Federal Republic of Yugoslavia, at a ceremony boycotted by all EC nations except Greece and attended by China, Russia and a number of non-aligned countries. The former Yugoslav People's Army, the JNA, became the Yugoslav Army, or VJ, and it was supposed in theory to operate henceforth only on Federal Yugoslav territory (that is in Serbia and Montenegro). The writer Dobrica Ćosić was elected President of Yugoslavia; the businessman Milan Panić, a United States citizen of Serbian origin, was made Prime Minister on 14 July. But the real power was in the hands of Slobodan Milošević, the President of Serbia. The others were there to provide him with some respectability and to head off sanctions. As soon as they quarrelled with him, he got rid of them. The Yugoslav media finished the job by launching slanderous campaigns against both Ćosić and Panić.[76]

The situation in the Third Yugoslavia, or 'Rump Yugoslavia', as it was sometimes called, was dominated in the early 1990s by the wars fought successively with Slovenia, Croatia and Bosnia. These had both a direct and an indirect impact. High military expenditure placed an impossible strain on the budget, and the sanctions imposed by the outside world cut off many trade links (although some of Yugoslavia's trading partners defied sanctions). As a result the Yugoslav economy suffered from large-scale unemployment (22 per cent in 1993), very heavy budget deficits (24 per cent in 1991, 52 per cent in 1992, 43 per cent in 1993), and an inflation which was practically off the scale (by 1994 the annual rate of inflation had reached 946 827 610 per cent).[77]

In addition to these economic problems, Milošević's Serbia had an awkward domestic problem: Kosovo. We have already noted the solution arrived at in 1989, which was to get rid of the autonomy that province had enjoyed since 1974 and reincorporate it into Serbia. Vojvodina, Serbia's other autonomous province, suffered the same fate at the same time, but caused far less trouble subsequently owing to both its much greater prosperity and the weakness of nationalism among the local Hungarian community, which in any case did not enjoy a majority position. Kosovo, in contrast, which was overwhelmingly Albanian, reacted strongly. On 2 July 1990 the Albanian delegates in the Kosovo provincial assembly declared political sovereignty for the province, demanding the same status within Yugoslavia as enjoyed by Serbia or any other republic. The Serbian reply came quickly: on 5 July the Kosovo Assembly was dissolved, and in September a new constitution confirmed the reduction of Kosovo's status to the level of an administrative district. The main political party of the Kosovo Albanians, the 700 000-strong Democratic League of Kosovo (LDK), led by Ibrahim Rugova, adopted a tactic of passive resistance to these Serbian measures, endeavouring to set up an illegal 'parallel state', the 'Republic of Kosovo' (7 September 1990).

This was remarkably successful for several years in running schools, hospitals and other institutions. The aim of the movement was originally autonomy rather than independence. As Rugova said in 1990: 'We are not separatists.'[78] But as time went by and Serbia showed no sign of conceding even autonomy, the possibility of other solutions started to be considered. By November 1993 Rugova had changed his position. The options for Albanians, he said, were now 'neutrality, independence or union with Albania'.[79] By the late 1990s both the tactic of passive resistance and the goal of national autonomy were seriously in doubt. Early in 1996 a shadowy 'Kosovo Liberation Army' appeared. It began a campaign of assassination against government officials. The murder of two Serbian policemen in March 1998 led to a big arrest operation by Serbian security forces, involving the death of 80 people. The crisis of March 1998 forced Rugova into calling for independence.[80] 'The majority of Kosovo Albanians', reports Matthias Rüb, 'see only one solution: full independence and separation from Serbia.'[81] Whether this will be achieved in the short term is problematic, for three reasons. First, the sentimental attachment of Serbs to Kosovo as the centre of their country in medieval times, which makes it politically difficult for Milošević to take this road, despite the continuing decline in the number of Serbs actually living in the province.[82] Second, the overwhelming military superiority of the Yugoslav Army. And, third, the insistence of the United States and the European Union that the best solution for Kosovo is autonomy within Serbia, not independence, and that the issue is pacification and the restoration of stability rather than constitutional change.

THE DIVISION OF CZECHOSLOVAKIA: HOW TO RESOLVE A PROBLEM PEACEFULLY

As we saw in Chapter 2, the division of Czechoslovakia was not desired by a majority either of Czechs or Slovaks. Separation was also painful in some ways, despite the lack of ill feeling. Slovakia received a guaranteed share of major state enterprises, which made future privatization more difficult even in the Czech Republic. The usual quarrels about the borders emerged as well. It took three years for the respective ministers of the interior to agree a border (on 4 January 1996) and even then the Czech Chamber of Deputies failed to ratify an exchange of territory with Slovakia (24 April 1996). But these were minor matters. They did not give rise to any ethnic conflict between Czechs and Slovaks.

Ethnic conflict did exist in both halves of former Czechoslovakia, however. In the Czech republic there was conflict between the Roma minority and the Czech population, especially in Northern Bohemia. In Slovakia there was conflict with the Roma, but also with the much larger Hungarian minority. After 1989, long-suppressed aspirations came into the open. The Hungarians began to demand minority rights, which had been formally recognized but in practice nullified under communism. The main Hungarian minority organization, Coexistence (ESWM), was founded in February 1990, and in theory it included all national minorities, though the Hungarian element was clearly dominant. Its programme involved cultural autonomy for all minorities, and 'political and economic self-administration' for Hungarian districts in southern Slovakia. It was careful not to play with separatism. It did, however, favour the retention of a federal Czechoslovakia, for the same reason that the Slovak nationalists wanted its dissolution: the Czechs' sense of fair play provided the Hungarians with some protection from the local Slovak majority. As Coexistence leader Miklos Duray said in 1990, 'Hungarians only feel secure within the framework of the present democratic republic, which makes it possible to control extremists' who are 'blindly anti-Hungarian'.[83]

The Slovaks, for their part, saw the Hungarians as an obstacle to the process of nation-building. Already in October 1990 a language law was passed, establishing Slovak as the official language, although it conceded the use of another language where the local minority population was over 20 per cent. This was not good enough for the Slovak National Party (SNS), which gained popularity by combining the two negative themes of Czech domination and Hungarian separatism. It claimed that Czech pressure was preventing the establishment of the

Slovak language in its full rights, and that Coexistence had hidden separatist aims. In the June 1990 elections the SNS received 14 per cent of the vote. Its nationalist drum-beating began to lose popularity, however, when it became clear that the charismatic Slovak leader, Mečiar, had himself decided to adopt the independence slogan. In the June 1992 elections the SNS's share fell to 7.9 per cent of the vote and 15 National Council seats. In 1994 it fell further, to 5.4 per cent. It has retained its position as a factor in Slovak politics for two reasons: Mečiar decided to include it in his government coalition after December 1994, and it retains its constituency by dint of anti-Hungarian demagogy. The leader of the SNS, Jan Slota, called for the 'outlawing of Hungarian politicians' because their aim was 'the destruction of the Slovak republic'.[84]

Slovakia has conducted a running battle with its Hungarian minority since independence, over the classic issues indicated earlier: Hungarian names on road signs and railway stations, the use of Hungarian in schools, the use of Hungarian personal names, the use of Hungarian in official institutions. The October 1990 language law was sharpened in November 1995, when Slovak was made sole official language. The Hungarian government was drawn into the conflict, accusing Slovakia in February 1997 of failing to respect minority rights. The Slovak reply (September 1997) was to suggest the solution of 'voluntary repatriation of minorities by both sides'. This proposal was naturally rejected by Hungary. The dispute continues.

THE POSITION OF MINORITIES ELSEWHERE IN EASTERN EUROPE

Ethnic tensions existed in communist Romania, but violent ethnic conflict was largely absent. This was paradoxical, given the government's efforts to suppress Hungarian cultural identity in the 1980s.[85] Intellectual dissidents in Transylvania produced an underground journal for a short period in the early 1980s, but the group was uncovered by Ceaușescu's secret police, and its members were arrested and expelled to Hungary.[86] Ordinary Romanians and Hungarians were too busy surviving austerity to get into conflict. The Romanian revolution of 1989 was started off in Timişoara by demonstrations of ethnic solidarity by Romanians, Serbs and Hungarians, who all opposed Ceaușescu's 'systematization' plans. The National Salvation Front government which took over after 1989 was committed to observing the rights and freedoms of ethnic minorities (according to the Ten Point Programme of 22 December 1989).

Despite these fine words, ethnic conflict did emerge in Romania after 1989.[87] The main events occurred in the town of Tîrgu Mureş in March 1990. The violence was 'artificially manufactured rather than being a spontaneous phenomenon'.[88] It was promoted by Radu Ceontea's *Vatra Românească* (Romanian Cradle), allegedly a purely 'cultural' organization. As we noted in Chapter 4, there were eventually two political parties of the extreme right, the PUNR (Party of Romanian National Unity) and Corneliu Vadim Tudor's PRM (Greater Romania Party). The PUNR combined nostalgia for Ceauşescu, hatred of Hungarians and hatred of foreigners in general. It had overlapping membership with *Vatra*. It was led after October 1992 by Gheorghe Funar, the controversial mayor of Cluj, and claimed to have six million supporters (certainly an exaggeration). The other nationalist party, the PRM, was distinguished from the PUNR largely by its greater extremism (it demanded the elimination of Hungarian minority organizations and the deportation of their members) and the broader range of its targets: it attacked Jews and Roma as well as Hungarians.[89]

Both parties were able to secure representation in the Chamber of Deputies in the September 1992 elections. Funar's PUNR with 7.7 per cent of the vote, and 30 seats, Tudor's PRM with 3.9 per cent and 16 seats. This was a sizeable voting bloc, and by 1994 the Romanian nationalists were part of the government coalition. There were three PUNR ministers in the cabinet. Their presence naturally made the solution of the Hungarian question more difficult and hindered President Iliescu's attempt to achieve reconciliation. As we shall see in Chapter 8, he decided in 1996 that they would have to be removed from the government. In subsequent elections, the PRM increased its representation to 19 seats and the PUNR declined to 18. Extreme nationalism, which has long traditions in Romania, is evidently not yet defunct there.

Bulgaria, where the Zhivkov regime had done its best to exacerbate tensions between Bulgarians and the ethnic Turks, was relatively free of ethnic conflict after an uneasy start in 1990. In that first post-communist year things did not look so good: there were several Bulgarian nationalist protests against initial moves to restore equal rights to ethnic minorities, above all in the southern district of Kărdzhali, where 80 per cent of the local people were ethnic Turks (1–2 January 1990 and again in June 1990). There were three Bulgarian nationalist organizations involved, and one of them, the Fatherland Party of Labour, gained a seat in the Assembly in the June 1990 elections. This success was not to be repeated.

Never again did Bulgarian nationalist support rise above the 4 per cent hurdle for political representation. Meanwhile, on the other side of the ethnic divide, a political party, the Movement for Rights and Freedoms (Dvizhenie za prava i svobodi) (DPS) was formed to represent the ethnic minorities (above all the Turks, but also the 300 000 Bulgarian Muslims, or Pomaks). The BSP endeavoured for a while to deprive it of the chance of registering as a political party, but the question had been resolved by 1991, and the DPS was able to play a part in political life, even entering government coalitions. The Bulgarian nationalists could only represent a credible threat with the support of the Socialists; but after their defeat in the October 1991 elections the latter decided to co-operate with the DPS, which clearly implied the abandonment of any attempt to play the nationalist card. Despite its tremendous economic and social problems, the country has so far not returned to the harsh ethnic confrontations of 1990.[90]

A country where large-scale ethnic conflict might have been expected to occur but did not was Albania. That remote and mountainous land had been notorious for inter-tribal feuding as late as the early twentieth century; and there was a very clear division between two broad ethnic groups, the Gegs and the Tosks.[91] Moreover the communist power base was in the south, among the Tosks, and the communist victory of 1944 was in some sense a conquest of the north by the south, of Gegs by Tosks. So the materials for ethnic discord were present. But the subsequent policy of the Albanian Workers' Party under Enver Hoxha was directed at erasing divisions between ethnic groups and creating an Albanian nationality. The absence of inter-Albanian ethnic conflict after 1991 is a testimony to their success. Subsequent divisions revolved around the personality of President Berisha, and the collapse of pyramid schemes, not tribalism. One can speak at most of a geographical division between north and south.[92]

Where ethnic conflict did occur it arose from the presence of a fairly small Greek minority in the south (1.9 per cent of the population in 1989). It was not too serious. The new Albanian government used a certain amount of constitutional chicanery against the Greek minority parties in 1992, banning all parties of an 'ethnic, regional or religious character', which meant that the *Omonia* Sociopolitical Organization was unable to participate in the elections of March. But another Greek party, the Unity Party for Human Rights, was allowed to participate, and it won two seats. Efforts by Greek minority activists to promote separatism in the far south of the country resulted in some repression by the Albanian authorities in 1993. Security forces clashed with Greek minority protesters near the town of Gjirokastër in June 1993, setting off a temporary crisis in relations with Albania's southern neighbour.[93] Some ethnic Greek activists were given prison terms in September 1994, but they were released five months later, and the Organization for Security and Co-operation in Europe (OSCE) reported at the time that Albania had 'no case to answer on alleged persecution of the Greek minority'. Berisha signed a pact of friendship with Greece in March 1996, by which the status of respective minorities was settled.[94]

The big problem for Albania lay not in the south but in the northeast: Kosovo. In communist times the Albanian government had tried to keep out of Kosovan affairs, despite the worsening of the Kosovo Albanians' position after 1981. There was no change in this attitude even after Milošević came to power and destroyed Kosovo's autonomy. The coming to power of Sali Berisha's Democratic Party in 1992 produced a certain increase in Albanian interest in Kosovo, but in view of the tremendous military preponderance of Serbia, it would have been foolish to encourage irredentism. Albania's intervention was limited to the establishing of contacts with the moderate Kosovan leadership of Ibrahim Rugova. In August 1995 Berisha criticized Yugoslavia for settling Serb refugees from Croatia in Kosovo, and appealed to the outside world to put pressure on Belgrade to restore Kosovan autonomy, but in the next few years Albania was far too concerned with its own internal problems to pay much attention to what was happening to the north-east. Non-intervention continues to be the Albanian government's position; although in 1998, with Berisha out of office, the new socialist government has been unable to exercise enough authority in the north-east, which is Berisha's political stronghold, to prevent him from collaborating with the Kosovo Liberation Army. So the possibility exists that Albania may still be drawn into conflict with Serbia over Kosovo.

Finally, some brief comments on the position of the Roma, who have taken the place of the Jews as the target of racist agitation in Eastern Europe. The collapse of communism presented both an opportunity and a danger for this ethnic group. The communists, though not hostile to them in principle, found in practice that their attempt at total social control came up against traditional nomadic customs. Everywhere, except in Yugoslavia, they were forced to settle, and attempts were made to assimilate them.[95] After 1989 they had the opportunity to move again, and to form their own organizations; but increased freedom of expression was also utilized by the extreme right in the host countries. Roma were one obvious scapegoat for the embittered victims of the post-1989 economic collapse. Anti-Roma graffiti appeared on the walls, racist attacks were made on them in Albania, Bulgaria, the Czech Republic, and Slovakia. They also suffered from economic discrimination (in Romania Roma unemployment stood at 50 per cent in 1997). In response, Roma parties and organizations have been formed, but whether they will be able successfully to combine the goals of ending injustice, protecting their traditional customs (including nomadism) and improving their economic position is a matter for the future.[96]

6 The Economic Underpinnings: Tearing down the Old, Building up the New

DIFFERENT APPROACHES TO TRANSITION

There were many different approaches to the problem of how to make the transition from the economic system that prevailed under communism; but about its desirability and necessity there was practical unanimity within Eastern Europe (if not in the Soviet Union and its successor states). Moreover, the international financial institutions, such as the World Bank and the International Monetary Fund, and their regional counterpart the European Bank for Reconstruction and Development (EBRD), generally made the granting of loans conditional on the implementation of radical economic reforms.

The kind of economic reform that was regarded as desirable was indicated clearly by the EBRD in its *Transition Report* for 1995. It picked out seven features that were essential for a successful transition in the economic sphere. These were:

1. growth of private enterprise, which could occur through both the privatization of existing enterprises and the entry of new firms into the economic arena;
2. hardened budget constraints to promote enterprise restructuring; this would compel an increase in the efficiency and profitability of enterprises; for restructuring to be successful, changes in the bankruptcy laws would be needed, allowing the liquidation of non-viable firms;
3. 'price liberalization', that is the freeing of prices from state intervention; this would imply the abolition of subsidies; but the authors of the *Transition Report* conceded that 'direct government control of prices may be occasionally needed on a limited basis';[1]
4. wage liberalization; this would imply the abolition of controls over wages and the creation of a purely market-determined wage;

5. trade and foreign-exchange liberalization; this would imply the removal of tariffs to ensure that domestic prices adjusted to world price levels;
6. restructuring of the banking sector; this would involve privatization, the entry of new banks, and the imposition of market discipline on banks, with the result that some would fail; and
7. establishment of non-bank financial institutions such as investment funds and securities markets; but the report stresses that these must be subject to a 'sound regulatory framework' to prevent swindles.

It would be advisable to add an eighth feature of a successful transition, not mentioned by the EBRD in this report: outside financial assistance. Ultimately, of course, the countries of the East were expected to stand on their own feet. The integration of the former communist bloc into the world economy was expected to occur in the long run through a flow of direct outside investment, but this would not happen immediately. In the interim clearly financial assistance was necessary, in the form of both outright grants and loans. We shall examine the record in this respect later in this chapter.

The above-mentioned features, taken together, constitute an 'ideal type' of a transition economy; in practice they have not often been present simultaneously. But initially transition governments were keen to attempt the necessary reforms. Owing to the convergence between right and left on the need for economic and political liberalization there was effectively a consensus within the political class, challenged only by critics from outside. Even in the Balkans the former communist parties at least paid lip-service to the need for change, though they took no immediate steps to achieve it. In the first stage of the reform process there was a high level of popular acceptance of sacrifices such as job losses, and a consistent degree of support for privatization, private entrepreneurship and profit-making by private individuals.

That was the position at the outset, in 1990. But the initial consensus tended to break down as the reforms started to bite and their deleterious social effects began to emerge. After all, Eastern Europe was now passing through an economic crisis whose manifestations were at least as severe as those of the depression of the 1930s. After a few years, the decline in support for liberal reforms was displayed in the results of elections. The former communist parties now benefited from a protest vote everywhere in Eastern Europe, which they cleverly exploited by calling for more moderate and less socially damaging economic policies, which they had no intention of implementing once returned to power.[2] Election results, however, do not bring this change of attitude into as sharp a focus as do the opinion polls, because the competing political parties tended to support some variant of the market model, and most were committed to accepting the policy prescriptions of Western financial institutions, whether they proclaimed themselves to be on the 'left', the 'right' or in the 'centre'.[3] The arguments within the political class in Eastern Europe were thus not about the desirability of transition but its modalities. We shall now move on to examine the policies of economic transition, first in outline, then in detail.

SHOCK THERAPY VERSUS GRADUALISM

The Polish shock therapy method of transition can be contrasted with the procedure adopted in Czechoslovakia. In the latter case the endeavour was made to carry out changes without imposing sacrifices. At first the distance between the two approaches did not seem great, since Václav Klaus, the leading figure in the Czechoslovak economic transition in its early years, used the phraseology of market liberalism for international consumption. Here is an example of his rhetoric: 'Whatever the impact, rapid transition to a free market system, with a minimum of inflation, is clearly the proper strategy.'[4] In reality, however, there was an element of social democracy about his policies, which made them very different from those applied in Poland. Klaus administered homoeopathic doses of liberalization and deregulation, rather than the strong market medicines favoured by his northern neighbours. He froze energy prices rather than allowing them to find their own level; he refused to make the Czechoslovak crown fully convertible. He maintained a high level of spending on social services.

He did not compel the banks to exert financial discipline on the state enterprises. Overemployment continued to be a feature of Czechoslovak industry; this is how Czechoslovakia's uniquely low rate of unemployment (3–4 per cent) was maintained. In this respect, Klaus cushioned the effects of transition, albeit hesitantly and in an *ad hoc* fashion.[5] Despite his flamboyant proclamations in favour of the free market, he did not 'dismantle the social safety net' in Czechoslovakia.[6] This was reflected in the unusually high proportion of GDP accounted for by state expenditure.

Right-wing Polish critics like Janusz Lewandowski saw the Czech financial crisis of 1996 as due punishment for this 'unprincipled moderation', and a sign of Klaus' political bankruptcy,[7] but he soldiered on, and weathered the crisis, although he was forced out of office a year later by a corruption scandal. It would, however, be an absurd exaggeration to view the Czechoslovak transition as a failure. Similarly, the economic transition in Hungary was marked by a high degree of gradualism, yet it too can hardly be seen as a failure from the perspective of 1998. It seems clear that it was not the *method* of transition that counted but the *point of departure*. The Polish, the Czechoslovak, the Hungarian points of departure were favourable to transition; elsewhere, as we shall see, the situation was different.

METHODS OF PRIVATIZATION

Not whether, but how to privatize was the question being asked in Eastern Europe in 1989 and subsequent years. There were four possible methods:

1. Restitution to former owners, on the ground that they had been illegally dispossessed in the 1940s. This was applied most vigorously in Czechoslovakia, where 70 000 properties were restored to their former owners, and also in Bulgaria.[8]
2. Sale to new private owners. This was a slow method, adopted in Hungary. The problem here was lack of capital; as a result, enterprises were sold either to members of the former *nomenklatura* or to foreign investors, except where there were restrictions on this (as in Poland, where there was a 10 per cent maximum for foreign purchasers of shares).
3. Free distribution of shares to the population via a voucher scheme. This was used in Czechoslovakia, and in varying degrees in other places. The method looked fair, but in Czechoslovakia investment funds bought up most of the coupons for speculative purposes.
4. Distribution or sale of shares to employees of the enterprise. This was a development from the idea of self-management, and there was strong pressure for it from the Solidarity trade union in Poland. The Polish path to privatization, in principle, was a combination of three methods: sale of shares to private owners, use of vouchers, and allocation of shares to employees.

We shall now proceed to review the economic changes in detail, first by examining the decisive and exemplary measures of economic transformation undertaken in Poland at the beginning of 1990. Poland's economic example was subsequently followed, in essence, by the other countries of Eastern Europe. We then examine some particular cases of privatization, both in industry and in agriculture, where different conditions gave rise to very different approaches.

THE TRANSFORMATION OF THE POLISH ECONOMY: THE BALCEROWICZ PLAN

The Balcerowicz Plan was more than a just a plan; it was actually put into practice, in all its details, in the last quarter of 1989 and in January 1990. Its author himself subsequently described it as a 'step into the unknown'.[9]

The main measures, adopted by the Sejm on 27 December 1989, involved:

1. Price Liberalization. All that was needed in this case was simply to continue the price-raising policies already adopted by the communist government in its final months in office. Annual retail price inflation ran at over 10 per cent in Poland throughout the early 1980s, then accelerated after 1986, rising to 17.5 per cent in 1986, 25.3 per cent in 1987, 61.3 per cent in 1988 and 243.8 per cent in 1989. By the beginning of 1990, 90 per cent of all prices had been freed. This led to a further surge in inflation, but it was assumed correctly that the other measures of reform would restore price stability in the medium term.
2. Devaluation of the Currency. Between October and December 1989 the value of the złoty had fallen from 1775 to 5200 per US dollar. Now (1 January 1990) the exchange rate was set at 9500 per dollar.[10]
3. Reduction of Subsidies. The proportion of subsidies to GDP was cut from 15 per cent in 1989 to 6 per cent in 1990.[11] Farmers no longer received guaranteed prices for their products.
4. Reduction of Income Growth. The decision to restrict wage increases was the most controversial aspect of the package, partly because this was a clear case of economic intervention by a government otherwise committed to reducing the role of the state in the economy. Wage rises were restricted, first by abolishing the wage–price indexation introduced in July 1989, which had contributed to the inflationary spiral, and second by imposing a tax on wage increases paid by state enterprises to their employees. State managers

were thus given a positive incentive to keep wages down. This tax, known as the *popiwek*, was set to come into force when a state firm raised wages by more than 30 per cent of the current rate of inflation. In February it was made more severe by lowering the threshold above which it came into operation to 20 per cent. The *popiwek* was naturally unpopular, as the real value of wages paid in state enterprises would inevitably fall as a result. It was opposed unsuccessfully from within the government by the Solidarity veteran Jacek Kuroń, who was Minister of Labour, and acted very much as the spokesperson of labour's interests.[12]

5. Liberalization of foreign trade. This involved reducing the average level of tariffs from 13.3 per cent to 8 per cent, and abolishing restrictions on the import of manufactured goods. Despite these measures of liberalization there was no flood of imports into the country. The home consumer could at first afford to buy very little, since the combination of rapid inflation (78.6 per cent in the month of January 1990 alone) and restrictions on wage increases wiped out the monetary overhang that had developed in the 1980s. Production was diverted towards exports, with the result that in 1990 Poland recorded a $668 million trade surplus.[13]

The extraordinary character of these measures, introduced practically simultaneously, was marked appropriately by the Polish economic weekly *Zycie Gospodarcze* when it called them a 'sprint marathon' of reform.[14]

From some points of view the Balcerowicz Plan was entirely successful. The typical queues for basic items of consumption disappeared. Inflation was rapidly brought under control (by August 1990 monthly inflation had fallen to a mere 1.8 per cent, and annual inflation fell from 352 per cent during 1990 to 70 per cent during 1991.[15] So the objective of price stabilization was clearly in the process of being achieved. There was, however, a heavy price to pay, heavier than had been expected by the advocates of 'shock therapy'. There were severe declines in industrial production (it fell by 24 per cent during 1990 and by 12 per cent during 1991) and in GDP (the decline in this indicator was less precipitous: 12 per cent in 1990 and 8 per cent during 1991). Unemployment grew substantially (it rose to 6 per cent by the end of 1990 and 12 per cent by the end of 1991). For those still in work, average real wages fell by 24 per cent during 1990.[16]

The new rulers of Poland quickly realized that the results of 'shock therapy' were worse than they had expected; they decided to attenuate its rigours somewhat. The base lending rate to commercial banks was reduced from 4 per cent to 2.5 per cent; the interest rate was reduced to 34 per cent; the *popiwek* threshold was raised to 60 per cent in April, and to 100 per cent in July, reverting back to 60 per cent in subsequent months.[17] Moreover, a number of firms were now exempted from the tax. These measures of relaxation led, however, to renewed inflation in the second half of 1990, which the Polish National Bank countered with tighter monetary controls. The rate of interest was raised from 34 per cent to 43 per cent in October, 55 per cent in November and 72 per cent in January 1991.[18]

The only omission from the Balcerowicz Plan was a fairly glaring one: no attention was paid to privatization. No progress was made in privatizing large firms, and the method chosen to promote the growth of the private sector – financial incentives – created its own problems. The decision to raise taxes largely from the state sector (through the *popiwek* and a tax on assets called the *dywidenda*) meant that budget revenues were linked to a declining sector of the economy. Seventy-seven per cent of the November 1991 budget deficit of $2.7 billion resulted from a failure by state firms to pay their taxes, because they were either bankrupt or on the point of bankruptcy.[19]

Accordingly, the privatization process advanced at a crawl. By January 1991 only five large state firms had been sold. Responding to criticism, particularly from President Wałęsa, the Bielecki government announced a privatization offensive, to be organized by Janusz Lewandowski, the head of the Ministry of Ownership Transformation (February 1991). Lewandowski's 'mass privatization' programme of June 1991 envisaged that 400 large firms, currently producing 25 per cent of total industrial output, would be privatized. Shares in these firms would be divided three ways, in a compromise which reflected the importance attached by the government to various sections of Polish society. The workers themselves would receive 10 per cent, which was a nod towards Solidarity's left wingers; the state would retain 30 per cent. The remainder, 60 per cent, would be handed over to investment funds. Shares in these would be distributed free of charge to each of the 28 million adult inhabitants of Poland.

As yet, this was only a plan of action. It took four years before the measures actually came into effect. There were three obstacles to overcome: the budgetary shortfall which would result from wiping out such a large slice of tax revenue (as we saw earlier, tax receipts came predominantly from the state sector); the fear that inflation would arise from the creation of so many new paper assets; and the suspicion that the investment funds would become too powerful. Parliamentary approval was not achieved until April 1993, and it was not until 22 November 1995 that mass privatization was actually launched, with the sale (rather than the free issue, as originally planned) of share certificates in the investment funds. In the meantime, a form of pseudo-privatization had already taken place in Poland: privatization through liquidation. Enterprises were purchased not for money but for debt. Creditors, usually banks, who held at least 30 per cent of an enterprise's debt were given the right to convert their claims into shares, thereby 'automatically triggering transformation into joint-stock companies without the legal consent of the enterprise's workers'.[20] This was the method used in approximately 90 per cent of enterprises privatized between 1990 and 1992. Ben Slay has described privatization through liquidation as 'one of the success stories of the Polish privatization effort'.[21]

MOVING FORWARD AT A STATELY PACE: THE HUNGARIAN EXAMPLE

Privatization went as slowly in Hungary as in Poland, but here there was no 'shock therapy' either. The delay in starting to privatize was initially due to the interventionist tendencies of the Hungarian Democratic Forum (MDF) government of 1990 to 1994. A privatization law was approved by the National Assembly in September 1990. It gave the State Property Agency (ÁVÜ) the threefold task of offering shares in privatized companies, opening the way to competitive bidding and introducing employee share ownership. Enterprises scheduled for privatization would be managed in the mean time by another agency, the State Holding Company. On 29 March 1991 the Hungarian Ministry of Industry and Trade proposed that the state should retain a 51 per cent stake in all utilities. In fact no energy privatization took place, despite a promise of 14 November 1990 to 'privatize existing monopolies using domestic and foreign capital'. Only one enterprise had been fully privatized by the end of August 1991. The MDF government then announced that 160 big companies in the strategic areas of telecommunications, energy and transport would remain in state hands. This did not mean that the private sector failed to grow under the MDF. But it grew mainly by the foundation of completely new enterprises, which were more efficient and profitable than the state sector. By the end of 1994 an estimated 55 per cent of Hungary's GDP was produced in the private sector.[22] Paradoxically, the socialists (MSZP), who took the reins of power in 1994, were more strongly committed to privatization than the democrats, but there were still some obstacles to overcome before Hungary could move effectively in this direction.

The MSZP–SZDSZ coalition government set up in July 1994 decided that restructuring should precede privatization and that the two privatization agencies should be merged. This merger (9 May 1995) opened the way to the privatization of the utilities. The new Minister for Industry, Imre Dunai, said on 24 August 1995 that the privatization of electricity, oil and gas would raise $1 billion by the end of 1995. But the price of electricity would be raised by 100 per cent to make the sales attractive to Western investors. This was good news for the latter, but bad news for the poorest third of the population: they would now have to pay 35 per cent of their income for energy.[23] There was some opposition by residual socialists within the MSZP to this; left-wing opponents of the policy were able to force Dunai's resignation (15 August 1996) and the postponement of the price increases, but ultimately the government continued on its course, notwithstanding scandals over corruption in the privatization process.[24]

CZECHOSLOVAKIA: PRIVATIZATION THROUGH VOUCHERS

The method of privatizing large-scale enterprises chosen in Czechoslovakia was the issuing of vouchers. The intention was that the ordinary Czech or Slovak would thereby be given a stake in what was formerly public property. Either the vouchers could be used to buy shares in privatized firms or they could be sold to investment funds. In fact private investment funds were able to buy up roughly six million out of the eight million voucher books issued in the first tranche. These funds appealed to people's greed and ignorance of the normal operation of the financial markets by promising very high returns on their investments.[25] Hence 'large privatization' simply meant handing over the companies to investment funds. But the latter could not run without capital, and this was provided by the banks, still state-owned, which thereby gained control of the privatized companies. The 28 per cent of citizens who kept their vouchers had their chance to buy shares in May 1992 when the first round of 'voucher privatization' took place. In the course of the next four years, privatization was completed, except for 56 'strategic enterprises', including the banks, which remained within the portfolio of the National Property Fund.[26]

THE FORMER GDR: PRIVATIZATION AT LIGHTNING SPEED

The former German Democratic Republic was a special case, because the objective here was to sell off the former economy as rapidly as possible, without considering the economic or social consequences. The agency set up to handle privatization, the *Treuhandanstalt*, originally had the mandate to 'manage and restructure East German holdings and attract joint-venture capital from the West',[27] but this was redefined in the summer of 1990. Now the aim was simply to find purchasers for the enterprises it was administering. The large units (the *Kombinate*) were broken up and sold piecemeal, and any that could not be sold were simply shut down. For instance, the Pentacon camera works in Dresden, employing 3000 workers, the Wartburg car plant in Eisenach, with 20 000 workers, and the Trabant plant in Zwickau all closed in the autumn of 1990. By the end of 1990 the *Treuhandanstalt* had got rid of all but 350 of the 13 789 former East German enterprises under its control. This involved the loss of 80 per cent of the country's industrial capacity, and a rise in unemployment to 30 per cent.[28] The man in charge, Detlev Rohwedder, was murdered in April 1991 by Red Brigade terrorists. But his successor, Hanna Breuel, continued the policy. Her aim, she said, was to 'find new owners as rapidly as possible'.[29] By the end of 1994 the process was complete. The last item to be sold was the rolling stock manufacturer *Deutsche Waggonbau*, which went to a company based in Boston, Massachusetts.[30] With that, the privatization agency could be wound up. East Germany's short period of state control of industry and agriculture was now definitively at an end.

THE TRANSITION IN AGRICULTURE

In this sphere, the ideal goal of the advocates of economic transition was clear: the establishment of an efficient farming sector by the conversion of state and collective farms into private property. There were certainly objections raised to this, both on grounds of economic efficiency and social justice, and there was a clear distinction between the situation in Russia and most other former Soviet republics, where decollectivization remained on paper, and Eastern Europe, where there was a consensus in favour of privatization, and it was pushed forward energetically during the period after 1989.

There were various ways in which privatization could come about in agriculture. There was a choice to be made between sale to new private owners and restitution to former owners dispossessed by the communists during the post-1948 collectivization drive. The restitution route was at first the most popular. This popularity was based on what Conte and Giordano call 'the myth of reversible history', the idea that 'the forty five years of communism were a kind of black hole'.[31] But most post-communist governments were constrained by practical difficulties, by the opposition of existing collective farm members and by the lack of interest displayed by young, urbanized heirs to land in recovering what their forebears had lost.[32]

Two countries alone decided to go forward with restitution in the full sense: Czechoslovakia and Bulgaria.[33] In Czechoslovakia the law of 21 February 1991 provided that all agricultural property which was confiscated in 1948 or subsequently would be restored to its original owners, or heirs, if they could be found. This category covered 10 per cent of the land in the country. Much of it had belonged to the aristocratic landowners of a previous epoch; the renowned Kinsky, Lobkowicz and Colloredo families received back the land they had owned since the seventeenth century. There were some protests about this.[34] But restitution was successful, at least economically, because it was not done too hastily or ruthlessly. Several years were allowed to elapse before the legal transfer took place. In the intervening period steps were taken to protect agriculture. Before 1989, Czechoslovak agriculturalists, whether they were in the co-operative or the private sector, had been accustomed to selling their produce to the state at subsidized price levels; under free market conditions this had to come to an end. But the Czechoslovak government eased the transition by temporarily continuing subsidies (July 1991).

In the Czech Republic the major restitution measures took place in 1992–3, the result being to raise the proportion of land in private ownership from 4.4 per cent to 35.6 per cent; in Slovakia it happened two years later, and was very thoroughgoing, with the proportion of private farms rising from 8.5 per cent in 1994 to 79 per cent in 1995.[35]

The Bulgarian government's restitution measures were less successful. The law of 22 February 1991, supplemented by the law of 20 March 1992, provided for the dissolution of all producers' co-operatives and the restitution of property rights existing in 1946. This had a disastrous effect on the agrarian economy. A return to 1946 meant a return to fragmentation of property. Six million Bulgarians became private farmers overnight, on twelve million parcels of land . Most of the land (91 per cent) was covered by minute farms measuring between a tenth of a hectare and one hectare apiece. Moreover, the law of 20 March 1992 also abolished the leasehold rights of collective farm members, who had used their leased plots very efficiently in the 1980s, producing between 30 per cent and 40 per cent of the total agricultural product from 15 per cent of the land area.[36] This decision on leasehold rights failed to take into account the legal changes of the 1980s, which had raised the importance of the private sector by letting peasants lease land from the collectives. By the end of the communist era the private sector was already playing a decisive part in Bulgarian agriculture. The hastily introduced and ideologically inspired agrarian policy of the Popov and Dimitrov governments of 1991–2 did not cause, but it certainly worsened, the economic decline of the mid-1990s. Agricultural production fell by 35 per cent between 1991 and 1994; agricultural exports collapsed completely, falling by 77 per cent between 1990 and 1993. Tobacco cultivation was particularly hard hit, falling from an index level of 100 in 1988 to 73 in 1991, 64 in 1992 and 46 in 1993. Tobacco exports fell correspondingly, from 55 000 tonnes in 1988 to 27 000 tonnes in 1991 and 15 000 tonnes in 1993. The overall contribution of agriculture to Bulgaria's national income fell from 15.5 per cent in 1991 to 11.5 per cent in 1992, 9.2 per cent in 1993 and 8.5 per cent in 1994;[37] the living standards of the population fell in proportion; by 1993, 59.4 per cent of the population were below the poverty line.[38]

Georgi Tanev, Minister of Agriculture in the government that followed Dimitrov summed up the impact of the latter's reforms in this way: 'The situation is pretty well catastrophic. I am bitter about the condition of agriculture. The collapse is so severe that I am astounded. A policy of Thatcherism has been carried out here, involving the complete withdrawal of the state from agriculture.' When the peasants heard that they would lose their land 'they slaughtered 72 % of their chickens, 38 % of their sheep and 7 % of their pigs in the course of 1992'. The Russian peasants of the early 1930s slaughtered their livestock in reaction to forced collectivization; the Bulgarian peasants of the early 1990s did the same thing in reaction to forced decollectivization.[39]

The Bulgarian socialists made a lot of political capital out of this disaster. In September 1993 they demanded 'the unconditional restoration of the property of the agricultural collectives'. This helped them to gain extra support in the countryside. But it was just propaganda. When they returned to power in January 1995 they did not change previous policies or dispossess the new private owners, who now accounted for 76.3 per cent of total agricultural production. Agricultural productivity went on falling under the BSP government: it fell from 2841 kg of wheat per hectare in 1994 to 2000 kg in 1996, with corresponding falls in all other crops except rice and dry beans.[40]

The inability of the BSP government to reverse the sharp decline in Bulgarian agriculture clearly indicates that the reasons for it went far beyond the restitution policies of the Union of Democratic Forces. They included: loss of markets owing to the collapse of CMEA trade; rising relative import prices; and the continuing monopoly position of state purchasing agencies (rather than being privatized they were regionalized, with grain being purchased after 1994 by 74 regional buyers instead of 1 national buyer, and tobacco bought by 22 buyers instead of *Bulgartabak* alone).[41]

In the rest of Eastern Europe restitution of agricultural land in the full sense did not occur. In Hungary the method chosen was monetary compensation for loss of value (June 1991), and even then a limit equivalent to $70 000 per person was placed on the amount. This reflected the political defeat of the Smallholders (FKGP) who had called for the total restitution of all landed property expropriated since 1949, and was a victory for the cautious approach of the MDF government, which was more concerned with the welfare of the small property owner than with abstract historical justice.[42] Land could also be bought with 'property coupons', and by May 1994 484 000 people had taken advantage of this possibility. But they then rented the land back to the co-operative farm which had previously cultivated it.[43] Not until the socialists came into office – another paradox of Hungarian socialism – was there a significant rise in the amount of land held privately (up from 26.5 per cent in 1993 to 43.3 per cent in 1994) and a corresponding fall in co-operatively owned land (down from 53.3 per cent to 37.7 per cent). The state farms, too, were left untouched until the Socialist–Free Democrat coalition took office. Agrarian restructuring in Hungary was accompanied (as elsewhere) by a decline in agricultural production (between 1990 and 1994 this fell by 23 per cent, a better result than in Bulgaria but worse than other parts of Eastern Europe).[44] The situation was worsened by a flight from the land: between 1990 and 1993 the agricultural labour force fell by 59 per cent.[45]

In Romania the National Salvation Front created a particularly confused legal situation by privatizing the land but simultaneously giving substitute plots to previous owners whose land had been converted to non-agricultural uses during the communist period. As result there were 300 000 court actions pending in 1995 over questions of landownership.[46] Nevertheless, by 1997, 74 per cent of the land was in private hands.[47]

Poland had already got rid of its collective farms in the late 1950s. But the country retained a fairly large state farm sector throughout the communist period. Dismantling the state farms was not easy, because the issue was bound up with the question of the restitution of Church property. Given the strong clerical influence on the first post-1989 governments there was strong pressure for restitution, but deep divisions between the President (who wanted Church property restitution alone), the Right (who wanted it applied to all property expropriations whatever the date) and the alliance led by the formerly communist SDRP (who wanted restitution limited to illegal expropriations) delayed any decision. So the state farms, which the Sejm voted to abolish on 4 October 1991, still retained 10 per cent of the land in 1994.

THE PROBLEM OF THE FINANCIAL SECTOR

The transition from state to private banking after 1989 was managed particularly badly. The desire to withdraw the state as completely and quickly as possible from any role in the economy meant that very little attempt was made either to build up new, sound financial institutions or exert adequate control over lending by existing banks.[48] The few financial reforms that were attempted 'remained at the formal level'.[49] An example is the Czech Republic, where the Klaus government, despite its enthusiastic commitment to market reforms, was deeply divided over the question of banking privatization. Jan Kalvoda, head of the Civic Democratic Alliance (ODA) wanted it to go ahead. Klaus wanted to postpone it because he feared banking instability. It was the Prime Minister who had his way; the banks were not privatized. As a direct result, banking crises blew up in 1996 and 1997.

The collapse of banks and the resulting scandals have been a feature of the situation in most of the post-communist countries. The banks have tended to pile up bad debts and to issue excessive amounts of money. This has sometimes been associated with corruption. In Poland senior officials at state banks were arrested, and the head of the central bank was suspended, for passing large sums of money to a private organization known as APT-B (7 August 1991). There have been two major corruption scandals in the Czech Republic. The Koženy–Wallis affair arose out of the mushroom growth of a company called Harvard Investment and Consulting, which had been set up to take advantage of the voucher privatization scheme.[50] Its founder Viktor Koženy bought secret information on the development of the economy from a certain

Václav Wallis, who was an agent of Czech intelligence. This enabled him to promise a tenfold profit to anyone who handed over their privatization voucher to his company; a million people did so. Wallis was later indicted by a military court (28 July 1993). Two years later, the former head of voucher privatization, Jaroslav Ligner, received a seven year sentence for accepting bribes (18 October 1995).

Inability to collect on bad loans has resulted in numerous bank collapses all over Eastern Europe. Given the close connection between the banks and the political elite it is not surprising that the fall of a bank sometimes entailed the fall of a government. In Lithuania the insolvency of the Lithuanian Joint-Stock Innovation Bank (LAIB) on 20 December 1995 led to the fall of the government of Adolfas Slezevičius and his replacement as Prime Minister by Česlovas Stankevičius in April 1996. In the Czech Republic, the way privatization was managed, through investment funds, meant that the banks often owned the firms on which they had to make financial judgments; they therefore tended to prop them up with unsound loans.[51] The Kreditní Bank collapsed in August 1996, because Motoinvest, a Prague investment group, was unable to repay its debts. This did not result in the fall of the government, but shortly afterwards Prime Minister Klaus was forced to move towards banking privatization by pressure from the EU. This brought further problems: since the state-owned banks had lent unwisely, they needed bailing out (this was described euphemistically as 'financial restructuring') before privatization could take place.[52]

In Hungary three of the largest banks became insolvent in 1993; the state intervened to prop them up, spending $3 billion between 1993 and 1996, a sum which allowed the banks to write off $1.5 billion of bad debts and restructure financially. Having had their fingers burnt, the banks later pursued an ultra-cautious credit policy. Foreign capital (more freely available to Hungary than to most other countries) was seen as the answer, and by 1997 the majority of Hungarian banks were controlled by Western financial interests (for instance the K & H Bank[53] is 56 per cent Belgian-Irish).[54] In Bulgaria, the collapse of the value of the currency in 1996 was blamed on excessive money issues by the central bank, with the connivance of the government. The IMF and the World Bank insisted that the power to issue money should be taken out of the hands of the bank and given to a Currency Board. So far this solution has worked.[55]

In general the financial sector is weak in the Eastern European economies, and given the limited level of Western involvement this situation is likely to continue.

ENVIRONMENTAL PROBLEMS

The whole of the former communist sphere suffered from severe environmental problems, which were the result of a desperate search for expanded production unrestrained by any considerations of human welfare or the quality of life. The profit-driven degradation of the environment, at least in the developed capitalist world, was restricted in recent years in response to popular pressure; under communism, in contrast, environmentalist pressure-groups knew they were facing a system that would resist change to the very end. 1989 should have been a great victory for environmentalism. But one of the paradoxes of the post-communist era was that whereas the opponents of communism had often made the condition of the environment a major plank in their political agitation before 1989, once in power they felt compelled by economic necessity to continue programmes which were harmful to the very environment they wanted to protect.

One example of the failure of the new governments to fulfil the promise of the dissident ecological movements of the 1980s was environmentally friendly energy supply. Energy was of course essential to continuing industrial production, and the decision of the Soviet Union's main successor state, the Russian Federation, to charge full market prices for energy exports made it essential for Central and Eastern Europe to find alternative sources of supply. In Hungary the dilemma was particularly acute, owing to the rejection, specifically on environmental grounds, of the Nagymáros-Gabčikovo hydroelectric power project, and the reduction in the supply of crude oil from Russia. The rejection of the Nagymáros project gave rise to severe and continuing tension with Czechoslovakia, which refused to accept the Hungarian decision to cancel the project (22 April 1991). Subsequently, Slovakia brought the issue before the International Court of Justice, on the ground that Hungary had committed a breach of international law in unilaterally abrogating a signed contract. The Hungarians were compelled to admit defeat on this point; the dam will now probably go ahead.

Nuclear power was an obvious alternative to fossil fuels. Superficially attractive, but potentially more dangerous to the environment than either hydroelectricity or coal, it was promoted by the Hungarian government in 1990 when it invited Edward Teller, the Hungarian-born 'father of the hydrogen bomb' to talk on television about the advantages of this new form of energy.[56] The Czech government also favoured the nuclear alternative. Industry Minister Vladimír Dlouhý announced on 24 February 1993 that nuclear power 'would allow a forty per cent reduction in the capacity of lignite-fired power stations in Northern Bohemia', hence less environmental pollution. It was therefore right to complete the new nuclear power station which was under construction at Temelin.[57] Environmentalists both within the Czech Republic and internationally were not convinced. However, the need for cheap energy supplies was the most powerful argument of all, and every East-European country except Poland has kept its old and dangerous Soviet-designed reactors. In Bulgaria the existing plant at Kozloduy was retained and the head of the International Atomic Energy Authority, Hans Blix, supported the construction of another plant at Belene. In Slovakia the government insisted on retaining its old nuclear plant at Bohunice despite the fact that the EBRD had made a loan for completion of a new plant at Mochovce conditional on the closure of the old one. The money was obtained from Russia instead (31 October 1995).[58]

In general, therefore, problems with energy supply were solved in the 1990s by resorting to the rather risky nuclear option. Energy consumption, however, produced just as much pollution as supply did in the wasteful industrial environment of late communism. In this sphere, the new regimes benefited from a post-communist paradox. For the general industrial collapse which followed the fall of communism had a silver lining: the fall in industrial production brought with it a fall in industrial pollution. For example, the 29 per cent fall in CO_2 emissions registered in Central and Eastern Europe over the four years from 1989 to 1993 went far beyond the 5 per cent reduction agreed as a world target. On a global scale, the transition countries' contribution to cutting CO_2 emissions has counterbalanced continuing Western increases in emissions over the same period.[59] The post-communist collapse of the former Soviet Union's so-called rust-belt industries had a strong effect in this regard: there was a 17 per cent decline in the emission of harmful substances in Russia between 1990 and 1992.[60] In the nature of things, however, this could only bring temporary alleviation. The underlying environmental problems persisted. When production began to recover, as it did from 1994 onwards in Eastern Europe, pollution increased as well.[61] There is, moreover, every reason to expect a continuing worsening of the situation, particularly given the substantial increase in motor vehicle use; actually this occurred even during the economic depression of the early 1990s. The percentage rise in motor vehicles ranged from 25 per cent upwards over the five years between 1989 and 1994 (Bulgaria: 26 per cent, Hungary: 26 per cent, Poland: 48 per cent, Ukraine: 37 per cent).[62]

HELP FROM THE OUTSIDE WORLD AND ITS LIMITS

It was understood in the West from the outset that the economic transformation of the formerly communist East could not be accomplished without outside assistance. Already in July 1989 a summit meeting of the Group of Seven (the seven most industrialized countries) decided to help Poland and Hungary in moving towards a market economy; this was followed by the creation by the European Commission of PHARE (an acronym which stands for Poland, Hungary, Assistance to the Restructuring of the Economy). This aid programme was limited initially to Poland and Hungary, then extended to the rest of Central and Eastern Europe. A separate programme was set up after 1992 for the CIS, under the acronym TACIS (Technical Assistance to the Commonwealth of Independent States). A European Bank for Reconstruction and Development (EBRD) was set up in April 1991, for the specific purpose of promoting both economic and political transformation over the whole area (including the former USSR). Existing international financial institutions (such as the International Monetary Fund and the World Bank) also played an important part in disbursing financial assistance. Finally, direct arrangements (for providing bilateral credits) were often made with members of the Group of Seven and other interested parties.

All these institutions granted assistance for different reasons and with different conditions; the aid was unco-ordinated, it was generally tied to the meeting of targets such as low budget deficits and it came overwhelmingly in the form of loans rather than grants, thus increasing the indebtedness of the recipients. In terms of quantity, however, the flow of aid far outpaced direct investment throughout the period. Between 1990 and 1993 Central and Eastern Europe and the former Soviet Union received a total of $142 billion of aid, in contrast to $12 billion of direct investment.[63] The figures for Eastern Europe in percentage terms were; aid 72.2 per cent, investment 13.6 per cent, borrowing 14.2 per cent. In Russia investment played an even smaller role (5.6 per cent).[64] Subsequently, the proportion of direct investment in the transition countries increased somewhat, from 8.5 per cent between 1990 and 1993 to 28.1 per cent in the year 1994–5 ($18.9 billion of investment, 1994–5, as against $67.1 billion of aid). But there is still a tremendous contrast between the readiness of Western companies to invest in China, which is still a communist country, and, for example, Russia. In 1996, $6.7 billion were invested in Russia, $135 billion in China. One reason is continuing suspicion that Russian companies do not meet Western financial standards, and a continuing conflict between Western banks and Soviet-style industrial managers. Another reason for the relative lack of Western investment is the pervasive sense of financial and physical insecurity, at least in the countries of the former Soviet Union. Finally, some countries have displayed xenophobic attitudes which have not encouraged outside investment. A surprising example is Slovenia, otherwise a model transition country, which refuses to grant foreigners the right to own property in the country; this policy, largely directed against Italian investors, is strongly upheld by Janez Jansa, the charismatic leader of the Slovene Social Democrats.

Aid of various kinds, therefore, remains the main component in capital flows to the transition economies. One specific kind of aid, which always depends on the recipient's commitment to pursuing a consistent reform programme, is debt rescheduling. Russia, which inherited a debt of $103 billion from the Soviet Union in 1992, was able in 1996 to secure a rescheduling of $40 billion of this burden: this meant a reduction in interest payments from $8 billion a year to $2 billion.[65] It should be noted that the transition countries have not received any special favours from the world financial institutions: between 1990 and 1995, only 15 per cent of total capital flows from developed to developing and transition countries went to the latter, and only 13 per cent of direct foreign investment. There has been no new Marshall Plan for the post-communist epoch; the policies of the advanced industrial countries have been more reminiscent of the 1920s, when the answer found was to stick to the established liberal recipes.

THE INITIAL IMPACT OF MARKETIZATION AND PRIVATIZATION

The consensus view of economists and the governments which followed their advice after 1989 was that the state should withdraw from the economy 'as far as and as quickly as possible', because 'otherwise the old *nomenklatura* would try to restore the command economy'.[66] As the influential Hungarian economist János Kornai proclaimed in 1990: 'Right now, at the beginning of the transformation process, it is time to take great steps away in the direction of a minimal state.'[67] This had the disadvantage, however, of creating an 'institutional hiatus',[68] because it was thought to be sufficient just to remove the old command system without replacing it with any new mechanisms. Legal regulation of enterprise activities was considered unnecessary; and any attempt to smooth the transition through subsidies of various kinds was rejected as reintroducing distortions into the market.

Transition policies resulted in severe hardship and economic dislocation. We shall examine the social consequences of transition in detail in Chapter 7, but in this section attention will be focused on the economy. There were falls in industrial and agricultural production, in GDP, in per capita income, in real wages, and in employment during the years 1990–2. Foreign trade also collapsed, falling to less than half its 1989 value. When trade volumes did start to recover, from 1993, it was on the basis of a gradual increase in trade with the developed industrial countries of the West, rather than between the transition countries; the latter now accounted for between 15 per cent and 20 per cent of the total (except in Bulgaria), the former for between 65 per cent and 80 per cent.[69]

Once the consequences of transition became clear, the minimalist consensus faded away, to be replaced by a clamour of competing advice. Western critics of neo-liberalism argued that it would be absolutely impossible to repeat the successes of the East Asian miracle economies of the 1970s and 1980s, because they were based on active government involvement and buoyant domestic demand resulting from relative income equality, neither of which conditions prevailed in Eastern Europe. Alice Amsden bluntly remarked in 1993 that 'economic transition policies have failed', using as evidence a thumbnail sketch of the economy of 'the most promising nation – Hungary'.[70] The indictment looked fairly convincing at the time (although it is fair to say that most of the problems she mentions were temporary): a 40 per cent fall in industrial output, unemployment in double figures and rising, 'government violation of press freedom and other civil rights'.[71] The conclusion she drew, shared by other critics, was that governments should intervene more decisively now, especially by granting subsidies to ailing industries. In Czechoslovakia the government of Václav Klaus, despite its free-market rhetoric, proved sensitive to this point of view.[72]

Perhaps surprisingly, the post-communist parties which came to power in Poland and Hungary as part of the electoral backlash against the hardship and economic dislocation produced by an uncontrolled transition did not in fact pursue policies of greater government intervention. In Poland the SLD was strongly pro-market and anti-interventionist. The example of the Gdańsk Shipyards demonstrates this. They were of great sentimental value because they were the birthplace of Solidarity, but were constantly on the edge of bankruptcy, making losses equivalent to $50 million in 1994 and $35 million in 1995. The SLD Finance Minister, Grzegorz Kołodko, firmly rejected calls to step in to save them. The government would 'accept the market's decision' he said (18 March 1996). No further help was extended. Kołodko also called for lower taxes, less government spending, self-financing pensions and the closure of 15 loss-making coalmines. The main resistance to this line came from the SLD's coalition partners, the Agrarian PSL. The Treasury Minister in charge of privatization, Mirosław Pietrewɪcz, who was a member of the PSL, contradicted Kołodko on 25 November 1996, saying that the shipyards could still be saved.

In Hungary the policies of the post-communist MSZP followed a similar trajectory; it came to power by promising that it would soften austerity measures, and proceeded to do the opposite. There was some opposition from within the party to this. Ministers Pál Kovács and Béla Katona resigned in protest against what they saw as a betrayal (14 March 1995). But they were unable to change the government's course.

It should be noted, however, that the scale of poverty and hardship in East-Central and South-Eastern Europe after 1989 did in fact compel governments to transfer a greater proportion of GDP to the poor and needy than the governments of either the former Soviet countries or comparable middle-income countries in other parts of the world. In fact at 15 per cent of GDP their levels of cash transfer were equivalent to those prevalent in the rich industrialized countries of the OECD.[73] A considerable proportion of this expenditure took the form of pension payments, through state-run pension schemes which continued to operate after 1989 in the old way, despite reform proposals. In Poland, where pensioners did relatively well (pensions were set at 71 per cent of the average wage), government spending on pensions rose from 7.5 per cent of GDP in 1990 to 15.8 per cent in 1995. In other countries, where benefits were lower, the proportion of GDP swallowed up was lower too (Czech Republic 9.9 per cent in 1995; Slovakia 9.4 per cent; Hungary 11.5 per cent).[74]

In South-Eastern Europe, where pensions were less of a problem because the age-structure was more favourable, governments quietly operated what was in practice a system of subsidies by allowing the banks to make loans to enterprises without checking their viability too carefully. Another way in which governments could intervene in the economy was by selling the arms produced by what was left of their military-industrial complex. This point applies most strongly to Russia, but it is also true of both halves of former Czechoslovakia. Russian arms sales in 1996 amounted to $3 billion, making Russia second only to the United States as a source of armaments.[75] The Czechoslovak government insisted in 1991 that arms sales 'would have to continue until substitute industries were in place', and announced that tanks to the value of $200 million had been sold to Syria.[76] The Slovak government continued this approach after the breakup of the country in 1993.

THE SHADOW ECONOMY

There is reason to suppose that the economic decline of the 1990s in the transition countries was less disastrous than appears at first sight. This is because of the rise of the 'shadow' or 'hidden' economy. For example, on paper, since 1991, Russia's GDP has fallen by 65 per cent, her industrial production by 50 per cent, her real income by 40 per cent; but the shadow economy has grown from an estimated 12 per cent of economic activity in 1989 to an estimated 40 per cent of GDP in 1996 (whereas in the countries of the European Union the average size of the 'shadow', or 'black', economy is reckoned to be between 7 per cent and 16 per cent of GDP).[77]

Russia holds the record for the size of its shadow economy, but Hungary is not far behind. There it was estimated at 30 per cent of GDP in 1994, and 37 per cent of that total was ascribed to illegal trading activities.[78] Increases in the size of the shadow economy have been reported in many transition countries. It rose from 4.3 per cent to 16.8 per cent of GDP in Bulgaria between 1992 and 1994, and from 6.7 per cent to 10.0 per cent in Romania, and stood at 20 per cent in Estonia and Slovenia in 1994.[79] These are naturally estimates; in the nature of things no-one knows the precise dimensions of unofficial economic activities.

There are cases where the existence and magnitude of the shadow economy can be inferred by indirect methods. Thus in Poland real income allegedly fell by 20 per cent in the five years between 1988 and 1993, but at the same time there was a 65 per cent increase in the ownership of video recorders, a 90 per cent increase in colour televisions, and a 45 per cent increase in motor car ownership.[80] Much of this equipment was bought by Poles who were officially unemployed; in 1995 between 5 per cent and 7 per cent of all adults were mainly occupied in the 'grey sphere' of economic activity.[81]

THE BALANCE SHEET OF ECONOMIC TRANSFORMATION

It is not too much to say that in a number of countries of Eastern Europe a successful economic transition has now been achieved. An interesting attempt to quantify the degree of economic liberalization, taking into account internal prices, external markets, size of the private sector and openness to private sector entry has been made by Åslund and others on behalf of the World Bank. The following countries had already liberalized to an extent of over 80 per cent by 1994: Poland, the Czech Republic, Slovakia, Hungary, Estonia, Lithuania, Croatia and Slovenia. Bulgaria, Romania, Albania, Latvia and Macedonia were between 70 per cent and 80 per cent liberalized.[82] Since then, the trend towards liberalization has continued. Moreover, the abnormal pains of the process of transformation have by now largely been absorbed in East-Central Europe. The problems that remain are social rather than economic. While economies have either recovered to their pre-1989 level or are within striking distance of it,[83] the human victims of the process have by no means recovered. The level of unemployment remains high in the former GDR, Hungary, Poland, Slovakia and throughout South-Eastern Europe.[84] Real wages have risen from the nadir they reached in the years around 1992, but they are not back even to the pre-1989 level.[85] There are large sectors of the population which have not yet seen the benefits of the ending of communist rule. These matters will be examined in more detail in the next chapter.

Despite the generally favourable economic picture sketched above, there are still some weaknesses, particularly in the financial sphere. These have affected South-Eastern Europe most strongly, although other parts of the region are not immune. The currency of the transition countries has been subject to intermittent crisis. These are, on one view, the inevitable result of integration into the world monetary system. After all, the advanced industrial economies have not exactly been crisis-free in the late 1990s. But on another view a currency crisis reveals genuine weaknesses and deficiencies in an economy, which need to be remedied. The Bulgarian crisis of 1996 was a case in point. Here the government resisted the advice of international financial institutions; as a result the lev collapsed from 70 to the dollar in January 1996 to 160 to the dollar in May 1996. Emergency measures taken to deal with the crisis included the closure of loss-making enterprises, bringing redundancies and social distress. This scenario is likely to be repeated in the future in other places where governments have made only a half-hearted start towards economic transformation.

7 The Shock of the New: Social Consequences and Costs of Transition

THE LOSERS

In this section we shall endeavour to outline the various kinds of suffering and loss imposed on the populations of post-communist countries by the transition process, and the measures, if any, taken by governments to alleviate these problems.

The main direct costs of transition have been usefully classified by the International Child Development Centre attached to UNICEF:[1] (1) unemployment; (2) lower real incomes; (3) food shortages and lack of adequate nutrition; (4) inadequately maintained and contaminated water and sewage systems, leading to the spread of infectious diseases; and (5) psychological stress arising from economic uncertainty.

First, unemployment.[2] This has inevitably risen, given that full employment was an essential component of the previous system. Job losses were not generally counterbalanced by increased alternative opportunities, which had been the optimistic expectation of the reformers. Hence the rise of unemployment was accompanied by a severe fall in full-time employment. To give the most extreme examples, between 1991 and 1996 the proportion of the population in full-time employment fell from 49 per cent to 37.8 per cent in Hungary, from 55.4 per cent to 36.6 per cent in Bulgaria, from 60 per cent to 48.8 per cent in Estonia and from 63.3 per cent to 44.2 per cent in Romania.[3] Moreover, the impact of unemployment has been uneven in some places, creating pockets of extreme misery amid relative prosperity. In Poland, for instance, there was a great contrast between the 28 per cent–30 per cent level of unemployment in poorer districts such as Suvalki, Koszalin and Słupsk and the single-figure levels registered in Poznán and Warsaw.[4]

Second, falling real income. This is almost always one of the results of a fall in GDP, because the latter brings with it a fall in GDP per capita.[5] The income of the wage-earning section of the population, that is real wages, fell even faster and further than GDP during the period of transition, owing to the differential impact on wage-earners of faster than expected rates of inflation.[6] In Czechoslovakia and Poland falls in wages accounted for the greater part of the cumulative fall in incomes between 1989 and 1991.[7] This contributed to an increase in poverty, which we shall discuss in more detail later.

Third, food shortages, resulting from the severe decline in agricultural production during the first few years of transition everywhere except in Romania (between 1990 and 1994 there were falls of 32 per cent in Poland, 30 per cent in Bulgaria, 27 per cent in Hungary, 13 per cent in Czechoslovakia and 10 per cent in Albania).[8]

Fourth, a decline in standards of health care and in the maintenance of essential services, which brought with it a decline in the general health of the population as well as the recrudescence of many diseases previously considered to have been eradicated. Outbreaks of cholera, typhoid fever, malaria, tuberculosis, syphilis and diptheria all took place in the former Soviet Union in the years after 1990. In 1994 that region accounted for 85 per cent of the world's diptheria cases. Moreover, inadequate supplies of syringes and condoms helped the new killer, AIDS, to take an increased toll, above all in Romania, where there were 3852 cases diagnosed between 1990 and 1995.[9]

Fifth, the role of psychological stress in this situation should not be underestimated. The rise in psychological pressures associated with the period of transition has led to more frequent heart attacks and strokes. The link between stress and increases in male mortality can be shown by examining the cause of death statistics reported to the World Health Organization. It seems that females have been better able to stand up to the stresses of the transition period than males. Male life expectancy at birth, after rising slowly until 1989, began to fall and continued falling until 1992 in every transition country except Czechoslovakia. In the former Soviet Union (including the Baltic States) and in the Balkans the fall has continued. Female life expectancy generally did not fall. But even here, the figure remained roughly stationary rather than rising steadily as it had done in earlier decades.[10]

The greatest deterioration has been experienced in Russia and some other parts of the former Soviet Union. The fall in male life expectancy in the Russian Federation was such that by 1996 Russian men had less chance of living to the age of 60 (54 per cent) than they had had in 1897 (56 per cent): a truly catastrophic result. The main reason for this was a sharp rise in the mortality rate for men in their forties and fifties. In 1995, for the first time ever, excluding periods of war and famine, the number of deaths was higher than the number of births over the territory formerly occupied by the USSR: there were 3.7 million births and 3.8 million deaths, producing a natural population loss of 109 000.[11] In contrast to this, the picture for East-Central Europe (except Hungary) was rather more favourable. Here the Age 20–59 mortality rate declined after 1989, while male life expectancy, after falling between 1989 and 1992, actually began to rise somewhat, with the result that an overall increase was registered over the whole period up to 1996.[12] The countries of South-Eastern Europe, along with the Baltic States, have so far followed the Russian rather than the East-Central European trend: life expectancy there has fallen.

The women of Eastern Europe have reacted to these pressures of transition, not by dying sooner, but by having fewer children. Since 1989 a continuing decline in the birth rate has been observed in every single transition country. The decline has been particularly marked in the Baltic region – ranging between 29.8 per cent in Catholic Lithuania and 45.9 per cent in Protestant Latvia.[13]

These rises in mortality and declines in the birth rate have tended to reduce the rate of natural population increase all over the region. Where populations were declining before 1989, as in Hungary, the decline has accelerated; where populations were increasing, the increase has slowed (Poland, Slovakia) or turned into a decline (Bulgaria, Romania and all three Baltic countries).[14] This has been a cause for concern particularly in small, newly independent states, which feel that population growth is essential to national survival. In Latvia, for instance, which holds the record for falling birth rates (sadly, it also holds the record for rising infant mortality), the government has introduced incentives to encourage people to have more children. These were increased in 1997 to 196 lats per child. Spending on this item now amounts to 10 per cent of the national budget.[15]

Statisticians and demographers have put much effort into exploring the precise nature of the link between the process of transition from communism and population decline.[16] Ellmann and Cornia have both pointed out that excess deaths are directly related to economic stabilization programmes: cuts in government expenditure have meant a deterioration in health services, medical care and social security systems. There is one bright spot in this grim picture: the reduced number of babies that *were* born in Eastern Europe had a better chance of surviving their first year of life than ever before. Declines in infant mortality of the order of 25 per cent or more have been the norm in the 1990s (except in Bulgaria and Latvia).[17]

The view is sometimes advanced that the decline in population in several countries of Eastern Europe (Albania, Bulgaria, Croatia, Hungary, Romania, Slovenia) and the former Soviet Union (Estonia, Georgia,

Latvia, Russia) since 1990[18] is a natural result of adaptation to Western-style birth rates. This view is unconvincing, given that basic demographic trends did not continue after 1989 but suffered sharp changes.[19] Factors linked with the transition have had a far more significant impact: economic instability, social stress, a sense of hopelessness, and a lack of government intervention in health and welfare policy have all played their part in the tendency of the population to decline.[20] There was a drastic and unprecedented decline in the crude marriage rate between 1989 and 1994 (varying between 13 per cent and 51 per cent) and a similar decline in the total fertility rate (varying between 7.3 per cent, the Hungarian case, and 37.7 per cent, the Estonian). The decline in the total fertility rate was more rapid among older women, hence it could not have resulted from adaptation to a Western style of female career expectations because these women's careers were already drawing to a close. The real reasons are hinted at in a survey of the reasons given by women in Belarus for their unwillingness to have children. They placed the difficulty of combining childcare with a profession at the bottom of a list which included economic uncertainty, a bad housing situation, and the fear of deformity arising from the repercussions of the Chernobyl disaster.[21]

In any case, the rapid rise in the death rate has been an equally significant factor in population decline. This has occurred everywhere except in the Czech Republic (where the rate has fallen by 7.3 per cent), Slovakia (a fall of 6.0 per cent) and Poland (a fall of 0.4 per cent). The main reason for the rise in mortality[22] is the stress of living in the post-communist environment, which has produced an epidemic of heart disease among the middle-aged. There are certainly other factors involved in the higher rate of mortality, but they had little impact in the post-1989 period; as we have noted, environmental pollution actually declined owing to the overall industrial decline; and alcohol consumption declined between 1989 and 1994 everywhere in Eastern Europe except in the Czech Republic, Poland and Romania (where it remained roughly static).[23]

SOCIAL CONSEQUENCES OF TRANSITION: WINNERS AND LOSERS

If we now move on to consider the social consequences of transition, we find first a clear change in the distribution of income. This has become more unequal in all the countries where precise analyses have been made, except Slovakia. The countries of Eastern Europe and the former

Soviet Union all had low Gini coefficients[24] before 1989. They ranged from 0.20 to 0.26. The five years after 1989 saw an average increase of five points on the scale; this is the same annual change as occurred in the United Kingdom under Mrs Thatcher, and it brought Eastern Europe up to the OECD average of 0.27. If the former Soviet Union is included in the calculations, the index rises to 0.30.[25] The biggest rises in the Gini coefficient took place in Russia, where 15 points were put on between 1991 and 1994 (from 0.26 to 0.41),[26] Estonia, where the increase was 16 points, up to 0.39, Kyrgyzstan, where the figure may have risen by 33 points, to 0.50, and in Bulgaria, where 13 points were added between 1989 and 1993 (from 0.21 to 0.34).[27] Another way of examining the degree of inequality in income is by looking at the top and the bottom of the scale, and this confirms the drastic character of the changes in Poland and Bulgaria. In both countries the poorest 20 per cent saw their share of income fall from 10 per cent to 6.5 per cent, while the top 20 per cent gained by 3 per cent (Poland) and 7.5 per cent (Bulgaria).

Where resources are scarce an increase in inequality will result in increased poverty. Using a poverty line of $120 a month at 1990 prices, Branko Milanovic showed in 1994 that the number of people living in poverty in Eastern Europe had grown from 3.6 million to 18.7 million – or from 4 per cent to 19 per cent. This increase has been concentrated in Bulgaria, Poland and Romania. In 1994 only 500 000 of the poor (2.7 per cent) lived in Hungary, the Czech Republic, Slovakia and Slovenia taken together; by far the greater part lived in Poland (9.8 million), Romania (5.6 million) and Bulgaria (2.9 million). Poverty was concentrated among the farming population, unemployed people and those without education. The farmers suffered severely from the transition to the market; the unemployed became poorer firstly because unemployment benefit fell as a proportion of the average wage from 40–60 per cent in 1991 to 25–35 per cent in 1994, and secondly because the level of family benefit fell, for example in the Czech Republic from 10.4 per cent of the average wage in 1989 to 5.0 per cent in 1994, and in Hungary from 20.5 per cent in 1989 to 14.6 per cent in 1994.[28] Finally, the uneducated, who are generally limited to low-wage jobs, also suffered even when in work because the minimum wage, inherited from the communist era, was progressively reduced below the minimum subsistence level 'with the partial exception of Poland, the Czech Republic and Slovakia'.[29]

The direct relation between these changes and government policy is clearly illustrated by the case of Czechoslovakia (followed, after 1993, by the Czech Republic). Until 1992 Czechoslovak social policy was shaped by social democrats and labour leaders. Petr Miller at the Ministry of

Labour played an important part in promoting policies of social justice. In contrast to Poland, the social safety net continued to operate.[30] In 1992 Václav Klaus became prime minister of a right-wing coalition government. He cut subsidies on rent, heat, electricity and transport, so that by 1993 they were down to 5 per cent of GDP, and he also phased out compensation for the loss of food subsidies (this came to an end in 1995). These things had an immediate effect on the income of the poorest people in the country; at the same time the increased concentration of wealth facilitated by the free market began to be apparent. Before 1992 the Gini coefficient had certainly increased, but only slowly (from 0.19 in 1988 to 0.23 in 1992). Now it started to increase rapidly (from 0.23 to 0.28 in 1994 alone), and while the share of the top 20 per cent of the population in the national income rose from 34.3 per cent in 1992 to 37.7 per cent in 1994 the bottom 20 per cent saw their share fall from 11.1 per cent to 9.6 per cent.[31] It was not surprising that Czechs (and Slovaks) began to complain about an increased inequality they had initially embraced as a welcome change from the sham egalitarianism of communist times. Thus whereas in 1990, 57.8 per cent of those surveyed said wage differences should continue to increase and 49.7 per cent thought private enterprise should be completely unrestricted in its operations, the corresponding proportions for 1994 were 18.9 per cent and 21.2 per cent; a startling reversal of opinion.[32]

Whether this change in attitudes will find a political expression has yet to be seen; it has not happened yet in the Czech Republic, although the increasing strength of the Social Democrats in successive elections, culminating in 1998 in their assumption of the reins of power, has created a possibility that the Klaus government's policies may be reversed.

We have shown in this section that there have been plenty of losers from the transition process. Later on we shall examine attempts by the losers to protect themselves by organizing collectively through trade unions. First, though, we shall take a look at some of the winners, starting with the rise of crime, and continuing by examining the survival of the *nomenklaturists*.

THE RISE OF CRIME

The growth of the shadow economy in Russia and some other transition countries[33] has gone hand in hand with the rise of organized crime. This is less pronounced in Eastern Europe than in Russia, though by no means absent from the scene even there. There is also a frequent settling of accounts among rival mafia clans.[34] It is often linked with the struggle over economic advantages; in fact the view is sometimes taken that the people who have attained great wealth through various shady methods can be compared with the robber barons of American capitalism in the nineteenth century, and therefore that this situation must be accepted. Yet there are too many unexplained killings to permit a complacent attitude, especially as they tend to be linked to quarrels over commercial favours.

There are several ways in which the conditions of the transition from communism have promoted the rise of crime. The dismantling of the earlier harsh police controls over all aspects of life has made it easier to offend against the law with impunity. Organized crime has benefited from the creation of an open economy, because this has allowed illegal and semi-legal underground entrepreneurs to start open activities. They have 'brought a culture of bribery, theft and even violence from the underground economy into the world of legal private enterprise'.[35] Finally the overall fall in real incomes, alongside the increase in disparities of income all over Eastern Europe and the Former Soviet Union, is a factor in the rise of unorganized, individual crime. Violent crimes are committed by the many victims of the transition process, and this adds greatly to the insecurity of daily life. Even in some of the more successful transition countries there is clear statistical evidence of a rising crime wave. Crime rates in Hungary rose from 1748 per 100 000 in 1988 to 3287 in 1990 and 4900 in 1995.[36] In Poland they rose from 1255 per 100 000 in 1988 to 2289 in 1990 and 2324 in 1995.[37] There was a similar rate of increase in South-Eastern Europe.

THE SURVIVAL OF THE *NOMENKLATURISTS*

Another group which has gained from the fall of communism is, paradoxically, the old communist *nomenklatura* itself. It would be wrong to take too extreme a position on this. Some authors (for example Hankiss[38] and Staniszkis[39]) see the former elite as simply reproducing itself. Staniszkis refers to a system of 'political capitalism' whereby the former *nomenklatura* have used their political power to gain private wealth via the privatization process. But there is a distinction to be made between political and economic survival. In the political sphere the old *nomenklatura* was somewhat discredited, at least in East-Central Europe, in the immediate aftermath of the events of 1989; a new political elite was created along with the new political institutions. Statistical evidence for this point has been provided by the Szelényis and their collaborators. In 1993 only 23.7 per cent of the Polish elite came from the old *nomenklatura*, and 30.4 per cent of the Hungarian elite;[40] moreover, only 17.5 per cent of Polish parliamentarians had been communist party members in 1988; for Hungary the figure was 12.5 per cent.[41]

Despite this decline in political influence, there was a certain continuity of personnel in some branches of the administration; a rather amusing explanation for this was given by a leader of the MDF in an interview:

> We cannot wipe out the professionals of the former regime. There is no one else available to substitute for these people. You could kick out the people from the MSZP, but the Parliament building is too big, and we wouldn't know how to get from one room to another.[42]

This testimony is the more impressive in that the Hungarian Democratic Forum was precisely the party which tried hardest to achieve 'administered social mobility'.[43] In Poland, continuity in the military and police spheres was strengthened by the compromise of 1989 whereby Solidarity allowed former communists, from Jaruzelski downwards, to retain their positions. A later example is the appointment in February 1996 of Andrzej Kapkowski, a veteran of the communist era secret service, to head the Polish Special Services. But generally where the *nomenklaturists* retained political power it was in a subordinate position, with the top offices being held by former dissidents, or, increasingly, people who played no part at all in political life before 1989. Members of the former ruling group tended to withdraw from politics, especially in countries which carried out effective de-communization campaigns (for example the Czech Republic).

Things were different, however, in South-Eastern Europe. Here former *nomenklaturists* were able to paint themselves in fresh colours, particularly nationalist ones, and they showed a remarkable capacity for political survival. In former Yugoslavia members of the *nomenklatura* were able to make almost a seamless transition to the new state of affairs. This is obviously true in Milošević's Serbia and Gligorov's Macedonia; but it also applied further north. The leader of the Slovene League of Communists between 1986 and 1989, Milan Kučan, was elected President of Slovenia in 1990. The Prime Minister of Slovenia since 1992 has been Janez Drnovšek. He is politically a Liberal Democrat, but he is also a former federal president of socialist Yugoslavia, which places him right at the top of the old *nomenklatura*. In general in former Yugoslavia (as over most of the former Soviet Union), the transition process has meant that local national elites have taken control of their areas, under whatever political banner was appropriate. In 1993, 51 per cent of the Russian elite were from the *nomenklatura*, while 67.7 per cent of the previous Soviet elite had retained their positions under the new dispensation; any wastage was largely through early retirement. Conversely, only 19.6 per cent of the Russian elite had a non-elite background.[44] But outside South-Eastern Europe and the CIS the *nomenklatura* has as a rule lost political power.

In the economy, in contrast, the old elite has retained its position at the top even in East-Central Europe. As Kolosi and Róna-Tas have pointed out, 'the economic transition to the market follows a different logic from the political one'.[45] There can be no doubt about the existence of '*nomenklatura* capitalism', to use the phrase coined by Jan Olszewski for Poland. An obvious route taken by *nomenklaturists* everywhere was to use their connections and inside knowledge to turn state enterprises into their own private property: '*nomenklatura* privatization'.[46] There is, however, disagreement on the relative importance in the economy of old *nomenklaturists* and new capitalists. This is partly a matter of which country you take. Polish evidence leads Kurczewski to postulate the existence of a 'new business class' associated with the new private sector of the economy.[47] A different view has been taken by Eyal, Szelényi and Townsley, who adduce survey data from Poland, Hungary and the Czech Republic during 1993–4 to show that the new economic elite did not consist of 'new people' but rather of managers from the former state economy, who made up an average of 72 per cent of the total. Almost half of them were in low-level positions beforehand, and they rose rapidly up the social scale after 1989.[48]

The conversion of political power into economic wealth has been extremely successful in Romania, where according to a former FSN leader '80% of the new millionaires are members of the old *nomenklatura*'.[49] Here one of the mechanisms for elite survival was the conversion of top officials of the former communist youth organization into 'the new barons of Romania's emerging private sector', using their wide range of personal contacts.[50]

THE REVERSION TO FEUDALISM

A further feature of the new situation, largely on the territory of the former Soviet Union, but also perceptible in South-Eastern Europe, has been a certain *reversion to feudalism*, that is the tendency of local notables, whether *nomenklaturist* or not, to make themselves in practice

The Shock of the New 141

independent of the state they claim to belong to. This is a result of the decline in the power of the state and the central authorities since 1989. A particularly noteworthy example of this could be seen in Former Yugoslavia: the activities of Fikret Abdić. This Bosnian Muslim military commander was part of the communist ruling group in the 1980s. He was notorious at the time for his involvement in one of the biggest corruption scandals of the epoch (the Agrokomerc affair). When Bosnia started to move towards independence he was let out of jail, joined the SDA, and recovered control of his fief (Cazinska Krajina). But instead of obeying the central government in Sarajevo he made an alliance with the Bosnian Serbs, establishing in September 1993 what was in practice an independent state, the 'autonomous province of Western Bosnia'. He was not defeated by central government forces until 1995, when he and his followers were forced to take refuge across the border, in Croatia.

The power struggles among the Bosnian Serbs after 1995, between the Plavšić and Karadžić factions, are another example of this tendency towards feudalization, as is the situation in Albania in the aftermath of the collapse of President Berisha's authority (1997–8). In Montenegro, too, the traditional division of the country into five clans survived the communist epoch and has resurfaced since 1991. The two northern clans of Vasojevici and Bijelo Pavlovica are traditionally pro-Serbian, and they provided recruits for the Bosnian Serb militias during the civil war in Bosnia-Hercegovina. They also formed the basis for the power of Momir Bulatović, the pro-Serbian politician who was President of Montenegro until 1997. The three southern clans favour Montenegrin independence.[51]

The feudalization of power is conditional on the extreme weakness of the state (as was the original feudalism of medieval times). Generally, therefore, it has not been carried as far as in former Yugoslavia. But Vladimir Shlapentokh has recently drawn a direct comparison between the situation in present-day Russia and medieval Western feudalism.[52] There are naturally some differences. Business in Russia is based not on traditional family ties but on personal connections. But these have played a very important role in politics in the 1990s, and it remains to be seen whether the Russian state will recover sufficient power and independence to break their present stranglehold.

THE IMPACT OF THE END OF SOCIALIST PATERNALISM

For many people the post-communist epoch did not live up to expectations. This created a deep feeling of bitterness. One possible reaction was a search for scapegoats. The communists themselves were the first and most obvious ones, but the target soon shifted to Jews, Roma, Freemasons, and in general members of other nationalities than the one embraced by the speaker. Unscrupulous demagogues, such as Vladimir Zhirinovsky in Russia, took advantage of these feelings; and the reformed communist parties also benefited from what German journalists soon dubbed 'Ostalgie': nostalgia for the communist past. By 1994 this feeling was strongly present almost everywhere in Eastern Europe. Confidence in the new governments was running at an average of 28 per cent (highest in the Czech Republic and Slovenia), confidence in parliament at 22 per cent, confidence in the political parties at 14 per cent; and an average of 23 per cent of those polled yearned for the return of communism.[53] In Poland a poll revealed that between 48 per cent and 54 per cent of the sample saw the communist period as the happiest time of their lives.[54] Another reaction, more positive than this yearning for the return of the past, was for the disadvantaged to band together and try to exercise influence on the post-communist governments, by the classic method of trade union activity. We now turn to consider the role and effectiveness of trade unions in the transition period.

THE ROLE OF THE TRADE UNIONS AFTER 1989

Industrial workers, who had occupied a relatively privileged position during the communist era, and lost it afterwards, could well be regarded as a disadvantaged group after 1989. In any case, trade unions now had a choice between defending workers' interests through confrontation (as in Poland, Romania and Bulgaria, where they were ready to use the strike weapon fairly freely) or through social partnership (as in Czechoslovakia and Hungary). In the latter case, the union would work within the structure of *tripartite agreements*, which set up councils representing the trade unions, the employers and the government in equal proportions.

Czechoslovakia was the first country to set up a tripartite Council of Economic and Social Accord, first at federal level (2 October 1990), followed by corresponding institutions in Slovakia (13 October) and the Czech Republic (30 October). Each of these councils had 21 members, 7 drawn from each of the social partners. On the trade union side there were 6 representatives from the Czech and Slovak Confederation of Trade Unions (ČSKOS) and one from the Confederation of Art and

Culture (KUK), the smaller, right-wing cultural union, which opposed the idea of a minimum wage.[55] Each year a General Agreement was drawn up by these partners stating agreed objectives. These varied from year to year. In the 1991 agreement it was laid down that there would be 'increases in wages according to the cost of living' so as to 'prevent a decrease in real earnings of over 10%', and an indexed minimum wage, to be funded from the state budget for the public sector (Article 10).[56]

This rather generous approach reflected the continuing influence of moderate reformers in the Czechoslovak government. Klaus himself opposed the idea of tripartite councils at first, and it was pushed through by Petr Miller, the Minister of Labour and Social Affairs, who was later to join the Social Democratic Party (ČSSD), and Marian Čalfa, the communist party member who was prime minister at the time (1990). It should be noted, however, that these agreements were not legally enforceable. They were accompanied by a package of social policies aimed at softening the shock of transition, under the title 'Scenario for Social Reform', which was approved by parliament in September 1990. In this way 'social peace' was ensured in Czechoslovakia, allowing what Klaus later described as 'a painless and non-conflictual transition from communist society to a free and open society and a market economy'.[57] He eventually accepted the policy of consensus with the trade unions because it was a good way of emasculating them.

In fact the government scrapped the indexing of the minimum wage in July 1991, while the agreement was still theoretically in force. The 1992 agreement was a much vaguer document, and contained no commitments about wages. Ultimately, the unions had very little to show for their readiness to co-operate. Peter Rutland has commented that the Czechoslovak trade unions 'were disempowered by the sham corporatism' of the tripartite agreements.[58] The effect of this system of labour relations was that the Czech Republic was characterized by a combination of low real wages, lower than in Hungary or Poland, low unemployment and low inflation. The trade unions generally accepted Klaus's argument that wage restraint allowed marginal workers to remain employed. They therefore accepted the imposition of wage restrictions on workers in state enterprises, and an excess wages tax on private enterprise, with the result that in 1991 real wages fell by 40 per cent.[59] It was not felt that the Klaus government was pursuing anything other than the right policy. The head of the Czechoslovak trade union confederation, Vladimír Petrus, proclaimed in May 1992 that 'prosperity is only conceivable when a conservative and liberal government is in power'.[60]

There was a certain divergence between Slovak and Czech trade unionists over this point. The Slovaks tended to place their faith in Mečiar's Movement for a Democratic Slovakia, hoping that independence would allow them to increase their influence (the leading Slovak trade unionist, Roman Kovač, stood for parliament under Mečiar's party label). The first General Agreement of the independent Slovak Republic (1993) seemed to justify these hopes. It abolished wage controls, raised the minimum wage, and provided for wages to be increased every three months in line with the rate of inflation.

The General Agreements of 1993 and 1994 in the Czech Republic also provided for real wage growth, but this was cancelled out by a government decree of 22 December 1993 restoring wage controls over all private enterprises with more than 24 employees. This, in combination with certain other government measures such as the decision to raise the age at which pensions became payable, led to the first breach in the system of 'social peace', when 40 000 trade unionists attended a protest demonstration in Prague. Klaus called the demonstrators 'irresponsible extremists', but a poll showed 57 per cent support for the action.[61] A month later Petrus was replaced as President of the Czech chamber of trade unions (ČMKOS)[62] by the more radical Richard Falbr, although in practice both sides moved rapidly to defuse the situation, with Klaus accepting the need to continue negotiating through the tripartite council, and the trade unions abandoning the path of confrontation and protest. The first strike since 1989, leaving aside a 15-minute warning strike over privatization of pensions on 21 December 1994, was carried out not by trade unionists but by doctors (1 December 1995). The reason for the lack of trade union militancy in the Czech Republic was the combination of low unemployment and, after the decline of the first few years, a continuous rise in real wages. Only in regions hit by industrial decline, such as North Moravia and Ostrava-Karvina was there pressure for a more active trade union policy, and, equally, a tendency to vote for the extremes of right (SPR-RSČ)[63] and left (the communist party).[64]

Trade unions, thus, were not generally a vehicle for opposition to government policies either in the Czech Republic or Slovakia. In Hungary the trade unions were somewhat more active. There, the previous regime had already set up a conciliation council (in 1988). The coming of the new era brought a decline in the membership of trade unions (from 90 per cent of the labour force in 1989 to 50 per cent in 1992) and a lessening of interest in trade union activity among the members themselves (at the May 1993 trade union elections the participation level was a mere 38.9 per cent).[65] This worked to the advantage of the formerly communist National Confederation of Hungarian Trade Unions (MSZOSZ), which won most of the official posts (45 per cent). The MSZOSZ tended towards oppositionism, threatening a strike in autumn 1992, which compelled the Antall government to sign a 'social contract'.[66] When the Socialist Party came to power, the MSZOSZ continued to exert pressure. It boycotted the Interest Coordination Council in March 1995 in protest against the government's failure to consult the trade unions before imposing austerity measures, and it lent its support to a rally called on 14 March by the left of the MSZP and the Young Democrats (FIDESZ). The MSZOSZ continued to mount protests during 1995, though without success.

In Poland, where the trade unions were very strong, Solidarity was in an awkward position. It had started in 1980 as a movement of confrontation, counterposing the interests of the workers to the policies of a communist-run government. After 1989 it was faced with a Solidarity government and a Solidarity president. This made for splits in the movement and an uncertain policy direction. In 1990, Solidarność '80 was set up to continue the confrontational tradition of the 1980s; the 'official' Solidarity union, NSZZ–Solidarność, continued to exist side by side with it; while the old communist-era union, the OPZZ, itself retained considerable strength. The result of this rivalry between the Polish trade unions was that a tripartite council was not set up until 1994.

Official Solidarity's involvement with the government resulted in a tremendous decline in its standing among ordinary Poles. In 1993 opinion polls showed that 75 per cent of the population had less confidence in Solidarity than they had had in 1989.[67] The leaders of the movement thought the answer lay in a reversion to populism, so they refused to follow President Wałęsa when he endeavoured to bring the union in behind his presidential party the BBWR in June 1993. They decided to set up independent candidates at the elections.[68] The result was a disaster for both groups. Solidarity did not even get into parliament, while the BBWR, despite being the presidential party, secured only 5.4 per cent of the vote, just enough to scrape in.

The trade unions have not made much impact in East-Central Europe, then. There are three reasons for this. First, they are marginal to the new situation: trade unions are often regarded as survivals of the old communist order, or at least as fighting to preserve what remains of it. Second, they have been unable to achieve unity among themselves. The former communist trade unions have all continued to exist alongside the new professional associations that sprang up in the aftermath of 1989. Third, and most important, their efforts to defend their members have been hampered by the lack of an alternative policy. They have felt unable to challenge the current neo-liberal orthodoxy; in fact they continue to regard neo-liberal policies as the best hope for the future. Further south the trade unions have played more of a role in politics, but, as we saw earlier, their position has been highly contradictory; they have tried simultaneously to push governments towards more rapid market reforms, and to defend their members' immediate material interests, which were certain to be damaged by such reforms.

WOMEN IN THE TRANSITION

In some respects women suffered disproportionately from the ending of communism and the coming of a new epoch. Under communism it was always argued that a woman's duty was to engage in 'productive labour'; but in the subsequent era of economic restructuring women were often first to lose their jobs. Judit Acsady notes that post-1990 politicians 'vilified the communists for bringing women out of the home and into the labour force'.[69] There were also cuts in day-care subsidies, and in social welfare benefits, which hit women harder than men. Hence in several countries in the early 1990s women formed a greater proportion than men of the post-communist unemployed: 70 per cent in Russia, and 60 per cent in Czechoslovakia, Poland, Bulgaria and the former GDR.[70] Hungary was the exception: there, only 40 per cent of the unemployed were women.[71] The differential between male and female unemployment was still the same in 1995. Hence in the Czech Republic and Poland women continued to be more likely to be unemployed, while in Hungary the reverse continued to be the case.[72]

The turn against communism after 1989 was accompanied by a definite revulsion against feminism, which was seen to be somehow connected with the former system.[73] This meant not only a worsening in women's economic position and a reduction of women's economic role but also lessened political participation. This was in part a voluntary decision: many women regarded their enforced civic duties under communism as yet another burden imposed by the state, on top of the double burden of looking after children and home and going out to work. Everywhere there was a decline in female representation in parliaments. There is some evidence that this was a deliberate move by the politicians: in Czechoslovakia in June 1990 women were relegated to the bottom of the parties' lists of candidates, which under proportional representation meant that they were far less likely to be elected. The proportion of women in parliament accordingly fell from 30 per cent to 9 per cent. The picture is similar for other countries: in 1992, 7 per cent of the deputies in Hungary were women (the figure rose to 18 per cent after the socialist victory in the elections of 1994); in Croatia in 1994, 4 per cent; in Poland in 1991, 9.6 per cent; in Bulgaria in 1990, 8.5 per cent; in Romania there was a fall from 34 per cent to 4 per cent, in Russia from 16 per cent in 1989 to 5 per cent in 1990 (although the success of the 'Women of Russia' movement in the 1993 elections brought the proportion back up to 11 per cent).

There are, however, differences of opinion about the true significance of these changes. Western authors have tended to see them as a sign that women lost more than they gained in 1989. But a different view has been taken locally. In the political sphere, the relatively high level of representation enjoyed by women under communism resulted from the use of a quota system; it did not mean that the women involved had any political power.[74] In the industrial sphere, increases in female unemployment are also seen as less than tragic by the women of the region. The jobs that women did before 1989 were not always very stimulating or well paid. In Hungary women were paid an average of 20 per cent less than their male counterparts.[75] In Bulgaria 'the exercise of so-called labour rights...turned into a burden, compulsion, for most women had to work out of necessity; the men could not earn enough to make ends meet'.[76] The overall fall in female employment in Czechoslovakia can also be viewed positively, for it covers a fall of 50 per cent in the number of agricultural workers and a 10 per cent improvement in women's position in finance, trade and insurance. As a result some progress was made between 1988 and 1994 in closing the earnings gap.[77]

Similar differences of opinion exist over the more intimate spheres of personal life. To take the Czech example, the trend has been towards fewer marriages (down from 8.8 per 1000 population in 1990 to 6.4 in 1993), more divorces (up from 35.2 per 100 marriages to 45.8 in 1993), and a falling birth rate (down from 13.8 per 1000 population in 1988 to 8.8 in 1996). These trends have given rise to varying reactions. Is there an undesirable decline in family life? Or is this a sign of female emancipation from compulsory family roles? Even the commercialization of the female body, exemplified by the flood of pornographic material released onto the Eastern European market after 1989, has been viewed as a kind of emancipation from the desexualization characteristic of the communist era.[78]

There have inevitably also been deep disagreements in post-communist Eastern Europe about family planning and its relation to sexual behaviour. The level of contraceptive use and availability in Eastern Europe was low throughout the communist period (except in Hungary and the GDR),[79] and there has so far been little change in this respect. In Poland in 1993 only 11 per cent of women used modern contraceptive methods. In Bulgaria and Romania most women continued after 1989 to have no access to the contraceptive pill.[80] Condoms were used by between 10 per cent and 25 per cent of married couples. But the main means of family limitation in Eastern Europe before 1989 was abortion, and this is how it has remained. Liberalization of the abortion laws was one of the distinctive signs of de-Stalinization during the communist era; but this came up against strong religious objections from some parts of the population in predominantly Catholic countries, and once communist rule had ended the way was clear for attempts to outlaw the practice.

This gave rise to serious conflicts in Czechoslovakia, Hungary, former Yugoslavia and above all Poland (in Romania the issue did not arise, since the post-1989 period saw the reverse process: liberalization of an abortion regime which had been strongly pro-natalist beforehand).[81] In Serbia in 1990 the authorities attempted to restrict the right to abortion for nationalist reasons (because Serbian women were having fewer children than ethnic Albanian women in Kosovo). They were forced to back down by a strong feminist protest movement.[82] In Czechoslovakia an attempt to ban abortion was defeated in parliament on 9 January 1991; in Hungary there was considerable debate on the issue though the law was not changed;[83] in Croatia conservative and nationalist groups and the Catholic Church campaigned against abortion under the slogan 'The Unborn Are Also Croats'.[84] In Poland there was a head-on conflict between secular and religious forces over the issue. The two sides were pretty well evenly matched, which made for long drawn out and bitter conflict. On one side there was the power of the Roman Catholic Church, the church of the overwhelming majority of Poles; on the other side there was the urgent practical need felt by young Polish women to resort to this method of family limitation. The coming to power of Solidarity (which endorsed a total ban on abortion in March 1990, although there was some opposition to this stance from feminists within the movement) introduced six years of very highprofile debate on this issue.

Supporters of anti-abortion legislation argued that the practice was immoral, that there were too many abortions in Poland, that the country was becoming underpopulated as a result and finally that a ban on abortion was in line with the will of the Polish people; opponents stressed the 'need to control the causes of abortion by improving women's living conditions', the risks to health posed by illegal abortions which would inevitably ensue and finally the principle of 'a woman's right to choose'.[85] A first attempt to ban abortion was blocked by the Women's Parliamentary Circle, a cross-party group of feminist deputies (May 1991).[86] But the campaign continued, with strong Church backing, and in March 1993 abortion was made a criminal offence, if it took place later than the first three months of pregnancy (except in cases of rape or incest). Estimates for the number of annual abortions ranged from 300 000 to 600 000 (compared with 550 000 live births).[87] These figures may have been exaggerated for political purposes (the higher one would involve the assumption that there were five times as many illegal as legal abortions even during 1990, when legal abortions were freely available) but the problem was certainly serious. Despite the victory of the post-communist SLD in the 1993 elections it was not possible to pass a more liberal law for three years, owing to the opposition of both President Wałęsa and the SLD's coalition partner the post-communist peasant party (the PSL).[88] Eventually the Sejm passed an Abortion Liberalization Law (30 August 1996) over the furious opposition of the right and centre parties, and the Polish episcopate, which called the vote 'a crime against humanity'. This provided for abortion on 'personal and social grounds' up to the twelfth week of pregnancy.

Women fared better than men during the transition from communism in at least one way: their life expectancy improved everywhere in Eastern Europe, whereas men's fell or remained static.[89] Where female life expectancy did fall, as in Bulgaria, Latvia and Lithuania, it always fell less than men's. Between 1988 and 1996 female life expectancy increased by an (unweighted) average of 0.8 years in Eastern Europe, while male life expectancy fell between 1988 and 1996 by an average of 0.1 years. Many women certainly suffered during the period of transition; they were on the whole poorer than men and more likely to become unemployed; but they seemed better able to cope with the situation.

8 The Middle Years: Drifting towards the Millennium

EAST-CENTRAL EUROPE: CROSSING THE BRIDGE TO NORMALITY

By 1998 the countries of East-Central Europe were well advanced along the road to parliamentary democracy, free market-based economies and a homogeneous Western-style culture. One notable tendency of Western democracy which was quickly reproduced there was apathy among the voters. After the short period of enthusiasm induced by the end of communist rule, the participation rate in elections fell everywhere. In Czechoslovakia turnout fell from 97 per cent in 1990 to 85 per cent in 1992; this fell further to 76 per cent in both Slovakia (September 1994) and the Czech Republic (May 1996); in Hungary turnout fell from 66 per cent in March to 46 per cent in April 1990 (though it rose again to 69 per cent in 1994); in Poland turnout fell from 60 per cent in June 1989 to 55 per cent in December 1990 (presidential election) and 43 per cent in October 1991, rising to 57 per cent in September 1993 and falling again in 1997 to 48 per cent. Electoral apathy was a sign partly of disillusionment, certainly, but also of stability. There was no longer a sense that the victory of the adverse party would bring a change of system. In 1992 the veteran Hungarian dissident George Konrúd expressed a fear that 'tolerance in the new democracies could end, because there is no broad middle stratum, no economy and culture independent of the state, no individual ethic'.[1] These fears have turned out to be unjustified.

Alongside the growth in apathy there has been a decline in credulity; another sign of political maturity. In the first few years of post-communism there was a tendency to support political adventurers from the West who promised immediate material gains for the electorate. As we have seen, this political credulity had its financial counterpart further south in the rise of dubious 'pyramid schemes'. In Poland Stan Tymiński, an unknown Canadian who stood against Wałęsa on a purely demagogic programme, gained 25 per cent of the vote in the presidential elections of November 1990. This success was not repeated, however.

By the time of the next elections, for the Sejm, in September 1993, the challenge of Tymiński's 'Party X' had faded into insignificance. In the following sections, we shall illustrate these general remarks about East-Central European stability by examining the course of political development in each of the countries concerned.

1 POLAND

In Poland the transition from communism was made rapidly and successfully, despite the element of compromise contained in the 1989 agreement. The situation in Poland has been characterized by four underlying features: political stability; economic dynamism, after an initial dip in the early 1990s, shown by annual GDP growth of between 5 per cent and 7 per cent; a high level of foreign confidence and readiness to invest; and a number of social problems, such as unemployment in older, declining sectors of the economy, and pockets of poverty in some population strata, which though serious have not produced a level of discontent high enough to threaten the new system.

Poland's political stability was based on a genuinely democratic pluralism of opinion. This did not mean the absence of serious conflicts, but a readiness to fight them out within the given constitutional arena. As Tworzecki has commented, these 'political cleavages' were 'compatible with a democratic form of government'.[2] Poland was in fact divided along several lines: the communist era had, at first sight somewhat surprisingly,[3] not resulted in a homogenization of Polish society. Thus there was still a gulf between town and country, expressed politically in continuing tension between the PSL, which acted as an agrarian pressure group, and the more urban parties, including even its ally the SLD. There were divisions according to the level of income, with the more prosperous Poles favouring the KLD and the UD and the rest the more populist parties. Historical geography has also played a part: each election has shown a clear differentiation between the former Austrian south (Galicia), which tended to favour agrarian populism and the anti-communist Right, and the lands of former Prussian Poland in the west, which opposed populism, favoured market liberalism, and supported the post-communist SLD in all three elections (1991, 1993, 1997).

There were also ideological divisions, complicated greatly by a typically post-communist confusion between Right and Left: the SLD's enthusiasm for the market did not sit well with its 'left' image; and the advocacy of government intervention to soften the pain of transition to the market, which was practised by the KPN, contradicted the latter's right-wing line on other questions. Similarly, the polarization between religious and secular Poles over the abortion issue brought the market liberals of the KLD and the UD into an odd alliance with the post-communist SLD, although all three parties stressed their respect for the Church as such.[4]

Despite these divisions, the people of Poland have been in basic agreement on underlying national objectives. This has meant that though political battles have been fiercely fought, all sides have observed a shared framework of rules. Thus the considerable political instability of the period of SLD rule in the mid-1990s did not do more than disturb the surface of Polish life. Fears that President Wałęsa would take his struggle with a hostile parliamentary majority to unconstitutional lengths were not realized in the event. His active interventions into politics between 1993 and 1995 repeatedly came to nothing, precisely because he was limited by the constitution. He dismissed the head of the media control body, Marek Markiewicz (1 March 1994); the decision was overturned by the Constitutional Court. He threatened to dissolve the Sejm (16 April 1994); he was unable to carry out the threat. He pressed for a Concordat with the Vatican; the Sejm rejected it because it gave the Roman Catholic Church a privileged position. He vetoed a liberal abortion law (4 July 1994); it was reintroduced and passed two years later (30 August 1996). He constantly quarrelled with old friends and colleagues. On 12 October 1994 the Sejm voted by 305 to 18 in favour of a motion that he should cease 'activities that might threaten democracy'. He threatened again to dissolve the Sejm (9 January 1995); it replied by voting to impeach him if he did so; he gave way (12 February 1995). The list could be extended. By the time presidential elections were due (in November 1995) Wałęsa had done a very thorough job of 'destroying his own monument'.[5]

The predictable, but still astonishing, result, was his narrow defeat at the hands of the post-communist candidate, Aleksandr Kwaśniewski (who won in the second round by 51.7 per cent to 48.3 per cent). Kwaśniewski benefited from a professionally conducted campaign, and from the support of young voters[6] (his slogan was 'let us choose the future'); he was smooth, elegant, and slim and he resembled the star of a popular American television series; he was also, paradoxically, supported by older victims of the process of transition who were nostalgic for communist times;[7] finally, the hints of Archbishop Jozef Glemp that good Catholics should use their vote against 'neo-paganism' backfired. Many Poles saw this as unacceptable clerical interference in politics.[8]

Barbara Labuda, for instance, a deputy for the Freedom Union (UW), normally aligned with the Right, campaigned in favour of Kwaśniewski in the second round of the elections because of his stand in favour of permitting abortion.[9] The election of an SLD president removed the discord between president and parliament, but it did not end political instability. The SLD still had to stay in coalition with the PSL, and hard decisions on privatization, shipyard bankruptcy and abortion continued to give rise to conflict between the two parties and agitation among the population at large.

The final twist so far in the Polish political story has been the recovery of the post-Solidarity forces and the defeat of the post-communists. This has its roots in the recognition by the parties of the Polish Centre and Right that their proud independence and resultant political fragmentation was damaging them in the electoral competition with the far more unified Left. Failure to unite in time for the 1993 elections led to the exclusion of much of the Right from parliament, as none of the small right-wing factions was able to reach the 5 per cent threshold. Failure to unite in 1995 meant the Right had to fall back on Lech Wałęsa as presidential candidate, although his popularity as incumbent president had gone downhill continuously. By 1996, after repeated defeats, attitudes on the Right towards mutual co-operation had changed. In June 1996, Solidarity Electoral Action (AWS) was set up as a coalition of no less than 30 parties, under the aegis of the Solidarity trade union. Its leader was the new head of Solidarity, Marian Krzaklewski. The AWS was able to mount a successful challenge to the post-communist SLD because it possessed two inestimable advantages: political legitimacy, because it was the genuine heir to the Solidarity tradition; and grassroots support, through a network of seventeen thousand local branches, which organized the one and a half million members of the Solidarity trade union.

Solidarity accordingly played the dominant role in the AWS, receiving 50 per cent of the seats on its National Council. It was able to hold together the two main wings of the Polish Right: the 'liberal conservatives', the Thatcherite non-interventionist camp, who were divided among themselves, but successfully created a single party in January 1997 (the Conservative Peasant Party); and the 'traditionalists', 'right' on some issues, such as nationalism, but 'left' on the need for government intervention in the economy. The traditionalist group consisted of the KPN (which had abandoned its previous stance of complete political independence and renamed itself KPN – Patriotic Camp), the Christian National Union (ZChN) and Solidarity itself (ZS). Finally, one right-wing group refused to join the coalition forged by Solidarity: Jan Olszewki's Movement for Poland's Reconstruction (ROP), the uncompromisingly anti-communist party which was the clearest example of 'socialist conservatism' in Poland. As well as a thorough purge and exclusion of former communists it advocated protection for industry, restrictions on foreign ownership and the transfer of state property to the citizens of Poland.

The unification of the Right certainly reduced the complexity of the Polish political scene in 1997, but it by no means abolished it. There were four other major elements in the political spectrum: first, the post-communist SLD, which had governed the country since 1993, and could point to rising prosperity as a justification of its policies. Associated with the SLD in government was, second, the representation of the farming interest, the PSL, a party which was continually pulling the SLD away from its commitment to free market liberalism, because of its determined opposition to market reforms in the agricultural sector. The Fifth Congress of the PSL, held in November 1996, saw an attempt by Roman Jagielinski to move his party in the direction of agrarian reform. He failed, and in August 1997 the PSL showed its continuing strength by forcing the government to buy three hundred thousand tonnes of grain from domestic producers at subsidised prices;[10] this triumph was also its swan-song, as it turned out.

The other elements of the Polish political spectrum in 1997 were the Freedom Union (UW) and the Labour Union (UP). The UW, led by Leszek Balcerowicz, resulted from a merger of the Liberal Democratic Congress (KLD) and the Democratic Union (UD), and was the party of consistent pro-market liberals, strongly opposed to propping up the moribund state sector, but also opposed to the clerical and nationalist tendencies of other groups on the right. The UP, led by Ryszsard Bugaj, was the closest thing in Poland to a Social Democratic Party, and represented the more left-leaning strand of the Solidarity tradition. It was divided from the SLD by its more strongly developed social conscience and its rejection of the latter's communist past and evident roots in the *nomenklatura*.

The results of the 21 September 1997 elections showed that the unification of the Right had paid off: the AWS gained votes (from 3 286 000 in 1993 to 4 427 000 in 1997), at the expense of the PSL (that party's share of the vote dropped catastrophically from 2 124 000 to 956 000, while its representation in the Sejm fell from 132 seats to 27) and the UP (which lost 385 000 votes and just failed to reach the parliamentary threshold, thereby forfeiting all its seats). The SLD, meanwhile, also increased its voting strength, from 2 815 000 to 3 551 000, but lost a few seats (down from 171 to 164). Olszewski's anti-communist and populist campaign was unsuccessful: the ROP only just made it over the 5 per cent barrier, with 5.6 per cent and 6 seats. Balcerowicz's Freedom Union received slightly less support in 1997 than its predecessors in 1993 (14.4 per cent in 1993; 13.6 per cent in 1997) and fewer seats (down from 74 to 60).

2 HUNGARY

Three lessons were drawn by the victorious Hungarian Socialists from the political conflicts of the years after the ending of communist rule: the MSZP must resolutely look to the future, dissociating itself from its communist past, it must unify the nation rather than relying on its majority in parliament and it must do everything necessary to improve relations with its neighbours and bring the country closer to the West. A number of implications followed from this, spelled out very clearly on 14 July 1994 by the new socialist prime minister, Gyula Horn. In the domestic sphere a process of national reconciliation was needed; in foreign relations all territorial claims against Romania and Slovakia would be abandoned, in return for guarantees to ethnic Hungarians in those countries; and in social policy the people of Hungary should not expect any dramatic improvement in living standards (in other words, austerity would be the order of the day).

Horn's decision to attend a memorial ceremony for Imre Nagy (16 June) was a testimony to his concern to achieve national reconciliation, though the dismissal of the MDF-appointed heads of radio (László Csúcs) and television (Gábor Nahlik) on 7 July could be seen as part of the time-honoured tradition whereby the winning party puts its own people into key positions; it was followed by the return to work of the 129 journalists dismissed by Csúcs earlier in the year for criticizing the MDF government. The formation of a coalition government with the liberal SZDSZ (15 July) was a sign that the Socialists would be consistent in their support of the free market and financial orthodoxy. Money-saving and tax-raising measures of various kinds were now introduced. The 'World Expo' planned for 1996 was scrapped (26 July); VAT was raised to 12 per cent and the forint devalued by 8 per cent (21 September); an emergency budget was introduced with the aim of reducing the inherited deficit by 10 per cent. Finance Minister László Békesi noted that 'job losses would be necessary in state-run industries'

(18 October). The ideal solution was for these industries to be privatized, he added, but this would take time.

Although the MSZP was more strongly committed to privatization than its predecessor in power, its first decision was to abandon a privatization: in January 1995 the sale of the HungarHotels chain was cancelled.[11] This confused some observers, but there was a specific reason for the cancellation: the State Property Agency had raised the price to be paid from $57 million to $67 million, and the prospective purchaser, a US company, refused to raise its offer. Horn made it clear (29 January) that there was 'no question of slowing down privatization. Quite the contrary, we would like to speed it up. But we want to do it in a more well-founded way... The big strategic industries will be privatized.'[12] He was as good as his word; the Privatization Law passed by the National Assembly on 9 May 1995 allowed the sale of strategic companies previously kept in state hands and streamlined the process by merging the two state agencies previously responsible for privatization, the State Property Agency and the State Holding Company, into a single company, the State Privatization and Holding Company (ÁPV Rt.). In August the ÁPV Rt. announced that 275 firms would go to the highest bidder.

This line of policy was continued in subsequent years. Horn and the majority of the MSZP were able to overcome the opposition of some sections of the party, which would have preferred a less hard-nosed approach. Finance Minister Bokros announced further austerity measures on 12 March: job losses in the state sector, a 9 per cent devaluation of the forint, an 8 per cent surcharge on imports. This would reduce the budget deficit to $3 billion, or 3.5 per cent of GDP, not quite reaching the IMF's stipulation of 3 per cent of GDP, but close enough. The resignations of Pál Kovács (Minister of Welfare) and Béla Katona (Minister of National Security) in protest (14 March) were timed to coincide with a mass demonstration organized by the trade unions against austerity measures; the opposition MDF called for 'an economic policy which pays more attention to society's threshold of tolerance than the present one'. This was Horn's reply: 'This country faces state bankruptcy, with a $20 billion foreign debt. It needs foreign resources to pay its debts, boost growth and catch up. These foreign resources can be obtained if our affairs are put in order.'[13]

Further austerity measures were imposed on 26 July (an 8 per cent rise in energy prices and a further cut in government spending). This set off another protest resignation, when Magda Kovács left the Ministry of Labour (5 October 1995). The Constitutional Court added its voice to the chorus of opposition by ruling on two occasions (30 June and 13

September) that some of the government's measures (such as the reductions in the maternity allowance and sickness benefit) were illegal. The crisis over this issue culminated in the month of November 1995, which saw protests by public sector workers against the cuts, a further resignation (this time it was the Minister of Education, Gábor Fodor of the SZDSZ, who resigned in protest against cuts in his department) and a challenge from the left of the MSZP at the party's annual congress. The Horn government successfully rode out all these attacks without modifying its policies. The privatization of large strategic companies was begun in December with a number of sales: the Hungarian Telecommunications Company (MATAV) went to a US–German consortium, gas and electricity distribution was taken over by a West European consortium, and 75 per cent of the Hungarian Oil and Gas Company (MOL) was sold, half of it to foreign investors.

After the crisis of November 1995 the smooth course of the process of transition in Hungary resumed. It was punctuated by ministerial resignations and privatization scandals, neither of which seemed to matter very much. Lajos Bokros resigned in February 1996 as Minister of Finance; but his policy was continued; the Minister of Trade and Industry, Imre Dunai, resigned because he opposed the energy price rises insisted on by Western investors; the Minister of Public Welfare, György Szabó, resigned in November owing to the refusal of the government to allot sufficient funds to public health. The 'Tocsik Affair', a major privatization scandal, emerged in the autumn of 1996, when it was revealed that Mártá Tocsik, a private consultant, had received a 'success fee' of 800 million forints ($5 million) for negotiating with the ÁPV Rt. This led to the dismissal of the Minister of Privatization, Tamas Suchman (6 October) and the whole board of directors of the ÁPV Rt. Fraud charges were later brought against eight ÁPV officials, against László Boldvoi, the treasurer of the MSZP, and against Mártá Tocsik herself (6 June 1997).

The economic indicators generally remained favourable throughout this period, although Hungary's rate of recovery was somewhat slower than that of the other countries of East-Central Europe (GDP growth was 2 per cent in 1995, 1 per cent in 1996 and 3 per cent in 1997). Unemployment remained stationary at around 10 per cent. Real wages fell severely in 1995, the year of austerity, but recovered subsequently. Exports grew steadily (their value rose from $8.6 billion in 1993 to $13.1 billion in 1996). The budget deficit stayed within 4 per cent of GDP (for 1998 it is expected to be slightly higher, at 4.4 per cent of GDP). One indication of Hungary's success in making the economic transition was its admission on 29 March 1996 to the Organization for Economic

Cooperation and Development (OECD), the Paris Club of the world's most industrialized nations. Politically, there was little the 'right-wing' opposition could do but call on Horn to resign on account of his role in the period after 1956 (September 1997). But for most people what happened under communism was really a dead issue. It was clear that the Hungarian Socialists had succeeded in turning their back on the past while remaining an all-purpose governing party, ready to pursue whatever policies were needed to re-integrate their country into the West.

Their defeat in subsequent elections (May 1998) was above all a sign of the health of Hungarian democracy. It was a result in part, as in Poland, of the opposition's ability to coalesce. The MSZP itself retained most of its vote. In fact it was the largest party in the first round (32.9 per cent); the complicated electoral system, which combined proportional representation with constituency seats, was responsible for the victory of the opposition in the second round. The formerly liberal FIDESZ, which had shifted to the right in response to its disappointing showing in the previous elections, and had taken on the mantle of the conservative parties of the early 1990s, the MDF and the KDNP, gained 29.4 per cent of the vote in the first round, and 38.3 per cent of the seats (a relative majority) in the second round. The upshot, after long negotiations, was the formation of a centre-right coalition under Viktor Orban, leader of the FIDESZ (8 July 1998). The most right-wing element in this coalition was represented by the Smallholders' Party (FKGP) led by József Torgyan. A certain increase in nationalistic xenophobia can be expected, but there is no evidence that this change of government will mean much in terms of general policy.

3 THE CZECH REPUBLIC

Politically speaking, one could say that between 1993 and 1996 the Czech Republic did little, and did it well. There is an extraordinary dearth of major political events during this period. Prime Minister Klaus appeared to be running the country very successfully; it had already turned the corner economically, and the process of transition was smooth, at least on the surface. What was happening beneath the surface was, politically, a shift in the landscape, and, socio-economically, the growth of a new inequality which eventually had political consequences, and the weakening of a flimsy financial structure. The political shift involved a split in the communist party and the departure of a proportion of its supporters; the social shift both raised doubts about the wisdom of Klaus's Thatcherite approach to policy and created a less privileged stratum of Czechs who were concerned enough to turn out to vote in large numbers in 1996 (there was a higher level of participation than in Poland or Hungary although some decline in comparison with previous elections: 76.4 per cent of the electorate went to the polls); the financial weakness, finally, was to bring difficulties that ultimately ended Klaus's tenure of office.

The political and social shifts taken together resulted in a startling increase in the strength of Czech Social Democracy. In 1992 the ČSSD secured a mere 6.5 per cent of the vote; in 1996 it gained 26.4 per cent; the main victims of this process were not Klaus and his ODS, which stayed steady at 29.6 per cent, but the communists (KSČM), who fell from 14.1 per cent to 10.3 per cent, and the Moravian and Silesian regionalists, who vanished from the scene altogether. Votes for both the Social Democrats and the Civic Democrats (ODS) were spread out fairly evenly over the country; whereas support for the communists and the extreme right SPR-RSČ (which also did rather well, with 8.0 per cent) tended to be localized in centres of declining industry in northern and western Bohemia.[14] The ČSSD refused to form a new government after the 1996 elections, as any combination they could construct would have been an unprincipled alliance between the Centre and the extreme Left or extreme Right. In the event, Klaus was left to soldier on. He was now in charge of a minority coalition, consisting of his own ODS, the ODA and the agrarian and clerical KDU-ČSL. Since he was dependent on Social Democratic toleration Klaus was obliged to concede a slower pace of cuts in health and welfare expenditure. Some members of the ČSSD wanted to go further and halt a state property restitution decree, by which 175 000 hectares of state land were to be handed back to the Roman Catholic Church; but the party leader, Miloš Zeman, prevailed on his colleagues simply to abstain in the crucial vote (25 July 1996).

The result of the elections of June 1996 was to make the political situation inherently unstable. Klaus constantly had to reckon with the possibility of parliamentary defeat; but he was a man of strong nerves and great self-confidence, and he continued in office until the last possible moment. The 1997 budget was approved (9 October 1996) for one reason only: two ČSSD deputies defied their leader and voted in favour of it. They were expelled from the party the next day. A series of banking collapses and fraud scandals now weakened Klaus's position still further. The Credit Bank (Kreditní Banka) collapsed in August, and the Agricultural Bank (Agrobanka) lost 10 billion Czech crowns and was only saved from collapse by being put under state control (17 September). The managers of Trend VIF, an investment fund, were charged with fraud in March 1997 after the disappearance of one billion crowns; the managers of Agrobanka were charged with fraud in April; finally in May the Czech crown came under speculative attack. This forced the Czech National Bank to spend $3 billion on shoring it up. This amounted to a third of the nation's currency reserves. As usually happens in these cases, it was a waste of money. On 26 May the government gave up and allowed the crown to float on the exchange markets. It immediately lost 10 per cent of its value.[15] Leading members of Klaus's own party, the ODS, including Vladimír Dlouhý, the Minister of Trade and Industry, resigned at the end of May, calling on the government itself to follow their example and go. President Havel also intervened, saying on 25 May that the cabinet changes were an inadequate reply to the crisis: 'the cleanest solution would be the departure of the entire government'.[16]

Far from resigning, Klaus claimed that the economic and financial difficulties were caused by political instability, rather than the reverse, and he presented a programme for economic recovery which involved further cuts in government expenditure. The problem of the currency would be solved, he said, by linking it directly to the German mark. He won a vote of confidence by the narrowest of margins (101 to 99) on 10 June 1997, after the independent deputy Josef Wagner had been brought over to the government side by a promise not to undertake further privatization without the consent of the Chamber of Deputies. Klaus continued to hold to his policy of austerity and financial orthodoxy. The same day, the new Finance Minister, Ivan Pilip, introduced a cut of $20 billion Czech crowns ($620 million) in spending on welfare and education. This was denounced by the leader of the ČSSD as a 'barbaric and irresponsible' measure which would 'undermine the roots of our national future'.

The aim of the Pilip cuts was to wipe out the deficit completely in 1998, an achievement brought a step nearer by the passing of a budget in which revenue and expenditure were equal, at $16.3 billion (22 October). The political crisis continued to smoulder, though it was temporarily placed in abeyance by the intervention of natural forces: the floods of July 1997, an emergency which brought the nation together and required a considerable sum of money to be raised at short notice. The public responded well, purchasing 150 000 000 dollars' worth of emergency bonds (22 August 1997). Nevertheless, the government was forced to abandon a 'flood tax' which would have added 13 per cent to

the tax bill when the opposition won a parliamentary majority against it (16 September).
 Klaus was finally brought down in a classic corruption scandal. Josef Zieleniec, his foreign minister, resigned in October on the ground that the Prime Minister had done nothing in 1996 when he revealed the identity of a Czech businessman who had corruptly obtained control of the state steel company by giving donations to Klaus's party, the ODS. Klaus's coalition partners chose to believe Zieleniec's allegations, and their withdrawal of support brought the whole government down (30 November). A transitional government was formed under an independent, Josef Tosovský, with a mandate to continue in office until new elections, which were scheduled for June 1998. Subsequent political events were dominated by the approach of these elections. The ODS split, with supporters and opponents of Klaus lining up on either side. The party of Klaus's opponents, the Freedom Union, which was headed by Jan Ruml, former Minister of the Interior, won the support of 30 of the 69 ODS deputies; its combination of free market policies and dissociation from the financial scandals that had dogged Klaus in the previous two years proved popular, and made it likely that the ČSSD would be deprived of its expected electoral victory; the Social Democrats were also weakened by reports in the weekly *Respekt* that they had received money from the communists in 1990.
 The fall of Klaus did not end political uncertainty in the Czech Republic; it opened a period of heightened confrontation between rival policies. The left-leaning ČSSD wanted to soften the harshness of the orthodox financial approach of Klaus and his party, and the free marketeers, whether they belonged to the ODS or the Freedom Union, wanted to continue it.
 Against this background runs the subsidiary theme of racism and xenophobia, which increased considerably in the Czech Republic during the 1990s, and was exemplified by the murder in November 1997 of a Sudanese student by right-wing extremists, and the agitation of Miroslav Sladek and his party the Republicans (SPR-RSČ) against the Roma. Though unpleasant, these phenomena are of minor importance. All the indices for 1997, though they display a slight deterioration over 1996, which is understandable in view of the combined impact of the floods and the currency crisis, show an economy which has successfully made the transition. In 1997 real wages rose by 4 per cent; unemployment stood at 5 per cent; annual inflation was 9 per cent; the budget deficit was low, at 1.6 per cent of GDP; the balance of payments deficit fell from $4.5 billion in 1996 to $3.7 billion; the only unsatisfactory aspect

of the country's economic performance was the slow rate of growth of GDP, which fell to 1.2 per cent.[17] These relatively favourable economic figures are reflected in a continuing stolid acceptance by the population of the sacrifices imposed on the less well off by Klaus and his successors, and the evident rise in social inequality.

The parliamentary elections, which were held on 21 June 1998, produced a political deadlock. The Social Democrats, who had hoped to win decisively, received 32.3 per cent of the vote against the ODS's 27.7 per cent.[18] The smaller parties, such as the KDU-ČSL and the Freedom Union, with 9 per cent and 8.6 per cent respectively, were possible coalition partners for either large party, but the Freedom Union, which was on the neo-liberal right, refused to have anything to do with the Social Democrats. After a month of discussions, it was decided that the only solution was for the ČSSD to form a minority government, which would receive a vote of confidence thanks to the deliberate absence of Klaus's party from the Chamber of Deputies on the day in question. The ambiguous verdict of the electorate in 1998, and the tremendous premium it has placed on inter-party tolerance and co-operation, only strengthens the likelihood that continuity will be the order of the day. The Czech Republic will continue its slow but sure advance towards re-integration with the advanced industrial economies of the West, while retaining its democratic political traditions.

4 SLOVAKIA

Generally speaking in Eastern Europe, economic recovery has coincided with successful political liberalization. There was, until recently, one exception to this rule: Slovakia. Commentators have found it difficult to account for this. One suggestion was that after 1992 the reform path 'split in two', so that two separate roads were taken, a road of economic reform and a road of failed democratic consolidation, owing among other things to the authoritarian behaviour of Vladimír Mečiar.[19] It might be more accurate to speak rather of an *incomplete* degree of liberalization in both spheres, the economic and the political. There has been no liberalization of rents, or of energy prices; there have been extensive government programmes of road and oil pipeline building; there have been increasing links with Russia.

This mixture of policies was given ideological coherence by one leading member of the HZDS, who described it in 1997 as a 'third way': 'We are against importing the liberal model with its millions of unemployed' he said, adding 'We shall not follow the IMF's advice, which has a minimal success rate in the rest of the world, and we do not want to be dominated by transnational companies'. The distinctive Slovak method would be 'to set up our own giant companies'. In line with this view, the state continues to put money into infrastructural projects like motorways and oil pipelines; strategic enterprises are not sold off; foreign capital investment is not particularly encouraged: Jana Černa, an adviser to Prime Minister Mečiar, says 'they [meaning the Western institutions] don't like us because we have refused to sell everything'. This policy allegedly involves 'refusing to follow the lines laid down by the IMF or to import the liberal model' of the economy.[20]

However, such statements are made for public, particularly for domestic, consumption. When one examines actual policies Slovakia starts to look rather less original. There has in fact been a considerable amount of privatization: in 1996 the private sector produced 76.8 per cent of GDP. The former state enterprises have been sold to Slovaks rather than foreigners. More specifically they have gone to people enjoying connections with Prime Minister Mečiar and to a lesser extent also his coalition partners from the SNS and ZRS. The head of the National Property Fund, Stefan Gavorník, who was in charge of many of these insider privatizations, had this rather disturbing comment to make to a French journalist: 'I would never write a book on privatization because I would be dead before the end of the first chapter'. So the firms have gone to insiders, and the other half of the programme of privatization applied elsewhere in Eastern Europe – freedom of entry for small firms – is conspicuous by its absence. The number of private entrepreneurs has remained static at 280 000 over the whole period of independence so far.

It was not in economics but in politics that Slovakia differed from its neighbours. The regime of Prime Minister Mečiar was authoritarian in many ways. He regarded the ruling party, the HZDS, as his own private fief: he boasted that he himself was 'the strongest faction in the HZDS'. His political rhetoric was not particularly subtle: his way of reacting to hostile Constitutional Court decisions was to describe the Court as a 'sick institution'. His methods could on occasion be brutal. His way of conducting a struggle for power with his rival, President Michal Kováč, was to have his son kidnapped temporarily (in August 1995), using the secret service (the Slovenská Informačná Služba, Slovak Information Service, SIS), which was staffed by his supporters.[21] When a police investigator found evidence of SIS involvement in the kidnapping he was dismissed (October 1995). However, Mečiar had a lot of popular support, and even the opposition hesitated to qualify Slovakia as an autocracy, since elections remained free. The tendency of the outside world to reject Slovakia as a candidate for NATO or the EU increased the strength of Slovak isolationism and support for nationalist-inclined parties in the short term, though in the long term Slovakia became tired of going it alone.

There can be no doubt of at least the temporary success of the Slovak compromise between the market system and continuing state intervention in the economy. The Gross Domestic Product, after undergoing the characteristic post-communist decline in the early 1990s, began to recover in 1994, and rose continuously thereafter.

Slovakia's way of managing the transition has been to retain large enterprises in the hands of the Slovak ex-*nomenklaturists* who run the political system, to export more to transition economies than to advanced market economies (the proportion of exports to transition economies rose abruptly from 34 per cent in 1992 to 61 per cent in 1993[22] and was still at 55 per cent in 1995) and to expand trade with Russia (imports from Russia rose from 7.4 per cent of the total in 1992 to 16.6 per cent in 1995; direct negotiations between Mečiar and Russia's Prime Minister Viktor Chernomyrdin led to Slovakia's being given the job of producing aircraft engines for the Russian air force; Slovakia is entirely dependent on Russia for gas and 80 per cent dependent for oil).[23]

This mixture of policies seems to have worked so far. Slovakia's economic performance since independence has been little short of astonishing: GDP has grown continuously since 1993, faster than anywhere else in Eastern Europe: it increased by 6.8 per cent in 1994, by 7.4 per cent in 1995, and by 6.9 per cent in 1996, slowing to an estimated 5.3 per cent[24] in 1997, still a respectable figure. As a result, Slovakia is closer now to its 1989 level in terms of GDP per capita than any other country in Eastern Europe (1989 figure: $7851; 1997 figure: $7267).[25] This has coincided with a slight fall in unemployment (from 14.5 per cent in 1994 to 13.9 per cent in 1995), a result in part of a deliberate policy of increasing the number of people employed in industry (full-time employment as a proportion of the population rose by 4.1 per cent in 1995, while across the border employment in Czech manufacturing industry fell by 10 per cent). Inflation has also fallen (from 13 per cent in 1994 to 9.9 per cent in 1995 and 5.8 per cent in 1996). Budget deficits since 1994 have been uniformly low (between 1.4 per cent of GDP and none at all). The exchange rate has been steady (since 1993 the Slovak crown has stood at 31 per dollar). Exports were buoyant, amounting to 49 per cent of GDP in 1995 and 47 per cent in 1996.[26] All this took place with very little direct foreign investment – a cumulative inflow between 1989 and 1996 of 144 dollars per person, in contrast to the Czech Republic's 642 dollars.[27]

How did Slovakia achieve this, under the rather undemocratic rule of Vladimir Mečiar and his extreme right-wing nationalist and extreme left nostalgic communist allies? One reason is the good starting position the newly independent state inherited in 1993. Former Czechoslovakia had a fairly low level of international debt, and its Slovak component accordingly had a debt of $3.2 billion in 1993, which fell to $2.6 billion in 1994 and $2.4 billion in 1995. The only Eastern European country with a lower per capita debt at this time was the Czech Republic. Czechoslovakia as a whole was also closest to Western levels in the 1980s in terms of GDP per capita (55 per cent of the Austrian level; only the GDR's figure of 59 per cent was higher at that time).[28] So Slovakia could afford not to worry too much about the world financial institutions' reaction to its unorthodox measures.

The second advantage Mečiar and his allies had was the strength of national feeling: this was a young country, and the fear of international isolation, which affected many other older countries, was not a factor. Rather the reverse: a defensive reaction to international pressure strengthened the position of the ruling political group. This, at least, is what happened at the elections of the mid-1990s. Mečiar's HZDS, the ruling party, only dropped 2 per cent of its vote in the first post-independence elections (1994) as compared with 1992. The beneficiary was the left-wing Association of Workers (ZRS), which came from nowhere to gain 7.3 per cent of the vote; the best performance anywhere in Eastern Europe by an avowedly leftist party. The 'red–brown' coalition which ruled Slovakia until October 1998 was held together by a common commitment to 'defend the Slovak nation'. Hence Mečiar was able to use the demagogic tactic of accusing the democratic opposition, the 'Slovak Democratic Coalition', of 'conspiring with the Hungarian minority to grant autonomy to the Hungarians as a preparation for transferring southern Slovakia to Hungary'. The only basis for this absurd accusation was the fact that the Hungarian minority parties formed part of the opposition coalition, but it was good vote-winning propaganda.[29]

The third factor favouring Mečiar was the relative weakness of liberalism in Slovakia; some authors ascribed this to the long-term influence of an authoritarian political culture, with Slovak political subjection lasting at least until 1918. This argument appears to underestimate the development of democracy in the period after 1918. But, in any case, it must be admitted that Slovakia was characterized in the 1980s by an extremely weak opposition: only about 10 of the 1000 signatories of

Charter 77, the founding document of Czechoslovak dissidence, came from Slovakia, and the majority of Slovaks never really supported the 'velvet revolution' of 1989: supporters of transformation never constituted more than 49 per cent of the sample polled in public opinion surveys, and the figure actually fell to 41 per cent in 1994. When living standards began to fall after 1989 Slovaks blamed this on the fall of communism, and withdrew their confidence from democratic institutions. Confidence in parliament, for example, fell from 57 per cent in 1994 to 41 per cent in mid-1995 and 25 per cent in late 1995.[30] Moreover, to be a member of the former communist elite was not as much of a stigma in Slovakia as it was elsewhere: a popularity poll in 1990 revealed that the top nine politicians were all members or former members of the communist party; and in 1992, 25 per cent of those polled regarded the communist period as the best in the whole of Slovak history.

One must beware of over-stressing the differences between Slovakia and her neighbours; we have already pointed out that there is a considerable difference between the words of Slovak representatives and the actions of the government. The private sector is now dominant, despite the rhetoric; and if we examine the level of government spending, something liberal market theorists want to bring down as far as possible ('better and slimmer government' is the desired goal of the international financial institutions) the Slovak government has actually been more ruthless than its Czech counterpart, bringing the ratio of government expenditure to GDP down from 60 per cent to 46.7 per cent. The Czech figure is 50.4 per cent.[31] This is one reason for Slovakia's low budget deficits. Moreover, when the pressure was really on, Mečiar knew how to bend: as in June 1996 when Slovakia scrapped a 10 per cent import surcharge in response to a complaint from the World Trade Organization. Even Slovakia's initially strong Eastern trade orientation was progressively reduced: the proportion of exports that went to transition countries fell from 61.4 per cent in 1993 to 46.7 per cent in 1997, and exports to advanced industrial countries (that is essentially the West) rose from 31.8 per cent (1993) to 50.4 per cent (1997).

So the reasons for Slovakia's success under Mečiar were twofold: first the political atmosphere of nationalist defensiveness and sensitivity, which allowed him to ride roughshod over the opposition using classic demagogic tactics without meeting much resistance; and second the fact that Slovakia's originality in economic policy was more apparent than real: in many respects her policies were those of orthodox market liberalism. The defeat of the HZDS in the September 1998 elections and the coming to power in October of the opposition will undoubtedly bring changes in Slovakia's relationship with the West, ending five years of dissonance between her politics and her economics.

THE BALKANS: TRAVELLING IN AN UNCERTAIN DIRECTION

1 Post-Dayton Yugoslavia

The Dayton Agreement was originally a temporary truce, made on 21 November 1995, between rivals who really did not want to stop fighting but were forced to do so by pressure from outside; from the United States, and from Serbia. So far it has lasted. In theory Dayton reunited Bosnia, under the name 'Federation of Bosnia and Herzegovina'. But it also divided Bosnia into two 'entities': the Muslim-Croat Federation, comprising 51 per cent of the territory, and the Serbian Republic (*Republika Srpska*), comprising 49 per cent. The complexity of this operation is indicated by the cartographic appendix to the Dayton Agreement: there are 102 maps in it! There were surprisingly few questions left unresolved. The deadline for the transfer of control over the outskirts of Sarajevo to the Muslim-Croat Federation was met successfully (19 March 1996) although the departing Serbs destroyed whatever they could before leaving. The only outstanding issue was the status of Brčko, a district in the north of the country the possession of which was seen by the Bosnian Serbs as the key to effective communication between the two halves of their territory. The President of *Republika Srpska*, Biljana Plavšić, warned that there would be 'war if the arbitrators award Brčko to the Federation' (16 December 1996). Instead, the arbitration commission placed Brčko under temporary international supervision. The Bosnian Serbs remain in control of the town on the ground.

The competence of the political organs of 'Bosnia and Herzegovina' was restricted to foreign affairs. Most state functions were to be carried out by the two entities separately. This was a compromise between the Serbs' insistence that the central authorities be as weak as possible and the wish of everyone else that there be some move towards unity.[32] The two entities were separated by a four-kilometre zone to be patrolled by an international implementation force (known as IFOR).

In reality, however, post-Dayton Bosnia consisted of three entities not two, because the Muslim-Croat Federation existed only on paper. Haris Silajdžić, an opponent of narrow Muslim nationalism, who upheld a multi-cultural approach, was forced to resign in January 1996 as prime minister of Bosnia-Herzegovina and replaced by Hasan Muratović, also a member of the main Muslim party, Alija Izetbegović's SDA. It was significant that the new government of the Muslim-Croat Federation had no joint members with the government of Bosnia-Herzegovina. The Croats for their part held onto their self-proclaimed 'Republic of Herceg-Bosna' and refused to reunite the divided city of Mostar. A political party set up by Silajdžić in April, the Party for Bosnia-Herzegovina, which was intended to transcend ethnic divisions, made a certain amount of headway among Muslims, but not enough to make any difference. At the parliamentary elections of 14 September 1996 it secured 11 seats out of 140 in the House of Representatives of the Muslim-Croat Federation. With this exception, the elections were simply an ethnic plebiscite: Serbs voted for Serbian nationalist parties, Muslims voted for the SDA, and Croats voted for the HDZ.

In Federal Yugoslavia itself (the federation of Serbia and Montenegro set up by the Constitution of April 1992) there have been signs that the ending of the civil war in Bosnia is allowing genuine political differentiation to take place. In Serbia in November 1996 the opponents of President Milošević won local municipal elections; he annulled them, but the opposition replied with a long series of street protests, and the OSCE increased the pressure from outside by demanding recognition of the opposition's success. In Montenegro the domination of Milošević's ally and counterpart Momir Bulatović, head of the local successor party to the SKJ, the Democratic Socialist Party of Montenegro, and President of the republic, was brought to an end in July 1997 when he was expelled from his own party by the Prime Minister, Milo Đukanović. Đukanović, who went on to win the presidential elections in October, is trying to free Montenegro from the Serbian embrace, which is beginning to look like a stranglehold. He hopes to achieve at least a genuine autonomy for his country.[33]

Croatia was able to restore its territorial integrity after the beginning of serious Western intervention against the Bosnian Serbs and Milošević's decision to abandon their cause. As we saw in Chapter 5, Krajina was reconquered in August 1995, and a large number of local Serbs fled or were driven out of the area. Those that remained had to accept that they had little hope of securing autonomy. On 20 September the Croat parliament suspended the existing law that gave the Krajina Serbs special minority rights.

Further north, the region of Eastern Slavonia, conquered by Serbia from Croatia in 1992, could now be regained by negotiation. The agreement of 12 November 1995 provided for its 'eventual re-integration into Croatia'.[34] For the present, an international body (the UNTAES, or United Nations Transitional Administration in Eastern Slavonia) was set up to supervise the process (January 1996). Goran Hadžić, former President of the Serbian Republic of Krajina, became President of the Regional Council of Eastern Slavonia. This was acceptable to Croatia because he promised to work for re-integration; progress in this direction made it possible to normalize relations between Croatia and Yugoslavia (by the agreement of 23 August 1996). Local elections, described by OSCE observers as 'largely free and fair', were held in April 1997. They resulted in a victory for the Independent Democratic Serbian Party in 11 out of 28 cases. The UN Security Council voted in July 1997 to extend the mandate of UNTAES to allow the return of refugees; the process was completed in January 1998 when Croatia resumed control and UNTAES withdrew. With this Croatia finally recovered all its former territory and returned to peace with its eastern neighbour.

2 Bulgaria

We left Bulgaria in Chapter 4 with the setting up of the Popov cabinet. This was the first Bulgarian government to be dominated by forces consistently opposed to the old system, despite the fact that only five ministries were in anti-communist hands (three SDS, two BZNS), against the BSP's eight.[35] Prime Minister Popov was determined to take steps to bring Bulgaria into the post-communist epoch. He was able to carry through some of the reforms delayed by the political infighting of 1990. Interest rates were raised from 15 per cent to 45 per cent. 'Rapid and extensive privatization' was promised for the future. A step was taken towards price liberalization by the removal of subsidies (1 February 1991). This resulted in tremendous increases in the price of electricity (raised by 600 per cent) and basic foodstuffs (raised by 700 per cent). The trade unions promised on 8 January not to call any strikes, partly because wages were to rise by the equivalent of $90 a month in compensation, partly because this was a transitional government of national consensus; there were material reasons for going on strike but political considerations outweighed economic ones. The two main Bulgarian trade union federations, the CITUB and *Podkrepa*, jointly signed a 'social peace' agreement with the government (13 June 1991). In return for guarantees of minimum wages and social benefits they promised not to strike.

The Union of Democratic Forces (SDS), which set the tone in Popov's cabinet, was a heterogeneous coalition of democrats and others. But it was dominated by conservatives, whose explicit aim was 'the immediate and definitive liquidation of communist and neo-communist structures and tendencies'.[36] They soon began to overreach themselves, and to begin a series of extreme and in fact counter-productive measures, the common feature of which was the attempt to stamp out communism once and for all. They wanted to take revenge for all that the Bulgarian people had suffered in previous years. They began at the top with Zhivkov. He was put on trial for embezzlement (25 February 1991). They exposed 32 deputies as secret police informers. They forced through a land law which immediately restored the property rights of the pre-1946 owners of land expropriated since then. They forced out the liberals in their ranks who advocated a more moderate policy towards the BSP, and who formed a separate party. The impact of this new party on the situation was very limited: it only managed to secure 2.8 per cent of the vote at the October 1991 elections, thereby failing to pass the 4 per cent threshold for parliamentary representation.[37]

These elections, which had been called to end the instability inherent in a situation where one party was still in office and the other was master of the streets and the major cities, in fact solved nothing. They merely confirmed the existing balance of forces. It is true that the BSP lost the absolute majority it had enjoyed in 1990; but the SDS was only a fraction ahead (with 34.4 per cent of the vote, against the BSP's 33.1 per cent). It was forced to rely for its parliamentary majority on the mainly Muslim Movement for Rights and Freedoms (DPS), which had 7.6 per cent of the vote and 24 seats.

The elections of October opened the next phase of post-communist political history: the period of unstable SDS rule. This lasted from November 1991 until October 1992. The cabinet of Filip Dimitrov, approved on 18 November by 128 votes to 90, was a minority government propped up by the DPS, although the latter party was not given any seats in the cabinet, which was dominated by the SDS. The DPS was prepared to enter this arrangement because its former allies, the socialists, had squandered any political capital they had gained from the initial reforms of the early months of 1990 by reverting to the anti-Turkish course of the 1980s and using anti-Muslim demagogy as a means of gaining an artificial popularity: for instance the socialists had repeatedly endeavoured over the previous two years to ban the DPS on the specious ground that it was an 'ethnic association' rather than a political party.[38]

The new government of Filip Dimitrov was continuously engaged during 1991 and 1992 in a confrontation with its socialist opponents and the communist past. At the same time, it pushed ahead with implementing the standard programme of privatization, price liberalization and marketization required of all the Eastern European transition countries. Unfortunately this approach involved conflict with the SDS's erstwhile supporters amongst the urban workers. The 'shock therapy' policies embraced by the SDS resulted by the end of 1991 in 15 per cent unemployment, 85 per cent inflation, falling real wages, and (according to trade union claims) poverty for 60 per cent of the population. The *Podkrepa* trade union federation, which under Konstantin Trenchev had performed sterling services to the SDS in the fight against communism and socialism throughout 1990 (as in the physical attack on the BSP's headquarters, and numerous political strikes), was nevertheless unable to stray far from its working-class base. Hence it behaved rather like the Solidarity trade unionists had in Poland. In February 1992, *Podkrepa* withdrew from the 'Social Peace' agreement; in March it encouraged the miners to go on strike; in April it joined the ex-communist trade union federation, the CITUB, in walking out of talks with the government in protest against price liberalization policies.

Other groups were also offended by the SDS. Religious believers, collective farmers and members of the Turkish minority all had their grievances. An ecclesiastical dispute arose between the government and the supporters of the former Patriarch Maxim. Maxim had been head of the Bulgarian Orthodox Church since 1971: to the SDS it was clear that he was too closely linked with the past, and he was removed. The Constitutional Court ruled that this was illegal (11 June 1992).

More serious than this, because of its far-reaching ramifications, was the Dimitrov government's handling of the land problem. Its Land Restitution Law (5 February 1992) provided for the return to the original owners of all property nationalized between 1947 and 1962. We have already discussed the damaging impact of this measure on agricultural production.[39] But it had wider implications: it particularly affected tobacco growing and mining, two branches of industry in which the ethnic Turkish minority was heavily represented. Worse was to follow. The Law of 30 March 1992 abolished the preferential rights of owners and lessees of adjoining lands to purchase land put onto the market. It also restored property relations precisely as they had existed in 1946, before the setting up of the collectives, and abolished all collective farms and agricultural cooperatives, including those set up since the fall of communism. These measures, apart from creating uncertainty about the ownership of agricultural land, largely had the effect of excluding the ethnic Turks from the privatization process. The fairly large Turkish population (9.7 per cent of the total in 1992)[40] had possessed no land in pre-1946 Bulgaria; with the return of the land of the collectives to private property they lost what they had gained under communism. They also suffered disproportionately from the abolition of collective farm members' leasehold rights. This was not deliberate, as the SDS were free of the chauvinism the communists and their successors the BSP had exploited, but it was bound to antagonize the representatives of the ethnic Turks.[41] The leader of the DPS, Ahmed Dogan, decided to cast an individual vote against the Dimitrov cabinet as a warning that his party might be forced to change sides (24 July 1992). Dogan's constituents reacted in another way. Ethnic Turks from the district of Kurdzhali began to flee the country. By September 1992 at least 70 000 refugees had crossed the border (the Turkish government claimed the true figure was 160 000). These people were largely landless labourers driven out by the dissolution of the collective farms, which had produced an unemployment level of 40 per cent in the border districts.[42]

The President of Bulgaria, Zhelyu Zhelev, also had reason to be dissatisfied with the Dimitrov government, even though he was himself one of the founders of the SDS. Zhelev had wanted a non-party vice-president, to aid national reconciliation; instead he was forced to accept Blaga Dimitrova, a poetess closely associated with a radically anti-communist faction of the SDS (January 1992). Zhelev finally lost patience, and in August 1992 he intervened publicly. He called upon the SDS to end its 'war against everyone: the trade unions, the press, the whole of the democratic opposition and the Orthodox Church'. The party must correct its course, he said, and adopt a policy of 'national consensus'. Ahmed Dogan backed up Zhelev's views on 6 September by saying that the government must either change its political approach radically or be replaced altogether. Dimitrov rejected this and other appeals. The natural result was that the party of the Turkish minority abandoned him and he was overthrown on a vote of confidence in October 1992.[43]

There followed a return to political and economic gradualism, with the establishment of a non-party cabinet of experts (30 December 1992), headed by Professor Lyuben Berov, Bulgaria's most eminent economic historian, and more recently economic adviser to the President. The next phase of Bulgarian history stretches from then until the victory of the SDS in the general election of April 1997. It falls into two periods: the first is marked by non-party government under predominantly BSP influence (December 1992 to December 1994), the second by direct BSP rule, fairly stable until December 1996, then under conditions of political and economic crisis, culminating in loss of office by the BSP in February 1997 and an SDS election victory in April.

The Berov cabinet started off under favourable auspices; it aimed to continue the transformation process started by the SDS but to smooth off some of its sharper edges, while calling a halt to the Dimitrov government's anti-communist radicalism and obsession with symbolic gestures. The generally favourable atmosphere for this endeavour was reflected in the tremendous vote of confidence received by Berov at the outset (124 to 25). The main body of the SDS abstained from voting, despite its view of the Berov cabinet as 'a shady deal between the DPS and the BSP'. Two moderate factions of the SDS, the Alternative Social Liberal Party and New Choice, were inclined to give Berov the benefit of the doubt. Ironically, the only people actually to vote against him were 25 hard-line Marxist deputies from the BSP, led by Alexander Lilov. Berov received a further boost in March 1993 when 19 dissident SDS deputies crossed the floor, setting up the New Union for Democracy as part of the government coalition.

In terms of policy, the new prime minister tried to steer a middle course between the prescriptions of the IMF and the clamorous demands of various domestic pressure groups which felt they would suffer from rapid reforms. The success of the Berov programme depended on the readiness of the international financial institutions to relax their strict rules. They refused. The World Bank withheld a sum of $250 million in 1993 because of Bulgaria's failure to make genuine progress towards large-scale privatization; the IMF refused to approve Berov's request to allow a budget deficit of 10 per cent of GDP, which was admittedly far beyond the prescribed maximum of 6 per cent.[44] He presented his 1993 budget to parliament anyway (9 February 1993). Bulgaria had to wait over a year, until 11 April 1994, for the next loan from the IMF, which was granted on condition that 'Bulgaria continues to guarantee the pursuit of economic reform'.

The Berov cabinet also suffered from serious domestic problems in its endeavour to balance between the Bulgarian factions and pressure groups. It was criticized by President Zhelev on both political and economic grounds. He said it was 'excessively dependent on the BSP'. Moreover, it was 'failing to attract foreign investment' and conducting privatization at 'too slow a pace' (30 March 1994). But Berov continued his balancing act. He tried to keep the BSP sweet by including Rumen Gechev in his cabinet as Minister of Economics, but he also introduced

VAT at 18 per cent, raised fuel prices (1 April), defied strikes called by the CITUB against these measures (4 May and 18 May) and started a mass privatization scheme on the Czech model (28 June). Under the Berov scheme, all Bulgarian adults were to be sold vouchers at nominal prices, which could be invested either in state enterprises or private investment funds. An initial list of 340 enterprises earmarked for privatization was approved in August. This was more than the Dimitrov government had achieved, for all its self-proclaimed radicalism. The reward from the international institutions came quickly: on 29 June the London Club decide to write off 47 per cent of Bulgaria's debt to foreign commercial banks.

Despite these successes, Berov was compelled to resign on 2 September because both the BSP and the SDS now thought it was to their advantage to hold early elections. These elections, held on 18 December 1994, at last brought a clear political decision. The BSP and its allies, who had formed an electoral coalition under the name of the Democratic Left, won a decisive victory. With 43.5 per cent of the vote, the Democratic Left received 125 seats in parliament out of the total of 240, giving it an absolute majority. The SDS vote fell to 24.2 per cent, which translated into 69 seats.

There were many reasons for this defeat. The SDS lost because of the costs of transition, which were very severe in Bulgaria. The collapse of Comecon was a severer blow to Bulgaria than to any other state of Eastern Europe, because its economy was the one most integrated into the eastern trading network. No less than 83 per cent of Bulgaria's exports went to communist-bloc countries in 1989, but by 1993 this had fallen to 38 per cent. Attempts were made to gain alternative markets in the West, but this did not prevent an overall decline in the volume and value of trade.[45] Loss of exports involved loss of jobs, and the move to the market economy brought lower real pensions for the elderly and extreme social polarization for the whole population, 17 per cent of whom received 40 per cent of the national income in 1994, as compared with 30 per cent in 1992. In a public opinion survey conducted in 1994, 85 per cent of the respondents thought the income gap was too big in Bulgaria.[46] The BSP benefited from the general swing of the electoral pendulum to the left all over Eastern Europe in 1993–4; and they could rely on the political traditionalism of older people and the rural population. They also gained support from the provincial towns.[47]

The election of December 1994 marks the start of the next phase of post-communist history – the phase of direct socialist rule, by the cabinet of Zhan Videnov. Videnov decided against continuing the coalition of the previous two years, and simply appointed his colleagues and allies to ministerial office. The resulting cabinet had the misleading appearance of a coalition, however, because it included a satellite peasant party, the AS – BZNS, as well as Ecoglasnost (the pro-socialist wing of the environmentalists). Both these parties had run in the election on joint lists with the BSP under the Democratic Left umbrella. For the next two years, for the first time since 1990, a Bulgarian government appeared to rest on the firm foundation of an unassailable parliamentary majority. It soon became clear that Videnov intended to halt the reform process, and retain a large state sector with elements of a planned economy.

It turned out that in the new global political and economic climate this was impossible. The international institutions (particularly the World Bank and the IMF) required a commitment to thorough structural reform, fiscal discipline and a guarantee that pressures from sectional interests would be resisted. A firmly pro-Western foreign policy was also needed, at least implicitly. The Videnov government, in contrast, preferred to look eastwards. Exports were reoriented again, this time from West to East, with the result that the proportion of Bulgaria's exports going to transition countries rose from 28 per cent in 1994 to 43 per cent in 1996. Boris Yeltsin's offer to enter negotiations for economic union with Russia caused great concern in the West (29 March 1996). It would be wrong to ascribe the disastrous outcome of the Videnov episode purely to his uneasy relationship with the IMF, but this certainly played a part. It was not until July 1996 that that body felt able to approve a standby credit of $582 million, to be used over the next 20 months. In the intervening period, Bulgaria received almost nothing from the outside world. In 1994 there was a net resource inflow to Bulgaria of a mere 0.1 per cent of its GNP.[48] Moreover, there had been very little direct foreign investment: at $69 per capita Bulgaria received less than any other country in Eastern Europe.[49]

By 1996 the country's economic position had been seriously compromised. Unwise government measures were partly to blame. In February 1995 the privatization process was in effect frozen by limiting the amount of shares available in each large company to 25 per cent.[50] Insolvent companies were subsidised, so that $5 billion of bad debts piled up. The interest on external debt payments was $1.25 billion in 1996, but the Bulgarian National Bank's reserves were down to $600 million. Nothing seemed to go right. In a desperate search for hard currency the government continued to allow grain to be exported during

1996 even though it was clear that the harvest would not suffice to feed Bulgarians themselves. Cereal production had been falling ever since 1989. By 1996 it was at 50 per cent of the 1989–91 level.[51] In the autumn Bulgaria suffered a grain supply crisis more reminiscent of the situation in eighteenth-century France than in late twentieth-century Europe.[52] There was a fall of 38 per cent in real incomes between December 1995 and September 1996. Now ordinary Bulgarians began to lose patience. Protests began, not just in areas of SDS strength but in Burgas, a Black Sea port which was previously a socialist stronghold. A 'tent city of protest' was set up there in September.

Videnov's way of dealing with the situation was to execute a complete change of policy. He outlined the terms of his surrender to the outside world on 4 May 1996. In view of Bulgaria's huge debt servicing problem, he said, it was impossible to do without the support of the international financial institutions. This required structural reform, and a reduction of losses by state-owned industry, which were the main cause of the collapse of the lev on the foreign exchange markets. Videnov was able to push his reforms through the BSP's Supreme Council, despite the opposition of Mincho Minchev's Marxist Platform faction. The Marxists condemned Videnov as a 'Rightist' and demanded the introduction of the 'Chinese model' of market socialism. Stefan Proderon, the editor of the party newspaper, who was opposed to the change of line, warned that the World Bank and the IMF wanted to 'break our national spirit and bring us to our knees'.[53] During the summer of 1996 the Videnov government carried out some reforms and promised more. It raised petrol prices by 80 per cent, and other energy prices by 22 per cent. It proposed the closure of 64 loss-making companies, which would mean the loss of 40 000 jobs (12 May). It raised the rate of interest to 108 per cent to curb inflation. It promised to begin mass privatization in the autumn. Certain strategic sectors would be excluded (banks, arms production, railways, electric power), but the total number of firms privatized would rise from 309 to 467.

It is difficult, but not impossible, for a government to change course and stay in power. The Videnov government was in fact unable to do this, because its change of course came when the agrarian crisis was reaching its height. It was announced on 15 August that the grain harvest would amount to 1 800 000 tonnes. This was the worst result since 1951, and reflected a fall in yield from 3500 to 1850 tonnes per hectare since 1989. Bulgaria would need to import another 1 800 000 tonnes to feed the population. The SDS blamed the BSP; the BSP blamed the restitution measures carried out by the SDS, claiming for instance that 60 per cent of the land returned by the SDS to its former owners had fallen out of cultivation.[54] But the immediately relevant political point was that people on the verge of, or fearing, starvation, would not be likely to vote for Videnov in any free election. The Bulgarian Ambassador to the United Nations, Slavi Pashovski, added more pressure by denouncing his own government: 'The ghost of communism is hovering over Bulgaria', he said, adding somewhat melodramatically 'This means it is also hovering over the Balkans and over Europe'.[55] The economic crisis got progressively worse in the autumn of 1996. Inflation began to accelerate, forcing the Central Bank to raise the rate of interest to 300 per cent (23 September). This in turn increased the burden of foreign debt repayments; it was thought Bulgaria would become the first country to default on a debt restructuring deal. Nine Bulgarian banks were on the verge of collapse as a result of issuing excessive credits: 41 per cent of the loans the banks had made were found to be non-recoverable.[56]

The BSP had just one advantage left: its control of radio and television, which was strengthened by a law pushed through parliament in September. Bulgarians could still read a free press, but often they could not afford to buy the newspapers, so they were dependent for information on the state-run media (twice as many people – 363 out of every 1000 – had television sets as bought newspapers). Unusually for Eastern Europe, the BSP's control of the media did not produce the expected result. People knew what their daily lives were like, so when the presidential elections took place they gave strong support to Petur Stoyanov of the SDS (he secured 59.9 per cent of the vote in the second round, on 3 November 1996, against his BSP opponent's 40.1 per cent).

The new president-elect of Bulgaria stressed that he would 'get a broad debate going over how Bulgaria can get out of the economic crisis' and 'restore confidence in the national banking system so that people's savings will remain safe'.[57] But Videnov and the BSP still hung onto power, defeating a no-confidence motion by 87 to 69 on 12 November 1996. Even when Videnov was forced out of office (December) he was replaced temporarily by another BSP member, Minister of the Interior Nikolai Dobrev. When Stoyanov took over from Zhelev as President (23 January) the BSP leader made it clear that he expected a mandate to form a government. It took a further financial crisis and a collapse of the foreign exchange rate (the lev fell from 495 to 1730 to the dollar during January 1997) before the BSP was forced out of office. After all, it could still command a parliamentary majority; it had every reason to resist the holding of fresh elections.

As had happened in 1990, the opposition made use of extra-parliamentary mass pressure to get rid of the BSP government. On 10 January SDS protesters broke into the National Assembly and were only ejected after a running battle with the police; the oil-refinery workers and dockers struck work on 13 January; the formerly socialist-run, but now independent, CITUB threatened a general strike unless the BSP capitulated and held immediate general elections, and on 30 January it carried out its threat.

The BSP was forced to promise early elections, and to hand over the government to its rivals in the meantime. In March the new SDS government announced a reform programme agreed with the IMF, under which price controls would be lifted on all items except eight staple foods, and 160 000 jobs in the state sector would be eliminated by the end of the year. The reward came in the shape of an IMF loan of $627 million (11 April) and an EBRD loan of $300 million (23 May).

The Bulgarian socialists' lack of success during their period of office can be accounted for by a combination of social and economic factors. Their starting point was not favourable. They were too clearly tied to the old order of things; it was commonly said that in the BSP the 'red grandmothers' always predominated over the 'red mobile phones'. They also inherited an agrarian crisis, owing in part to the unfavourable impact on agriculture of the restitution policies of the Dimitrov government, though the collapse of the market for agricultural products was also a contributory factor. They failed to exert control over the banks, allowing bad loans to be made to failing state sector companies. They were faced with a tremendous foreign debt of $13 billion. One reason for the 1996 food crisis was the BSP's decision to go on exporting food to reduce this debt. The problem of servicing the foreign debt was exacerbated by the decline in exports, the value of which fell from $6.6 billion in 1989 to $4 billion in 1994. After 1994 the cost of debt servicing regularly soaked up over 20 per cent of exports (27.9 per cent in 1994, 21.5 per cent in 1996).

As Videnov himself put it on 4 May 1996: 'Given the foreign debt problem it is impossible to do without support from the international financial institutions. This means structural reform and cutting state industry's losses.'[58] And his economic adviser Ivan Angelov underlined the point two days later: 'Our society has not perceived that the symbol of real industrial power is not factory chimneys belching out smoke. The production of goods and services at any price is an irresponsible policy.'[59] President Zhelev summed up the situation in an interview on 22 May: 'Foreign policy isolation is one of the main reasons for the 1996 crisis. In 1995 we rejected the IMF and now we are clutching at it.'[60] The example of Bulgaria demonstrated that it was in the long run impossible for a transition government to challenge the world consensus on economic policy.

3 Romania

Events in Romania in the mid-1990s followed a somewhat similar course to those in Bulgaria. As in Bulgaria, the party in power was largely post-communist: it was made up of members of the old political class who had managed to hold on to power despite the efforts of the democratic opposition. Electoral fraud played a larger part in Romania, although the repeated victories of the FSN under Iliescu also reflected strong support from industrial workers and collective farmers. Iliescu's economic policy resembled Videnov's: he favoured a very slow movement towards privatization, and in general economic policy an awkward balancing act between the recommendations of the IMF and domestic pressures exerted by the trade unions and other interest groups.

The differences between the two countries arose essentially from the events of the previous decade. In 1989, Romania was in better shape than Bulgaria to face the period of transition. Ceauşescu had imposed great sacrifices on the population in his endeavour to reduce the level of foreign debt; Zhivkov, in contrast, had been prepared to let it mount ever higher, so the corresponding sacrifices in Bulgaria took place after the fall of communism. Other measures by the Romanian government in the 1980s, such as the 'systematization' of the countryside, and the prohibition of abortion, lacked any economic rationality, and could be dropped immediately by the FSN government without causing any more damage. Romania was far less dependent on trade with the eastern bloc, hence better able to weather the collapse of Comecon. The problems that remained were still great, but manageable. This is part of the explanation for the success of the former communists in the FSN in fending off opposition. Other reasons include Iliescu's own political astuteness, and the instinct for survival displayed by his colleagues. The economic indices also generally improved after 1994, leading some observers to suggest that Romania had successfully turned the corner under FSN auspices.[61]

As it turned out, this claim was somewhat exaggerated. Romania's economic recovery was rather hesitant, except for 1995, which was a good year. Political stability was fragile, depending as it did on an alliance with extreme nationalist parties, whose agitation against the ethnic

Hungarian minority made it difficult for President Iliescu to achieve the reconciliation with Hungary which was so important to Romania's international standing. An Education Law passed on 24 July 1995 restricted Hungarian-language teaching to primary and secondary schools. On 20 September the display of foreign (that is Hungarian) flags and the singing of foreign national anthems was prohibited. Members of the Hungarian minority demonstrated in protest; the Hungarian Foreign Minister said agreement was out of the question until these 'contentious issues' had been settled (22 September). Iliescu finally turned on his nationalist coalition partners, denouncing Tudor and Funar as 'Romanian Zhirinovskys' (28 September) and following up by severing all links with the PRM (19 October). The extreme-left Socialist Workers' Party (PSM) withdrew its support from the government at the same time, over the decision to privatize the banks. The final step to agreement with Hungary could not be taken, however, until September 1996, when the three ministers of Funar's PUNR were dismissed from the cabinet. By the treaty of 16 September 1996 Hungary agreed to renounce all claims to Transylvania, and Romania agreed to implement a range of ethnic rights. But this foreign policy success did not save Iliescu and his Social Democratic Party of Romania (PDSR) from defeat.

There were two reasons for this: firstly, severe inflation, accompanied by a fall in real wages, cut away their mass support; this resulted in a wave of strikes in the summer of 1996; secondly, the democratic opposition were able to combine their forces. They found a moderate party leader, the trade unionist Victor Ciorbea, to replace the rather rightwing and nationalistic Corneliu Coposu at the head of the Democratic Convention alliance (CDR). They settled on a presidential candidate with a realistic chance of winning: Emil Constantinescu, a pro-Western economic reformer, who was the leader of the PNTCD, the main component of the CDR. In the first round of presidential elections the votes were evenly divided between Iliescu (32 per cent), Constantinescu (28 per cent) and the former FSN-backed prime minister Petre Roman (21 per cent). But in the run-off, most of Roman's supporters shifted to Constantinescu, so that he came out on top with 54 per cent to Iliescu's 46 per cent. Constantinescu, who took over from Iliescu in December 1996, was immediately dubbed 'clean hands Constantinescu' because of his anti-corruption programme.[62] But he also guaranteed that there would be 'no witch-hunt' against former communists. After all, he too was a former communist. He had been a party member from 1965 to 1989 and at one time occupied the post of party representative in his university faculty.

Legislative elections were held simultaneously with the elections for president (3 and 17 November 1996). They were won by the Democratic Convention. On a 76 per cent turnout the CDR won 122 seats to the 91 of the Iliescu Social Democrats (PDSR). The other successful parties were the Social Democratic Union (USD), set up by Roman (53 seats), the Hungarian minority party the UDMR (25) and the Romanian nationalist parties, Tudor's PRM (19) and Funar's PUNR (18). The parliamentary arithmetic necessitated a coalition, which required delicate negotiations because Roman's party were unhappy with the monarchist element within the CDR. But both sides finally agreed to enter a government, and Victor Ciorbea of the CDR became prime minister.

There had thus been a thorough political changeover in Romania. Both the president and the prime minister were members of the same party, and they were committed to thoroughgoing reform. Ciorbea announced a radical package on 17 January 1997. It included cutting the budget deficit from 5.7 per cent of GDP to 3.5 per cent. This was to be achieved by reducing government spending rather than increasing taxes. Privatization would be pushed forward vigorously. The policy of reconciliation with the Hungarian minority, already begun under Iliescu, was given clearer shape by the inclusion of two members of the Hungarian minority party, the UDMR, in the cabinet. Ciorbea signed an Agreement on Co-operation and Good Neighbourliness with the Hungarian prime minister (12 March 1997).

The decision to privatize six banks (comprising 75 per cent of the banking sector), along with ten large loss-making state enterprises (on 14 and 17 April respectively) brought rewards, in the shape of a resumption of an IMF credit of $400 million, which had been suspended in November 1996, to which the World Bank added a further $600 million (13 May). It also brought trouble at home. The trade unions began what they called a 'month of the yellow card' in May, in protest against the spending cuts in the budget. Industrial workers marched through Bucharest demanding cuts in energy and food prices and the abandonment of privatization plans. This was followed up by a miners' strike in June. In August protesting Romanian oil-refinery workers clashed with the police. These protests were not without effect. The government back-pedalled on privatization, and reversed some of its austerity measures. The projected budget deficit shot back up to 4.5 per cent of GDP.

The situation should have been ideal for reform, with no conflict between the president and the prime minister, and majority backing in parliament. But in fact Ciorbea was just as unable to master Romania's problems as the prime ministers of the early 1990s had been. He could control neither his government nor his party, and he was just as liable to bow to pressure from special interest groups as Văcăroiu had been. Under his aegis Romania's GDP fell for the first time since 1992, with no clear countervailing gains. He finally resigned in March 1998. His replacement was Radu Vasile, also a member of the PNTCD, an economist who hoped to govern with a coalition comprising his party, the Hungarian minority party, and the Iliescu Social Democrats. He proposed the same mixture as before: 'to accelerate privatization, restructure and modernize industry and prepare for entry to the European Union',[63] and his cabinet was largely inherited from Ciorbea (13 April 1998). The promised policies have so far not borne fruit. Romania's transition, delayed for six years by Ion Iliescu and the National Salvation Front, continues to be an issue for the future.

4 Albania

We saw earlier that President Sali Berisha of Albania, despite having come to power as a democrat in April 1992, immediately started using authoritarian methods to maintain his position. His excuse was the need to maintain stability while the transformation process was being implemented, and to defeat post-communist opposition to this. He used various techniques. One was to mount accusations of corruption against former communists, starting with Ramiz Alia, who was arrested in September 1992. Over the next few months most of Alia's former colleagues were also arrested. In July 1993 Fatos Nano, the leader of the formerly communist, now socialist, party, the PSSH, was put in jail on a charge of fraud for which no evidence was produced in court (3 April 1994). Former Prime Minister Vilson Ahmeti, who had headed the government in 1991–2, was also arrested, and convicted to two years in prison for 'wasting $1.6 million'. Another way of dealing with the post-communists was to ban them from public office: a Law Against Genocide and Crimes Against Humanity Committed Under Communist Rule, passed in September 1995, excluded anyone who held a position of power before March 1991 from public office or taking part in elections until the year 2002.[64]

Berisha's control of the media (through the Press Law of 18 October 1993, which was used to harass the independent press, especially the weekly *Koha Jonë*, banned for a month in July 1994[65]) meant that opposition to arbitrary actions was muted. Another way of silencing the opposition was the use of terror. A member of the Democratic Alliance was murdered after a political meeting in Shkodër in January 1994, allegedly at the instigation of Berisha's Democrats (PDSH). The murder was used as an excuse to ban further Democratic Alliance meetings. The wheels of government ran smoothly, thanks to reliance on family and clan ties. Berisha came from a well-established clan in the northeastern district of Tropoja. He promoted members of this and other northern clans. The family of Minister of Defence Safet Zhulali was particularly well entrenched.[66] Democracy in local government was abolished by the re-introduction of a system of centrally appointed prefects.[67] Ultimately of course, Berisha had to face elections. Warned by his abject failure in the referendum of November 1994, when the whole of the south and most major towns voted against Berisha's new constitution (84.4 per cent voted, and of those 41.7 per cent said yes, and 53.9 per cent no) he decided to conduct the forthcoming general election in a more traditional way, with harassment and beatings of oppositionists, and electoral irregularities. The parliamentary elections of 26 May 1996 were generally agreed to have been fraudulent. The opposition boycotted the second round, and the elections were declared invalid by OSCE observers.[68] After his expected victory (122 out of 140 seats) Berisha reappointed Alexander Meksi as prime minister, with an entirely PDSH cabinet (6 July 1996). He appeared to be firmly in control. But the period of presidential rule was destined to be cut short after one year.

In some ways this was surprising. Albania had benefited in the early years of Berisha's period of office (1992–3) from the outside world's correct perception that it was a poverty-stricken country on the verge of famine. Another source of financial support was the strong Albanian-American lobby in the USA. More food aid was provided to the Albanians in 1992 and 1993 than to any other country in the world (the figures are 4.7 per cent of the world total in 1992, 3.8 per cent in 1993).[69] Albania also delivered some impressive economic growth figures in the mid-1990s after the inevitable early decline: 11 per cent, 7 per cent, 6 per cent and 9 per cent. Real wages stopped falling in 1993 and rose by 14 per cent in 1994. Life expectancy, according to the Albanian Statistical Office, rose between 1989 and 1993 from 70.9 years to 73 years, at a time when it was falling almost everywhere else in the post-communist world.

The explanation for Berisha's ultimate failure lay not in politics but in economics. The political problems could be dealt with, as long as outside support remained strong.[70] The economic and social problems were much more intractable. Unemployment was high; and favourable growth figures could not hide Albania's basic poverty. Moreover, Berisha's success was based on fraudulent and illegal dealings of three kinds: money-laundering for criminal groups, smuggling and above all the expropriation of the population through financial pyramid schemes. The governor of the Bank of Albania, Kristaq Lunika, warned Berisha in 1995 of the danger posed by the pyramid frenzy; he was ignored. Nearly a third of the Albanians sank their meagre savings in these schemes, as well as selling their houses and fields to raise extra money for 'investment'. By the time of the collapse a total of $1 billion, or a third of Albania's annual GDP, had been invested in the funds; between a half and two-thirds of this money was transferred abroad by the recipients.[71] The Albanian pyramid schemes were an extreme case of the behaviour of populations exposed to modern capitalist methods of marketing for the first time; credulous and desperate to improve their living standards, they thought capitalism meant getting something for nothing. The founders of the schemes cleverly presented themselves as benefactors: Rappash Xhaferi, head of the Xhaferi Charitable Foundation, bought in expensive Latin American football players to train his local team in the town of Lushnjë.

When the inevitable collapse came the various houses of cards erected by the pyramid fraudsters fell to the ground, landing on the government, which was regarded by the public as responsible.[72] Nine pyramid schemes collapsed in January 1997; there was a further collapse in February. Unrest swept the south of the country. In March the local office of SHIK in the port of Vlorë was overrun by demonstrators; Berisha threatened to put down the revolt with an 'iron hand' and declared a state of emergency. But the defeat of his troops at the hands of the southern rebels on 4 March forced a rethink. He appointed a socialist prime minister, Bashkim Fino, who was previously the mayor of the southern town of Gjirokastër (11 March); he had Fatos Nano pardoned; he promised elections for June; the government started to pay compensation to the victims of the pyramid schemes. None of this was sufficient to calm the unrest. The rebels in southern Albania refused to disarm until elections had actually been held. Moreover, Berisha still hoped to hold on to power. He ignored a call by the socialist leader that he step down; he vetoed the socialist government's dismissal of his police chief (19 April); he rejected the socialists' demand for the presence of international observers to supervise the holding of the elections. Nevertheless, when the elections did take place (29 June and 6 July) they revealed the hopelessness of Berisha's position. The socialists gained 101 seats, an absolute majority, the democrats only 29. The results were declared 'acceptable' by the OSCE.

Fatos Nano became prime minister; Berisha stepped down as president and was replaced by Rexhep Majdani, also a socialist. Now the wheel turned full circle. The socialists took their revenge, purging the administration of Berisha's supporters and bringing back members of the communist-era Sigurimi to top positions in the police. But they cannot solve Albania's economic problems in this way, nor deal with corruption, especially as the Albanian Mafia, which is strongly entrenched in the south, is closely tied to local socialist leaders.[73] Political instability continues, and the position of the socialists as the new government is distinctly uncertain, given the readiness of the opposition to resort to force to overthrow them. The permanence of the latest solution (a five-party coalition including the socialists, but without Fatos Nano) is highly dubious.

IN PLACE OF A CONCLUSION: TOWARDS THE TWENTY-FIRST CENTURY

In the nature of things, no definitive conclusion is possible for a book which describes a process continuing from the present into the future. Here instead I shall put forward a number of speculations on the changes that have occurred in the last decade, and identify the main trends of development.

The degree and nature of change has varied in line with the geographical and cultural divisions indicated in the introduction: East-Central Europe; the Balkans; the former Soviet Union. There have also been some features common to all three regions, for example the tremendous reduction in the role played by the state, which has been partly deliberate, and partly an involuntary by-product of the end of communism. In this connection, Jacek Kochanowicz has gone so far as to write of the 'disappearing state'.[74] One result of the retreat, indeed the collapse, of the state, has been what numerous authors describe as 'a state of chaos'. This is present as a potential threat in many parts of the post-communist east. Perhaps one could go further and say that it is a postmodern phenomenon that afflicts the whole world.[75] The outlines of chaos are clearly visible in several transition countries: in Albania,[76] in the former Soviet Union,[77] in parts of former Yugoslavia.[78]

In what might be called the economic environment, the changes have been immense. Many sacrifices were made in the early years of transition, but it is clear from most of the economic indices that the rewards of transition, if they can be defined as a resumption of the pattern of growth after a period of decline, are already appearing strongly in some countries (essentially East-Central Europe plus Estonia and Slovenia), and weakly in others (South-Eastern Europe, the other two Baltic States). Countries which underwent exceptionally steep economic declines during the stabilization process (Russia, Ukraine, and the states that make up Transcaucasia and Central Asia) are now beginning to pull out of them, on the most recent evidence.[79]

There has also been a change in political structures and habits. The most obvious trend is that towards fully functioning and effective parliamentary democracies, underpinned by classic liberal institutions and constitutional arrangements: media freedom, freedom of assembly and public demonstration, freedom of movement, freedom of association, and of course the freedom to engage in commercial activity. All these democratic rights have been largely achieved (we have noted the exceptions in our country-by-country treatment).

The record of the 1990s on social rights is less clear. The new approach has usually been not to guarantee social rights but to create an economic environment in which these can effectively be protected. There are two problems with this approach: first, there are bound to be victims of the shift from one approach to the other, and second, everything depends on the success of the economic transformation. In East-Central Europe at least there are signs that the social costs have now been paid, and the benefits are being reaped, in the shape of increased real wages, a higher standard of life and a steadily increasing life expectancy. This is not to deny the existence of an underclass of more permanent victims, continuing pockets of poverty and a high level of disappointment and dissatisfaction among the less well-off. In the Czech Republic, for instance, a recent poll showed that 48 per cent of the population thought they were better off before 1989.[80] But nostalgia is not exactly unique to Eastern Europe. Moreover, any tendency to blame the costs of transition on economic policies should be held in check by the salutary reflection that the suffering has been greatest precisely in countries which have failed to carry out a consistent economic transformation (such as Bulgaria and Romania). There are other reasons as well, and it would be unwise to generalize from this point to cover the newly independent countries further east, which suffer also from specifically post-Soviet problems I do not propose to deal with here.

Somewhat counter-intuitively, changes in political personnel in Eastern Europe have not generally been profound. In many cases politicians of the former communist era have managed to retain their positions; where they have been challenged it has not generally been by former dissidents. The fate of the former dissidents is remarkable; instead of 'coming into their own' they have not been able to find a secure footing in the new era. In Czechoslovakia, the movements that emerged in November 1989, Civic Forum and Public Against Violence, split and lost elections (June 1992), subsequently disappearing from the scene. President Havel survives in Prague, but alone, since Petr Uhl, who was made head of the Czechoslovak news agency in February 1990, was dismissed in September 1992 by the new federal government of Jan Stráský. The self-dissolution of Charter 77 in 1993, suggested by Václav Havel himself, drew a clear line under the dissident past of the Czechs, much to the disgust of Peter Cibulka and other former dissidents: 'Vaska, you are a pig', they chanted.

In Bulgaria, the poetess Blaga Dimitrova resigned from the vice-presidency on 30 June 1993 as a protest against Zhelyu Zhelev's 'collaboration with the post-communists'.[81] In Poland, as we saw earlier, the period of Solidarity's parliamentary rule quickly came to an end, to be followed soon afterwards by the defeat of Lech Wałęsa in presidential elections. The veteran Solidarity activist Adam Michnik delivered the following verdict on this: 'We are the children of a past epoch, museum pieces and young people vote for Kwaśniewski because he's young and symbolizes the end of the struggle.'[82] John Torpey's conclusion on the fate of the dissidents, derived from a study of East Germany, can be applied more generally: 'Intellectuals have lost much of their cachet, as mass-market culture floods in from the West...They have been shoved aside in the post-revolutionary squabbling'.[83] The revival of Solidarity in Poland after 1997 is an exception to this rule, but only in part: the new government is mainly in the hands of people who were not prominent in the struggles of the early 1980s, though they did participate in them.

The people who rose to the top in politics during the 1990s were not active dissidents under communism. The post-1989 political elite either came from the 'grey zone' of sympathizers who for prudential reasons never made any open protest against the communist system or they emerged from the lower and middle ranks of the former *nomenklatura*. Prime Minister Klaus of the Czech Republic is a clear example of the first group. Examples of the second group abound, given that the successor parties to the communists did very well politically over most of the region in the mid-1990s. Recent governmental changes in Poland, Bulgaria and Romania have not significantly altered this situation.[84]

The overall result of the developments since 1989 in Eastern Europe has been to strengthen the historical division between the East-Central group, or northern tier, of more advanced countries, and the

South-Eastern, or southern tier, of less advanced countries, which was outlined in Chapter 1. The gap between north and south is reflected in recommendations issued by the European Commission in July 1997: negotiations for admission to the EU can be started immediately with Hungary, the Czech Republic, Poland, Estonia and Slovenia; Slovakia is excluded on political grounds; the rest are excluded on economic grounds.[85] The resulting split in the region has been described succinctly by Centeno and Rands: 'A new wall has been created: it begins in Estonia in the north and divides Poland, Hungary, the Czech Republic and Slovakia from the rest.' On one side of the line there are viable market economies, while on the other side 'the transition has yet to produce a coherent alternative'.[86]

Appendix: Statistical Tables

Table A1 Population of the post-communist states

Country	1987	1997	% change, 1987–97[1]
1 East-Central Europe			
Czech Republic	10 349 000	10 299 000	**−0.48**
Hungary	10 486 000	10 135 000	**−3.35**
Poland	37 664 000	38 660 000	+2.64
Slovakia	5 224 000	5 388 000	+3.14
2 South-Eastern Europe and Former Yugoslavia			
Albania[2]	3 076 000	3 170 000	+3.06
Bosnia-Herzegovina[2]	4 360 000	4 570 000	+4.82
Bulgaria	8 971 000	8 310 000	**−7.37**
Croatia[2]	4 740 000	4 600 000	**−2.95**
Macedonia[3]	1 990 000	2 160 000	+8.45
Romania	22 940 000	22 526 000	**−1.80**
Slovenia	2 000 000	1 985 000	**−0.75**
Yugoslavia (FR)[4]	10 340 000	10 600 000	+2.51
3 Baltic States			
Estonia	1 546 000	1 460 000	**−5.56**
Latvia	2 627 000	2 480 000	**−5.60**
Lithuania	3 616 000	3 710 000	+2.60
Total	129 929 000	130 053 000	+0.10

1. Rates of decline are given in bold.
2. 1996 population figures are given for Albania, Bosnia-Herzegovina and Croatia.
3. Official title: Former Yugoslav Republic of Macedonia (FYROM); population figures for 1995.
4. Comprises the former Yugoslav republics of Serbia and Montenegro.

Source: United Nations, Statistics Division, *Monthly Bulletin of Statistics*, 50, 12, pp. 1–10, and 52, 6, pp. 1–6.

Appendix

Table A2 Birth rates, 1989–96 (per 1 000)

Country	1989	1990	1991	1992	1993	1994	1995	1996	% fall 1989–96
1 Eastern Europe									
Albania	24.6	25.2	23.8		23.3	22.6	22.4		8.9
Bulgaria	12.5	11.7	10.7	9.9	10.0	9.4	8.6	8.6	31.2
Croatia	11.7	11.8	10.8	10.5	10.2	10.3	10.8	11.7	0.0
Czech Rep.	12.4	12.6	12.5	11.8	11.7	10.3	9.3	8.8	29.0
Hungary	11.9	12.1	12.3	12.2	11.4	11.3	11.0	10.4	12.6
Poland	14.8	14.3	14.3	13.4	12.8	12.5	11.5	11.1	25.0
Romania	16.0	13.6	11.9	11.4	11.0	11.0	10.4	10.2	36.3
Slovakia	15.2	15.1	14.9	14.1	13.8	12.4	11.4	11.2	26.3
Slovenia	11.7	11.2	10.8	9.9	9.9	9.8	9.5	9.3	20.5
Yugoslavia	14.8	14.7	14.6	13.5	13.4	13.1	13.3	12.9	12.8
2 Baltic States									
Estonia	15.5	14.2	12.3	11.7	10.0	9.5	9.1	9.0	41.9
Latvia	14.6	14.2	13.0	12.0	10.3	9.5	8.5	7.9	45.9
Lithuania	15.1	15.3	15.0	14.3	12.5	11.5	11.1	10.6	29.8

Sources: United Nations, *Monthly Bulletin of Statistics*, 51, 9, September 1997, pp. 7–8; United Nations, *Demographic Yearbook 1995* (New York: United Nations, 1997), pp. 324–5; United Nations, *Demographic Yearbook 1992* (New York: United Nations, 1994), pp. 326–9; national statistical yearbooks.

Table A3 Death Rates 1989–96[1] (per 1 000)

Country	1989	1990	1991	1992	1993	1994	1995	1996	(% rise or fall) 1989–96
1 East-Central Europe									
Czech Republic	12.3	12.7	12.1	11.7	11.4	11.4	11.4	10.9	−11.4
Hungary	13.9	14.1	14.0	14.4	14.6	14.3	14.2	14.1	+1.2
Poland	10.0	10.2	10.6	10.3	10.8	9.8	10.0	10.0	+0.0
Slovakia	10.2	10.3	10.3	10.1	9.9	9.6	9.8	9.5	−6.8
2 South-Eastern Europe and Former Yugoslavia									
Albania	5.7	5.6	5.5	5.1	4.9		5.7		+0.0
Bulgaria	11.9	12.1	12.3	12.6	12.9	13.2	13.6	14.0	+17.6
Croatia	11.0	10.9	11.5	10.8	10.6	10.4	11.2	11.3	+2.7
Macedonia				7.3	7.8	7.4	7.6	7.6	+4.1
Romania	10.7	10.6	10.9	11.6	11.6	11.7	12.0	12.7	+18.7
Slovenia	9.3	9.3	9.7	9.7	10.1	9.7	9.5	9.3	+0.0
Yugoslavia	9.5	9.3	9.8	10.1	10.2	10.0	10.2	10.5	+10.5

3 Baltic States

Estonia	11.8	12.4	12.6	13.0	14.0	14.8	13.8	12.9	**+9.3**
Latvia	12.2	13.0	13.1	13.5	15.2	16.4	15.9	13.8	**+13.1**
Lithuania	10.3	10.7	11.0	11.1	12.4	12.5	12.2	11.6	**+12.6**

1. Rising death rates are in bold.
Sources: United Nations *Monthly Bulletin of Statistics*, 51, 9, September 1997, pp. 9–10; United Nations, *Demographic Yearbook, 1995*, pp. 406–7; C. de Guibert-Lantoine and A. Monnier, 'La Conjoncture démographique: L'Europe et les pays développés d'outre-mer', *Population*, 52, 5, September–October 1997, pp. 1200–3; national statistical yearbooks.

Table A4   Rates of Natural Increase,[1] 1989–96 (per 1 000)

Country	1989	1990	1991	1992	1993	1994	1995	1996
1 East-Central Europe								
Czech Republic	0.1	**–0.1**	0.4	0.1	0.3	**–1.1**	**–2.1**	**–2.1**
Hungary	**–2.0**	**–2.0**	**–1.7**	**–2.2**	**–3.2**	**–3.0**	**–3.2**	**–3.7**
Poland	4.8	4.1	3.7	3.1	2.9	2.7	1.5	1.1
Slovakia	5.0	4.8	4.6	4.0	3.9	2.8	1.6	1.7
2 South-Eastern Europe and Former Yugoslavia								
Albania	18.9	19.6	18.3	18.5	18.4	18.0	16.7	
Bulgaria	0.6	**–0.4**	**–1.6**	**–1.8**	**–2.9**	**–3.8**	**–5.0**	**–2.3**
Croatia	0.7	0.9	**–0.7**	**–1.0**	**–0.4**	**–0.1**	**–0.4**	
Romania	5.3	3.0	1.0	**–0.2**	**–0.6**	**–0.7**	**–1.6**	**–2.5**
Slovenia	2.4	1.9	1.1	0.2	**–0.2**	0.1	0.0	0.0
Yugoslavia (FR)	5.3	5.4	4.8	3.4	3.2	3.1	3.1	2.4
3 Baltic States								
Estonia	3.7	1.8	**–0.3**	**–1.3**	**–4.0**	**–5.3**	**–4.7**	**–3.9**
Latvia	2.4	1.2	**–0.1**	**–1.5**	**–4.9**	**–6.9**	**–7.4**	**–5.9**
Lithuania	4.9	4.6	4.0	3.2	0.1	**–0.1**	**–1.1**	**–1.0**

1. Rates of population decline are given in bold.
Sources: As for Table A3.

Table A5   Infant Mortality (per 1 000 live births)

Country	1989	1996	% rise or fall, 1989–96
Albania	30.8		
Bulgaria	14.4	15.6	**+8.3**
Croatia	11.7	8.0	– 31.6
Czech Republic	10.0	6.0	–40.0
Estonia	14.8	10.5	–29.1

192   Appendix

Table A5 (contd)

Country	1989	1996	% rise or fall, 1989–96
Hungary	15.7	10.9	−30.6
Latvia	11.1	15.9	**+43.2**
Lithuania	10.7	10.1	−5.6
Poland	15.9	12.1	−23.9
Romania	26.9	22.3	−17.1
Slovakia	13.5	9.9	−26.7
Slovenia	11.4	4.7	−58.8
Yugoslavia (FR)	29.3	14.3	−51.2

Sources: national statistical yearbooks.

Table A6 Changes in Life Expectancy: Male and Female Expectation of Life at Birth, 1988–96

Country	1988	1990	1992	1994	1996	increment, 1988–96
1 East-Central Europe						
Czech Republic						
Male	68.1[1]	67.5	68.5	69.5	70.4	+2.3
Female	75.4[1]	76.0	76.1	76.6	77.3	+1.9
Hungary						
Male	66.2	65.1	64.6	64.8	66.1	**−0.1**
Female	74.0	73.7	73.7	74.2	74.7	+0.7
Poland						
Male	67.2	66.5	66.7	67.5	68.1	+0.9
Female	75.7	75.5	75.7	76.1	76.6	+0.9
Slovakia						
Male	66.9[1]	66.6	67.6	68.3	68.8	+1.9
Female	75.4[1]	75.4	76.2	76.5	76.7	+1.3
Slovenia						
Male		69.4		69.6	70.8	+1.4
Female		77.3		77.4	78.3	+1.0
2 South-Eastern Europe						
Bulgaria						
Male	68.3	68.0	67.7	67.1	67.1	**−1.2**
Female	74.7	74.7	74.7	74.9	74.6	**−0.1**
Romania[2]						
Male	66.5	66.6	66.1	65.7	65.7	**−0.8**
Female	72.4	73.1	73.2	73.4	73.1	+0.7
3 Baltic Countries						
Estonia						
Male	64.8	64.6	63.5	61.1	64.5	**−0.3**
Female	73.6	74.6	74.7	73.1	75.5	+1.9

Latvia						
Male	66.3	64.2	63.3	60.7	63.9	−2.4
Female	75.1	74.6	74.8	72.9	75.6	+0.5
Lithuania						
Male	67.7	66.6	64.9	62.8	65.0	−2.7
Female	76.6	76.2	76.0	74.9	76.1	−0.5

1. These data are for 1989.
2. All Romanian data except 1996 are three-year averages around the specified year.

Sources: United Nations, *Demographic Yearbook* (New York: UN Department of International Economic and Social Affairs), various issues; *Short Term Economic Indicators*, various issues; national statistical yearbooks.

Table A7   Gross Domestic Product, % Change (1989 = 100)[1]

Country	I 1990	II 1991	III 1992	IV 1993	V 1994	VI 1995	VII 1996	VIII 1997[2]	IX index
1 East-Central Europe									
Czech Republic	−1.2	−14.2	−6.4	−0.5	**2.6**	**4.8**	**4.1**	**1.2**	90.0
Former GDR	−15.5	−19.3	**7.9**	**7.2**	**8.5**	**5.3**	**2.0**	**2.0**	95.2
Hungary	−2.5	−7.7	−4.3	−2.3	**2.5**	**2.0**	**1.0**	**3.1**	91.6
Poland	−11.6	−7.0	**2.6**	**3.8**	**5.5**	**7.0**	**6.0**	**6.0**	111.1
Slovakia	−2.5	−14.6	−6.2	−4.1	**4.8**	**7.0**	**6.9**	**5.3**	94.7
2 South-Eastern Europe and Former Yugoslavia									
Albania	−10.0	−27.7	−9.7	**11.0**	**7.4**	**6.0**	**9.1**	−8.0	74.6
Bulgaria	−9.1	−11.7	−6.0	−4.2	0.0	**3.0**	−10.9	−7.4	61.3
Croatia		−15.1	−12.8	−3.2	**1.8**	**2.0**	**4.5**	**5.5**	75.7
Macedonia (FYROM)[3]		−9.8	−12.4	−12.0	−4.0	−1.5	**3.0**	**5.0**	63.9
Romania	−5.6	−12.9	−13.8	**1.3**	**2.4**	**7.0**	**4.1**	−3.0	79.3
Slovenia		−9.3	−5.7	**1.0**	**4.0**	**5.0**	**3.1**	**3.4**	92.8
Yugoslavia (FR)[4]	−8.4	−11.2	−26.2	−27.7	**6.5**	**6.1**	**4.3**	**6.5**	54.4
3 Baltic States									
Estonia	−7.1	−22.1	−21.6	−6.6	**6.0**	**4.0**	**4.0**	**5.2**	64.1
Latvia	−1.2	−8.1	−35.0	−14.9	0.0	**1.0**	**2.8**	**3.5**	53.9
Lithuania	−3.3	−13.1	−39.3	−16.2	**2.0**	**3.0**	**4.2**	**5.0**	49.1

1. Positive growth figures are given in bold.
2. Forecast.
3. Gross Material Product.
4. Gross Material Product.

Sources: for columns I–VI, World Bank, *World Development Report 1996* (Oxford, 1996), p. 173; for columns VII–VIII, *Economic Bulletin for Europe*, 49, 1997, Table 1.3.1, p. 22. The figures in Column VIII are October 1997 forecasts, except for East-Central Europe, Bulgaria, Romania, Slovenia and the Baltic States, where they are taken from *Transition* (World Bank newsletter about reforming economies), 9, 1, February 1998, p. 11. Column IX gives the 1997 index level of GDP, taking 1989 as the baseline, and is a measure of the degree of decline and recovery since then.

Appendix

Table A8 Gross Domestic Product per capita (in $, in 1997 rank order)

Country	1989	1993	1997	Index
Slovenia	7 851	6 310	7 267	92.6
Croatia	7 375	4 500	4 996	67.7
Estonia	4 740	3 040	3 631	76.6
Hungary	4 101	3 330	3 499	85.3
Czech Republic	3 578	2 730	3 242	90.6
Poland	2 942	2 270	2 800	95.2
Slovakia	2 476	1 900	2 382	96.2
Latvia	3 560	2 030	2 138	60.1
Serbia	2 752	1 700	1 833	66.6
Lithuania	2 450	1 310	1 502	61.3
Romania	1 681	1 120	1 327	78.9
Bulgaria	1 694	1 160	1 019	60.2
Albania	562	340	466	82.9
For comparison:				
Germany	22 890	20 990	22 853	99.8

Source: O. Hishow, 'Makroökonomische Politik und Reformfortschritte im östlichen Europa', *BBIOST*, 25, 1997, p. 9.

Table A9 Inflation[1]

Country	1989	1990	1991	1992	1993	1994	1995	1996	1997
1 East-Central Europe									
Czech Rep.	1.4	9.7	56.6	11.1	20.6	10.0	9.1	8.9	8.9
Hungary	17.0	28.9	35.0	23.0	22.6	19.1	28.5	23.6	18.2
Poland	264.3	585.8	70.3	45.3	36.9	33.2	28.1	19.8	15.0
Slovakia	1.3	10.4	61.2	10.2	23.1	13.4	10.0	6.0	6.4
2 South-Eastern Europe and Former Yugoslavia									
Albania	0.0	0.0	35.5	193.1	85.0	21.5	8.0	12.7	33.2
Bosnia-H.[2]	36.8	594.0	116.2			553.0	−12.1	−21.2	10.8
Bulgaria	9.2	50.6	338.5	91.3	72.9	96.2	62.1	123.1	1 000.0
Croatia	1 200.0	609.5	123.0	663.6	1 517.0	97.5	2.0	3.6	3.6
FYROM	1 246.0	608.4	114.9	1 505.0	353.1	121.0	16.9	4.1	3.6
Romania	1.1	5.1	170.2	210.7	256.2	147.1	32.2	38.8	125.0
Slovenia	1 285.3	549.7	117.7	201.3	31.8	19.8	12.7	9.7	9.2
Yugo.[3]	1 265.0	580.0	122.0	8 926.0			78.6	90.5	18.5
3 Baltic States									
Estonia	4.0	18.0	202.0	1 078.0	89.6	47.9	28.9	23.1	10.8
Latvia	5.2	10.9	172.2	951.2	108.1	35.7	25.0	17.1	8.5
Lithuania	2.2	9.1	216.4	1 020.5	410.1	72.0	39.5	24.7	9.2

1. This table gives the annual average percentage change in consumer prices.
2. Bosnia-Herzegovina's inflation rate, 1992: 64 218%; 1993: 38 825%.
3. Yugoslavia's inflation rate, 1993: 62 218%; 1994: 946 827 610%.

Sources: *Economic Bulletin for Europe*, 49, 1997, Table B.7, p. 106, and *Transition Report 1997* (EBRD, 1997). Inflation figures for 1997 are taken from *Transition* (World Bank), 9, 1, February 1998, p. 11.

Table A10 Trade Flows of East European Countries, 1989–96

	1989	1990	1991	1992	1993	1994	1995	1996	Change, %
1 Exports, in billion dollars US									
East-Central Europe									
Czech Republic					11.4	14.0	17.0	21.9	+47.9
Czechoslovakia[1]	14.1	11.6	10.9	12.3	(12.3	16.4	20.4	24.9)	+76.6
Hungary	9.7	9.6	10.0	10.7	8.6	10.6	12.9	13.1	+35.1
Poland	13.5	13.6	14.9	13.2	14.1	17.2	22.9	24.4	+80.7
Slovakia					5.5	6.7	8.6	8.8	+60.0
South-Eastern Europe and Former Yugoslavia									
Bulgaria[2]	2.8	2.1	2.1	2.5	2.4	3.4	5.2	4.5	+60.7
Croatia					3.9	3.5	4.3	4.5	+15.4
Romania	11.1	5.9	4.3	4.4	4.9	6.2	8.1	7.6	−31.5
Slovenia					6.1	6.8	8.3	8.3	+36.1
Yugoslavia (FR)					0.0	0.1	0.0	0.5	
Yugoslavia (SFR)	13.6	14.3	15.9	11.0					−19.1
Baltic States									
Estonia					0.4	0.8	1.3	1.8	2.1	+425.0
Latvia					0.8	1.0	1.0	1.3	1.4	+75.0
Lithuania					0.7	1.2	2.0	2.7	3.3	+371.4
2 Imports, in billion dollars US									
East-Central Europe									
Czech Republic					12.6	14.8	20.8	27.8	+120.6
Czechoslovakia	14.1	13.7	10.2	12.7	(14.4	17.3	24.5	33.3)	+136.2
Hungary	8.9	8.6	11.1	11.1	12.4	14.4	15.5	16.2	+82.0
Poland	11.4	9.0	17.1	15.2	18.8	21.6	29.1	37.1	+225.4
Slovakia					6.3	6.6	8.8	10.9	+73.0
South-Eastern Europe and Former Yugoslavia									
Bulgaria	5.1	3.4	2.7	4.3	4.5	4.7	5.5	4.3	−15.6
Croatia					4.7	5.2	7.0	7.8	+66.0
Romania	9.0	9.4	5.2	5.6	5.9	6.5	9.4	9.1	+1.1
Slovenia					6.5	7.2	9.5	9.4	+44.6
Yugoslavia (FR)					0.1	0.2	0.4	1.4	+1 300.0
Yugoslavia (SFR)	14.8	19.2	16.8	12.4					−35.4

Appendix

Table A10 (contd)

	1989	1990	1991	1992	1993	1994	1995	1996	Change, %
Baltic States									
Estonia				0.5	0.9	1.7	2.5	3.2	+540.0
Latvia				0.7	1.0	1.2	1.6	2.1	+200.0
Lithuania				0.6	1.4	2.4	3.7	4.4	+633.3

1. Figures for Czechoslovakia have been completed for the years 1993–6 by subtracting the mutual trade of the Czech Republic and Slovakia from their respective totals. The results are shown in brackets.
2. The sources give widely divergent figures for Bulgarian trade during the first two years. Lavigne for instance gives a figure of 1980 US $16.0 billion for Bulgarian exports in 1989 which if correct would place them at 62% of GDP (!) and would make Bulgaria, with the second smallest population, the largest exporter in the whole of Eastern Europe. The explanation for the discrepancy is that before the collapse of Comecon, trade within the Eastern bloc was measured in transferable rubles, which were given an arbitrary exchange rate with the dollar which varied from country to country. Since 83% of Bulgaria's exports went east in 1989, and since the ruble/dollar cross rate as applied to Bulgaria was 1.9 rubles to the dollar, Bulgaria's exports (and imports) were artificially inflated in value. This problem was not so severe for the other countries of Eastern Europe, which had already moved during the 1980s to more realistic rates (see M. Lavigne, *The Economics of Transition*, Table 6.3, p. 104).

Sources: *Direction of Trade Statistics Yearbook 1997* (Washington: IMF, 1997); *Direction of Trade Statistics Yearbook 1996* (Washington: IMF, 1996).

Table A11 Annual Percentage Changes in Real Wages

Country	1989	1990	1991	1992	1993	1994	1995	1996	1997
1 East-Central Europe									
Czech Republic	0.9	−6.3	−40.0	8.5	3.0	5.7	7.9	8.8	1.8
Hungary	2.2	−6.0	−9.4	2.9	2.2	2.7	−10.2	−5.0	4.9
Poland	10.4	−28.8	−5.4	−6.3	−4.0	5.4	0.4	6.1	7.3
Slovakia	0.9	−6.3	−44.7	10.1	−6.4	3.9	5.4	7.2	6.6
2 South-Eastern Europe and Former Yugoslavia									
Albania			0.3	−42.6	−26.0	−5.0	14.0	2.3	
Croatia				−44.0	−1.0	14.0	40.0	8.9	
Bulgaria			6.2	−42.3	17.3	−8.7	−23.8	−19.0	−28.1
Romania		2.8	5.4	−53.2	−40.9	−54.0	−1.5	21.8	9.2 −22.3
Serbia-Montenegro				−60.0					
Slovenia	27.6	−26.5	−35.2	−2.8	19.7	8.5	5.4	4.9	3.0
Yugoslavia			−22.0	−17.0					

Appendix 197

3 Baltic States

Estonia				−39.0	6.0	5.0	6.0	0.7	8.0
Latvia			−16.3	−15.7	1.0	12.0	−0.9	−2.8	13.1
Lithuania	8.1	7.3	−18.3	−32.8	−45.0	8.0	10.0	22.0	11.4

Sources: *World Employment 1996/97: National Policies in a Global Context* (Geneva: International Labour Office, 1996), p. 114; *Cestat Statistical Bulletin*, 1997/4 (Warsaw: ZWS, 1998); *Cestat Statistical Bulletin*, 1998/2 (Warsaw: ZWS, 1998).

Table A12 Unemployment (annual average, percentage of the total economically active population)

Country	1989	1990	1991	1992	1993	1994	1995	1996	1997
1 East-Central Europe									
Czech Republic		0.7	4.1	2.6	3.5	3.2	2.9	3.5	5.2
GDR (and former GDR)		10.3	14.8	15.8	16.0				
Hungary		1.7	8.5	12.3	12.1	10.9	10.9	10.7	10.4
Poland		6.3	11.8	13.6	16.4	16.0	14.9	13.2	10.5
Slovakia			6.0	11.4	12.2	13.3	13.1	12.8	12.5
2 South-Eastern Europe and Former Yugoslavia									
Albania		7.3	9.5	9.1	27.0	22.0	18.0	12.9	12.3
Bulgaria		1.7	11.1	15.3	16.4	12.8	12.5	10.6	13.7
Croatia	7.0	8.0	15.0	17.0	16.6	17.3	17.6	14.9	17.6
Macedonia	22.6	23.6	26.0	27.8	29.3	32.0	37.2	39.8	31.5
Romania			3.0	8.4	10.2	10.9	9.5	6.3	8.8
Slovenia	2.9	4.7	8.2	11.5	14.4	14.4	14.5	14.4	14.8
Yugoslavia					24.6	24.0	23.9	24.7	26.1
3 Baltic States									
Estonia				0.1	1.7	5.0	5.1	5.0	5.6
Latvia					2.3	5.8	6.5	6.6	7.2
Lithuania				0.3	3.5	3.5	4.4	7.3	6.2

Sources: United Nations, *Statistical Yearbook. Fifty-First Issue* (New York: United Nations, 1996), pp. 252–65; for the Czech Republic, Hungary and Poland: OECD, *Main Economic Indicators October 1997*; for 1997 figures, S. Hrib, 'Being Left Behind', *Transitions*, 5, 4, April 1998, p. 72, and *Cestat Statistical Bulletin*, 1997/4 (Warsaw: ZWS, 1998).

Appendix

Table A13 Election Performance of Communist and Post-Communist Parties (Where available, per cent of the valid vote; otherwise per cent of seats)

Country	1990	1991	1992	1993	1994	1995	1996	1997	1998
1 East-Central Europe									
Czech Republic	15		14				10		11
GDR	16								
Hungary	11				33				37[1]
Poland	9[2]	12			20			27	
Slovakia	13			15		18[3]			
2 South-Eastern Europe and Former Yugoslavia									
Albania		56	26				20[4]	65	
Bosnia		8					8/3[5]		
Bulgaria	47		33		44[6]			22	
Croatia	18			6			9		
Macedonia	26				79[7]				
Montenegro	66								
Romania			66[8]		31[9]			22[10]	
Serbia	48		61					46	
Slovenia	24		14				9		
3 Baltic States									
Estonia			21[11]			32[12]			
Latvia				7[13]		6			
Lithuania			52				9		

1. Including 4% for the extreme left Hungarian Workers' Party.
2. Presidential elections.
3. Comprises 10.4% for 'Common Choice', an alliance between the post-communist SDL' and two smaller parties, and 7.3% for the ZRS, a leftist breakaway from the post-communists.
4. Not regarded as a genuinely democratic election.
5. 'United List', which received 8% in the Bosnian Federation and 3% in *Republika Srpska*.
6. This is the vote for the 'Democratic Left', a coalition between the BSP, the Agrarians and Ecoglasnost.
7. This is the proportion of seats gained by the Alliance for Macedonia in 1994, as a result of a boycott by the main opposition party.
8. National Salvation Front.
9. Comprises 3% for the extreme left Socialist Party of Labour and 28% for Ion Iliescu's Democratic National Salvation Front (FDSN).
10. Vote for Iliescu's PDSR.
11. Comprises 4% strictly post-communist and 17% *Kindel Kodu* (Secure Home), a party based largely on the old communist *nomenklatura*.
12. This is the vote for an electoral coalition between the Party of Consolidation and the Rural People's Party; but the leader of the former, Tiit Vähi, denied that the election marked the 'return of the former communists'. In fact he insisted that he was leading a centre-right coalition.
13. Comprises 1% for a post-communist party and 6% for 'Equal Rights', based largely on ethnic Russians.

Table A14   Ethnic Composition of Former Yugoslavia (1991)

Republic or Province	Population	Ethnic Proportions
Bosnia and Herzegovina	4 365 000	43.7% Muslim; 31.4% Serb; 17.3% Croat; 5.5% Yugoslav
Croatia	4 700 000	77.9% Croat; 12.2% Serb; 2.2% Yugoslav
Kosovo Province	1 956 196	81.6% Albanian; 9.9% Serb; 3.4% Muslim; 2.3% Roma; 1.1% Montenegrin
Macedonia	2 034 000	64.6% Macedonian; 21% Albanian; 4.8% Turkish; 2.7% Roma; 2.2% Serb
Montenegro	615 000	61.9% Montenegrin; 14.6% Muslim; 9.3% Serb; 6.6% Albanian; 4.3% Yugoslav
Serbia (excluding autonomous provinces)	5 808 906	87.9% Serb; 3.0% Muslim; 2.5% Yugoslav; 1.3% Albanian; 1.3% Montenegrin; 1.2% Roma
Slovenia	1 963 000	87.6% Slovene; 2.7% Croat; 2.4% Serb
Vojvodina Province	2 013 889	56.8% Serb; 16.9% Hungarian; 8.7% Yugoslav; 3.7% Croat; 3.2% Slovak; 2.2% Montenegrin; 1.9% Romanian; 1.2% Roma
Yugoslavia (total)	23 455 991	35.6% Serb; 19.3% Croat; 9.8% Muslim; 9.1% Albanian; 7.3% Slovene; 5.5% Macedonian; 3.7% Montenegrin; 1.5% Yugoslav; 1.4% Hungarian

Sources: J. Bugajski, *Ethnic Politics in Eastern Europe*, pp. 4, 42, 76, 98, 132 and 172; for Serbia and Montenegro, *Statistichki Godishnjak Jugoslavije 1997* (Belgrade: Savezni Zavod Za Statistiki, 1997), p. 64.

Notes

INTRODUCTION: MAPPING OUT THE THEME

1. Actually, even this apparently clear-cut division fails to cover Mongolia, which is as 'post-communist' as most other states discussed here.
2. E. Hankiss, *East European Alternatives* (Oxford: Oxford University Press, 1990).
3. P.G. Lewis, *Central Europe since 1945* (London: Longman, 1994).
4. J. Rothschild, *Return to Diversity: a Political History of East-Central Europe since World War II*, 2nd edn (Oxford: Oxford University Press, 1993).
5. B. Fowkes, *The Rise and Fall of Communism in Eastern Europe*, 2nd edn (London: Macmillan, 1995).
6. Some examples: *Eastern European Politics and Societies*; *East European Quarterly*; *Eastern Europe Newsletter*; *Eastern Europe: the Fortnightly Political Briefing*; *Osteuropa*.
7. In his important book *Inventing Eastern Europe: the Map of Civilization on the Mind of the Enlightenment* (Stanford: Stanford University Press, 1994). The reference here is to p. 15.
8. C. Offe, *Varieties of Transition: the East European and East German Experience* (Cambridge: Polity Press, 1996), p. 151.
9. Greece is consistently excluded by R.L. Wolff from his highly regarded account, *The Balkans in Our Time* (Cambridge, Massachusetts: Harvard University Press, 1956), but included by L.S. Stavrianos, whose wider canvas is entitled *The Balkans since 1945* (New York: Holt, Rinehart and Winston, 1958).
10. J. Snyder, 'Introduction', in B.R. Rubin and J. Snyder (eds), *Post-Soviet Political Order: Conflict and State Building* (London: Routledge, 1998), p. 2.
11. K. Jowitt, *New World Disorder: the Leninist Extinction* (Berkeley: University of California Press, 1992).
12. This is yet another problem of definition. I shall consistently use the word 'socialist' in future without inverted commas, but the reader is advised to include them mentally each time the word is used. It would clearly be wrong to characterize these societies as 'socialist' *tout court*, following the French example, which is itself a reflection of the intellectual domination exerted by the French communist party over studies of the 'socialist world' until very recently.
13. B. Milanovic, 'A Cost of Transition', *Transition (WB)*, 5, 8, October 1994, pp. 1–4 (1).
14. This word is universally used throughout the post-communist world, and it is a useful shorthand expression for organized criminality.
15. Another useful shorthand expression; the term originally referred to the list of official positions for which Central Committee confirmation was necessary, and came to be used to cover people who had received, or would receive, such confirmation. Under Stalin's terror regime the

nomenklatura was unstable; but after the 1950s it tended to become a hereditary group, able to use nepotism to further its interests.

16. With the addition of Estonia, whose unique geographical position and linguistic affinity with Finland have enabled her to qualify for early membership of the EU. Slovenia and Croatia, geographically Central European lands which have over the last few years managed to extract themselves from their historical affiliation with the Balkans, may well also cross this barrier at some later date.
17. For an excellent comparative study of four countries in transition – Bulgaria, the Czech Republic, Hungary and Slovakia – see J. Elster, C. Offe and U. Preuss, *Institutional Design in Post-communist Societies: Rebuilding the Ship at Sea* (Cambridge: Cambridge University Press, 1998).

2 THE INHERITANCE OF THE PAST AND THE REVOLUTIONS OF 1989

1. J. Kochanowicz, 'The Polish Economy and the Evolution of Dependency', in D. Chirot (ed.), *The Origins of Backwardness in Eastern Europe* (Berkeley: University of California Press, 1989), pp. 92–130 (118–19).
2. This is the view taken by P. Gunst in 'Agrarian Systems of Central and Eastern Europe', in Chirot, *Origins*, pp. 53–91 (70, 76).
3. R. Brenner, 'Economic Backwardness in Eastern Europe in the Light of Developments in the West', in Chirot, *Origins*, pp. 15–52 (42–3).
4. Gunst, 'Agrarian Systems', in Chirot, *Origins*, p. 61.
5. J.R. Lampe, 'Redefining Balkan Backwardness', in Chirot, *Origins*, pp. 177–209 (184).
6. J.R. Lampe and M.R. Jackson, *Balkan Economic History 1580–1950* (Bloomington, Indiana: Indiana University Press, 1982), pp. 160–5.
7. A.J. Motyl, 'After Empire: Competing Discourses and Inter-State Conflict in Post-Imperial Eastern Europe', in Rubin and Snyder, *Post-Soviet Political Order*, p. 26.
8. Germany, France, Sweden, Belgium, Holland and Switzerland.
9. A. Janos, 'Continuity and Change in Eastern Europe: Strategies of Post-Communist Politics', in B. Crawford (ed.), *Markets, States, and Democracy: the Political Economy of Post-Communist Transformation* (Boulder: Westview Press, 1995), Table 7.1, pp. 150–74 (152).
10. Janos, 'Continuity and Change', p. 152.
11. The Polish figure is an underestimate, owing to the strength of the 'second economy' there and the severe economic downturn of the early 1980s.
12. P. Havlik, 'East–West GDP Comparison: Problems, Methods and Results', *Wiener Institut für Internationale Wirtschaftsvergleiche, Forschungsberichte*, 174 (Vienna, 1991), p. 37. Two similar calculations were carried out by Andrew Janos ('Continuity and Change', p. 152) using six advanced West European economies as the yardstick of comparison with roughly the same results. In one case all the countries concerned had fallen further behind by 1980; in the other case all except Poland and Bulgaria.

13. In communist countries outside the Soviet Union the ruling party was usually described under a different name, for example 'Workers' Party' or 'Socialist Workers' Party'. This reflected the forced mergers of the 1940s by which the Social Democrats were obliterated. In this book we shall generally use the term 'communist party', since the change of name had no practical meaning.
14. J. Batt, *East Central Europe from Reform to Transformation* (London: Pinter Publishers, 1991), p. 9.
15. W. Echikson, 'Bloc Buster', in L.H. Legters (ed.), *Eastern Europe: Transformation and Revolution, 1945–91. Documents and Analyses* (Lexington: D.C. Heath, 1992), p. 427.
16. I.T. Berend, *Central and Eastern Europe 1944–1993: Detour from the Periphery to the Periphery* (Cambridge: Cambridge University Press, 1996), p. 249.
17. C.S. Maier, *Dissolution: the Crisis of Communism and the End of East Germany* (Princeton: Princeton University Press, 1997), p. 37.
18. P. Kende and Z. Strmiska, *Equality and Inequality in Eastern Europe* (Leamington Spa: Berg Publishers Ltd, 1987), p. 177.
19. A. Bokor, 'Die Öffentliche Meinung im Zuge des Systemwandels in Ungarn', *Journal für Sozialforschung*, 31, 1, 1991, pp. 51–87.
20. S.P. Ramet, *Social Currents in Eastern Europe: the Sources and Consequences of the Great Transformation*, 2nd edn (Durham: Duke University Press, 1995), p. 25.
21. Hankiss, *East European Alternatives*, pp. 97–8.
22. T. Gallagher, 'The Balkans: Bulgaria, Romania, Albania and the Former Yugoslavia', in S. White, J. Batt and P.G. Lewis, *Developments in Central and East European Politics* (London: Macmillan, 1998), pp. 43–58 (58).
23. M. Todorova, *Imagining the Balkans* (Oxford: Oxford University Press, 1997), pp. 7, 59 and 156.
24. D. Hall, 'Albanian Identity and Balkan Roles', in D. Hall and D. Danta, (eds), *Reconstructing the Balkans: a Geography of the New Southeast Europe* (Chichester: John Wiley and Sons, 1996), pp. 119–33 (125).
25. This claim is described as 'fairly plausible' by A. Logoreci, *The Albanians: Europe's Forgotten Survivors* (London: Victor Gollancz, 1977), p. 183.
26. Rothschild, *Return to Diversity*, p. 180.
27. See Appendix, Table A14, for the results of the 1991 census.
28. According to the Croat geographer Mladen Klemencić the settlers were a mixed population who only became Serbs under the influence of Orthodox church propaganda ('Croatia Rediviva', in F.W. Carter and H.T. Norris [eds], *The Changing Shape of the Balkans* (London: UCL Press, 1996), p. 100).
29. G.E. Rothenberg, *The Military Border in Croatia 1740–1881* (Chicago: University of Chicago Press, 1966), p. 4.
30. The details of the partition of 1941 are outlined very clearly by Joseph Rothschild in *Return to Diversity*, p. 50.
31. S.G. Meštrović (with Slaven Letica and Miroslav Goreta), *Habits of the Balkan Heart: Social Character and the Fall of Communism* (College Station, Texas: Texas A & M University Press, 1993), pp. 50, 51, 61 and 65. Meštrović freely acknowledges his indebtedness for most of these ideas to an earlier Yugoslav sociologist, Dinko Tomašić.

Notes to Pages 18–27 203

32. SKJ: Savez Komunista Jugoslavije. This organization is known in the English-speaking world under the initials LCY.
33. S.L. Burg, *Conflict and Cohesion in Socialist Yugoslavia* (Princeton: Princeton University Press, 1983), p. 81.
34. W. Höpken, 'Yugoslavia's Communists and Bosnian Muslims', in A. Kappeler, G. Simon and G. Brunner (eds), *Muslim Communities Reemerge: Historical Perspectives on Nationality, Politics and Opposition in the Former Soviet Union and Yugoslavia* (Durham, NC: Duke University Press, 1994), pp. 214–47 (229).
35. F. Friedman, *The Bosnian Muslims: Denial of a Nation* (Boulder, Colorado: Westview Press, 1996), p. 162.
36. See Appendix, Table A14. This was an estimate by government statisticians; the Albanian population boycotted the census, and Albanian spokesmen claimed the proportion was nearer 90 per cent (See J. Bugajski, *Ethnic Politics in Eastern Europe* (Armonk, New York: M.E. Sharpe, 1994), p. 131).
37. M. Fulbrook, *Anatomy of a Dictatorship: Inside the GDR 1949–1989* (Oxford: Oxford University Press, 1995), p. 51.
38. *Keesing's, 1990*, pp. 37921–2.
39. J. Deimal, 'Bulgariens Kampf mit Vergangenheit und Zukunft', *SOE*, 46, 5–6, 1997, pp. 244–6.
40. J.F. Brown, *Hopes and Shadows: Eastern Europe after Communism* (London: Longman, 1994), p. 101.

3 HISTORY CHANGES GEAR: THE TRANSITION IN EAST-CENTRAL EUROPE

1. A. Horváth and Á. Szakolczai, *The Dissolution of Communist Power: the Case of Hungary* (London: Routledge, 1992), p. 213.
2. L. Bruszt, '1989: the Negotiated Revolution in Hungary', *Social Research*, 57, 2, summer 1990, pp. 378–9.
3. Hankiss, *East European Alternatives*, pp. 253–4.
4. A. Sajó, 'The Roundtable Talks in Hungary', in J. Elster (ed.), *The Roundtable Talks and the Breakdown of Communism* (Chicago: University of Chicago Press, 1996), p. 87.
5. Bruszt (who represented the Liga at the Roundtable talks) points out that even by September 1989 only 1 per cent of the adult population had joined the autonomous political organizations ('1989: the Negotiated Revolution in Hungary', p. 317).
6. D. Stark, 'Recombinant Property in East European Capitalism', *American Journal of Sociology*, 101, 4, January 1996, p. 998.
7. Berend, *Central and Eastern Europe*, p. 319.
8. Real wages fell by 6 per cent in 1990 and 9.4 per cent in 1991; inflation was 28.9 per cent in 1990 and 35.0 per cent in 1991; unemployment rose from 2 per cent in 1990 to 8 per cent in 1991 and 12 per cent in 1992.
9. Z. Szilagyi, 'Scenes from the Media War', *Transition (OMRI)*, 2, 8, 19 April 1996, p. 24.
10. As quoted in Brown, *Hopes and Shadows*, p. 88.

11. Jacek Kuroń points this out in his memoirs (*Moja Zupa*, Warsaw: Polska oficyna wydawnicza "BGW" 1991, p. 12).
12. R. Gortat, 'The Feud within Solidarity's Offspring', in M. Waller and M. Myant (eds), *Parties, Trade Unions and Society in East-Central Europe* (London: Frank Cass, 1994), pp. 120–1.
13. *OE*, 41, 1, January 1991, A 30.
14. D. Ost, 'Politics of Interest in Post-Communist Eastern Europe', *Theory and Society*, 22, 4, 1993, p. 211.
15. See below, p. 50.
16. See below, Chapter 7.
17. M. Jones, 'Polish Elections – a Shift to the Left', *Critique*, 26, pp. 165–70.
18. An attempt to reintroduce this tax, under the name *neopopiwek*, was vetoed in March 1994 by President Wałęsa.
19. M. Calda, 'The Roundtable Talks in Czechoslovakia', in Elster, *Roundtable Talks*, p. 161.
20. L. Brokl, 'Between November 1989 and Democracy', *Czechoslovak Sociological Review*, August 1992, pp. 23–36.
21. These are the figures for the Federal Assembly; in the separate elections for the Czech and Slovak National Councils there was a contrast between the strong showing of Civic Forum (49.5 per cent) and the rather weaker position of Public Against Violence (29.4 per cent). Apart from this, the separate republican elections produced very similar results, except that in Slovakia an extra party (the Democratic Party) got into the National Council with 4.4 per cent of the vote. (*Statistická Ročenka '91: České a Slovenské Federativní Republiky*, Prague: Statistické a evidenční Vydavatelství tiskopisů, 1991, pp. 629–30).
22. S.L. Wolchik, *Czechoslovakia in Transition: Politics, Economics and Society* (London: Pinter Publishers, 1991), p. 51.
23. M. Hrncir, 'Monetary and Credit Policies for Transition', *Prague Economic Papers*, 1, 2, 1992, pp. 109–26 (114).
24. J. Pehe, 'The Instability of Transition', *RFE/Report on Eastern Europe*, 2, 1, 4 January 1991, pp. 11–16 (15).
25. Wolchik, *Czechoslovakia in Transition*, p. 64.
26. J. Batt, 'The Politics of Economic Transition', in S. White, J. Batt and P.G. Lewis (eds), *Developments in East European Politics* (London: Macmillan, 1993), pp. 205–24 (219).
27. These are the figures for the respective National Councils. Federal Assembly results were in line with this, but were of little significance given the practical veto each nation could impose there. The source for all the figures is: *Statistická Ročenka České Republiký '93* (Prague: Český Statistický Úřad, 1993), pp. 439–41.
28. J. Juchler, *Osteuropa im Umbruch: Politische, wirtschaftliche und gesellschaftliche Entwicklungen 1989–1993. Gesamtüberblick und Fallstudien* (Zürich: Seismo Verlag, 1994), p. 342.
29. E. Mortimer, 'Ahead of the Pack', *FT*, 13 August 1997, p. 12.
30. In the November 1996 elections the TSLK won 70 seats, and the LDLP, the governing party, sank to a mere 12.
31. A.A. Michta, *The Government and Politics of Postcommunist Europe* (Westport, Connecticut: Praeger, 1994), p. 150.

Notes to Pages 48–55

32. N. Muiznecks, 'Latvia: Restoring a State, Rebuilding a Nation', in I. Bremmer and R. Taras (eds), *New States, New Politics: Building the Post-Soviet Nations* (Cambridge: Cambridge University Press, 1997), pp. 373–403 (392).
33. A. Lieven, *The Baltic Revolution: Estonia, Latvia, Lithuania and the Path to Independence*, 2nd edn (New Haven: Yale University Press, 1994), p. xx.
34. Between 1992 and 1994 Latvia's 'index level of economic liberalization' rose from 0.29 to 0.78 on the scale devised by Åslund, Boone and Johnson, placing the country among the 'radical reformers' of Eastern Europe (A. Åslund, P. Boone and S. Johnson, 'How to Stabilize: Lessons from the Post-Communist Countries', *Brookings Papers on Economic Activity*, 1, 1996, p. 221).
35. The election of 30 September–1 October 1995, at which no party gained more than 16 per cent of the vote, and nine parties cleared the 5 per cent hurdle to get into parliament.
36. *Keesing's, 1995*, p. 40695.
37. See his article with this title, in *Transitions (OMRI)*, 4, 2, July 1997, p. 30.
38. D. Ionescu, 'Former Communists on the March at Romanian National Radio', *Transition (OMRI)*, 2, 21, 1996, pp. 40–1 (40).
39. A similar sequence of events took place in Romania in 1997: Foreign Minister Adrian Severin was forced to resign (23 November) after he proved unable to substantiate his allegation that some politicians were collaborating with foreign intelligence agencies.
40. *Keesing's, 1991*, p. 38449. The specific issue here was the forced resignation of Václav Vales on 17 September 1991.
41. *SWB EE/2117/A/3/* 28 September 1994.
42. Original vote: 28 September 1995; Havel's veto: 6 October; parliamentary confirmation: 18 October.
43. *Le Monde*, 13 March 1996, p. 4.
44. This is V. Zubek's view ('The Phoenix out of the Ashes: the Rise to Power of Poland's Post-Communist SdRP', *CPCS*, 28, 3, 1995, pp. 275–306 (286).
45. K. Williams, 'New Sources on 1968', *EAS*, 48, 3, 1996, pp. 457–70 (457).
46. J. Juchler presents a useful comparative table of the relative strengths of parliamentary and presidential elements in post-communist political systems in 'Probleme der Demokratisierung in den osteuropäischen Transformationsländern', *OE*, 47, 9, September 1997, pp. 898–913.
47. See A. Bozoki, 'Intellectuals in a New Democracy: the Democratic Charter Movement in Hungary, 1991–1994', in *EEPS*, 10, 2, pp. 173–213.
48. Constitutional Court ruling of 13 September 1995 (*Keesing's, 1995*, p. 40740.)
49. H. Schwartz, 'Defending the Defenders of Democracy: a Judiciary under Threat', *Transitions (OMRI)*, 4, 2, July 1997, pp. 80–5.
50. A. Skolkay, 'Slovak Government Tightens Grip on Airwaves', *Transition (OMRI)*, 2, 8, 19 April 1996, pp. 18–21.
51. S. Fisher, 'Slovakia's Troubled Print Media', *Transition (OMRI)*, 2, 21, 18 October 1996, pp. 46–8 (47).
52. P. Sztompka, 'Looking Back: the Year 1989 as a Cultural and Civilizational Break', *CPCS*, 29, 2, June 1996, p. 120.

53. A. Smolar, 'The Polish Opposition', in F. Feher and A. Arato (eds), *Crisis and Reform in Eastern Europe* (New Brunswick: Transaction Publishers, 1991), p. 226.
54. A. Török, *Budapest: a Critical Guide* (Budapest: Corvina, 1997), p. 204.
55. W. Schlott, 'Kulturpolitik in Polen: Zwischen Neustrukturierung und anhaltender Notsituation', *OE*, 1, 1995, A32.
56. The Czech Minister of Culture, the well-known former exile Pavel Tigrid, was criticized for this in 1994. For the resulting debate over cultural policy, see I. Bock, 'Kulturpolitik: Tschechische Debatte', *OE*, 8, 1996, p. 791.
57. M.A. Centeno and T. Rands, 'The World They Have Lost: an Assessment of Change in Eastern Europe', *Social Research*, 63, 2, summer 1996, p. 387.
58. For the role of commercial television, see C. Sparks and A. Reading, 'Understanding Media Change in East Central Europe', *Media, Culture and Society*, 16, 2, April 1994, p. 268.
59. J. Topol, 'A Trip to the Railway Station', in A. Buchler (ed.), *This Side of Reality: Modern Czech Writing* (London: Serpent's Tail, 1996), pp. 205–8.
60. J. Cleave, 'Eastern Europe Holds on to Music Archive', *Transition (OMRI)*, 1, 24, 29 December 1995, pp. 66–9.
61. See Chapter 8 for the impact of their failure.
62. *Keesing's, 1994*, p. 40156. The whole episode has been analysed in detail by Katherine Verdery in a remarkable article, 'Faith, Hope and *Caritas* in the Land of the Pyramids: Romania, 1990 to 1994', *Comparative Studies in Society and History*, 37, 4, October 1995, pp. 625–69. This was later reprinted in *What Was Socialism, and What Comes Next?* (Princeton: Princeton University Press, 1996), ch. 7.
63. The words of the Romanian journalist Romulus Brâncoveanu, quoted by Verdery, 'Faith, Hope and *Caritas*', p. 669.
64. *International Herald Tribune*, 24 March 1994.

4 HESITANT BEGINNINGS IN SOUTH-EASTERN EUROPE: A 'BALKAN LAG'?

1. See above, Chapter 2.
2. J-Y. Potel, 'Singulière sortie du communisme dans les Balkans', *MD*, March 1997, pp. 12–13.
3. O. Hishow, 'Makroökonomische Politik und Reformfortschritte im östlichen Europa', *BBIOST*, 25, 1997, p. 9. Hishow's figures for Bulgaria differ from those given by the *United Nations Statistical Yearbook*, 41st issue (New York, 1996), pp. 149–66, which work out at $2790 per capita in constant 1990 dollars.
4. J.J. Linz and A. Stepan, *Problems of Democratic Transition and Consolidation* (Baltimore: Johns Hopkins University Press, 1996), fig. 18.1 on p. 352.
5. See the illuminating discussion of Bulgarian party structure in M. Waller and G. Karasimeonov, 'Party Organization in Post-Communist Bulgaria', in P.G. Lewis (ed.), *Party Structure and Organization in East-Central Europe* (Cheltenham: Edward Elgar, 1996), pp. 134–62.

6. The failure of the party liberals at the 39th BSP Congress (22–5 September 1990), owing to the strength of conservative rural groupings and the refusal of Lukanov to stand against Lilov, is examined in detail by K. Engelbrekt, 'The Bulgarian Socialist Party: Unity at Any Cost', in W. Höpken, (ed.), *Revolution auf Raten: Bulgariens Weg zur Demokratie* (Munich: R. Oldenbourg Verlag, 1996), pp. 83–116 (100–3).
7. The BZNS–NP was so named to distinguish it from the BZNS, the agrarian party left in existence by the communists after the execution of its leader Nikola Petkov in 1947, and closely allied to them ever since.
8. Engelbrekt, 'Bulgarian Socialist Party', pp. 96–7.
9. W. Höpken, 'Die unvollendete Revolution?', in Höpken, *Revolution auf Raten*, pp. i–xxi (viii).
10. The dominant role of the SDS is clearly outlined by R. Nikolaev, 'The New Coalition Government', *Report on Eastern Europe*, 2, 3, 18 January 1991, pp. 6–9.
11. D. Hall and D. Danta, 'The Balkans: Perceptions and Realities', Table 1.1, in Hall and Danta, *Reconstructing the Balkans*, p. 5.
12. M. Rady, *Romania in Turmoil* (London: I.B. Tauris, 1992), p. 127.
13. The decision to take part in the elections was made by the FSN on 4 January 1990.
14. Rady, *Romania in Turmoil*, p. 74.
15. M. Shafir, 'The Provisional Council of National Unity: Is History Repeating Itself?', *RFE/Report on Eastern Europe*, 1, 9, 2 March 1990, pp. 18–23.
16. Rady, *Romania in Turmoil*, p. 143.
17. J. Bugajski, *Ethnic Politics in Eastern Europe* (Armonk, New York: M.E. Sharpe, 1994), p. 213.
18. For a short account of the methods used in 1945, see B. Fowkes, *The Rise and Fall of Communism in Eastern Europe*, 2nd edn (London: Macmillan, 1995), p. 36.
19. Roman's programme was adopted by 988 to 58 (A.U. Gabanyi, 'Präsident Iliescu gegen Premier Roman: Frontenbilding in der "Front der Nationalen Rettung"', *SOE*, 40, 9, 1991, p. 436).
20. FDSN: Frontul Democrat Salvării Naţionale (Democratic Front of National Salvation). It was renamed yet again in 1993, becoming the PDSR (Partidul Democratiei Sociale din Româniu, or Social Democratic Party of Romania).
21. CDR: Convenţia Democratică din România (Democratic Convention of Romania); renamed Convenţia Democrată Română (Romanian Democratic Convention) in 1996.
22. T. Gallagher, *Romania after Ceauşescu* (Edinburgh: Edinburgh University Press, 1995), p. 126.
23. Forty-two out of the Democratic Convention's 82 seats were held by members of the PNTCD.
24. M. Shafir, 'Romania's Elections: Why the Democratic Convention Lost', *RFE/RFRR*, 1, 43, 30 October 1992, pp. 1–7.
25. See the statistical appendix, Table A11.
26. The Eleven Point Programme of 17 November 1993 is printed in *Keesing's, 1993*, p. 39746.

27. E. Biberaj, 'Albania, the Last Domino', in I. Banac (ed.), *Eastern Europe in Revolution* (Ithaca, NY: Cornell University Press, 1992), 188–206 (192).
28. These events are examined in detail in M. Vickers and J. Pettifer, *Albania: From Anarchy to a Balkan Identity* (London: Hurst & Company, 1997), pp. 33–52.
29. See the analysis by M. Schmidt-Neke, 'Die Albanische Parlamentswahlen vom 26.5 1996', *SOE*, 8, 1996, p. 568.
30. Vickers and Pettifer, *Albania*, p. 61.
31. The PPSH was renamed Socialist Party of Albania (in Albanian: *Partia Socialiste e Shqipërisë*, PSSH) at its 10th Congress, held in June 1991.
32. Vickers and Pettifer, *Albania*, p. 80.
33. Vickers and Pettifer, *Albania*, p. 86.
34. F.T. Lubinja, 'Pyramids of Slime', *Transitions (OMRI)*, 4, 1, June 1997, p. 67.

5 NATIONAL MINORITIES AND ETHNIC CONFLICT

1. Not everywhere. Poland had a population that was 97.88 per cent ethnically Polish; Albania was 97.96 per cent Albanian; the Czech Republic was 94.5 per cent Czech; Hungary was 91.4 per cent Hungarian (Bugajski, *Ethnic Politics*, pp. 268, 294, 360, 400).
2. For a brief discussion of the 'Russian question' in the Baltic states, see above, Chapter 3.
3. Hungary is the only country of Eastern Europe where Jews are still present in substantial numbers (eighty to a hundred thousand). They have not organized as a national minority, or made any special claims, relying instead on quiet support for democracy and membership of the main Hungarian political parties. Anti-Semitic groups exist, but have made little headway.
4. The proportions were: Hungarians in Slovakia, 10.8 per cent; Hungarians in Romania, 7.1 per cent; Turks in Bulgaria, 9.7 per cent; Russians in Estonia, 30.3 per cent; Russians in Latvia, 34.0 per cent; and Russians in Lithuania, 9.4 per cent. Official statistics understate the number of Roma. J. Druker ('Present But Unaccounted For', *Transitions*, 4, 4, September 1997, pp. 22–3) gives these minimum and maximum estimates: Romania 1 410 000–2 500 000; Bulgaria 500 000–800 000; Hungary 550 000–800 000; Slovakia 450 000–520 000; the Czech Republic 150 000–300 000; Yugoslavia (Serbia and Montenegro) 400 000–600 000; Croatia 18 000–300 000; Macedonia 110 000–260 000; Albania 10 000–120 000.
5. In his *Ethnic Politics in Eastern Europe* (1994). He omits the Baltic region, however.
6. *Keesing's, 1992*, p. 38735.
7. A. Janos, 'Continuity and Change in Eastern Europe', *EEPS*, 8, 1, p. 24.
8. A.J. Motyl, 'After Empire: Competing Discourses and Inter-State Conflict in Post-Imperial Eastern Europe', in B.R. Rubin and J. Snyder (eds), *Post-Soviet Political Order: Conflict and State Building* (London: Routledge, 1998), p. 14.
9. Here is Mark Thompson, for instance, writing in the Preface to his *A Paper House: the Ending of Yugoslavia* (London: Hutchinson/Radius,

1992): 'When I was travelling (in Yugoslavia) nations were almost all there was. This spared me certain illusions... Yugoslav hearts have fed too much on fantasy.'
10. S.P. Huntington, 'The Clash of Civilizations?', *Foreign Affairs*, 72, summer 1993, pp. 22–49 (30).
11. Statement made in an interview on 18 March 1991, quoted by L.J. Cohen, *Broken Bonds: Yugoslavia's Disintegration and Balkan Politics in Transition*, 2nd edn (Boulder, Colorado: Westview Press, 1995), p. 211.
12. See Susan L. Woodward, *Balkan Tragedy: Chaos and Dissolution after the Cold War* (Washington, DC: The Brookings Institution, 1995).
13. Catherine Samary, *La Déchirure Yougoslave: Questions pour l'Europe* (Paris: L'Harmattan, 1994).
14. See above, Chapter 2.
15. See Woodward, *Balkan Tragedy*, pp. 73–81.
16. A.N. Luk, 'The Linguistic Aspect of Conflict', in P. Akhavan and R. Howse (eds), *Yugoslavia: the Former and the Future* (Washington: The Brookings Institution, 1995), pp. 112–20 (119).
17. Cohen, *Broken Bonds*, pp. 56–7.
18. D. Janjić, 'Resurgence of Ethnic Conflict in Yugoslavia: the Demise of Communism and the Rise of the "New Elites" of Nationalism', in Akhavan and Howse, *Yugoslavia*, pp. 29–44 (35).
19. N.J. Miller, 'Reconstituting Serbia: 1945–1991', in M.K. Bokovoy, J.A. Irvine and C.S. Lilly (eds), *State–Society Relations in Yugoslavia, 1945–1992* (London: Macmillan, 1997), pp. 306–7.
20. Quoted by J. Udovički in the introduction to J. Udovički and J. Ridgeway (eds), *Burn This House: The Making and Unmaking of Yugoslavia* (Durham: Duke University Press, 1997), p. 9, n. 8.
21. C. Bennett, *Yugoslavia's Bloody Collapse* (London: Hurst Company, 1995), p. 116.
22. J. Udovički and I. Torov, 'The Interlude', in Udovički and Ridgeway, *Burn This House*, pp. 80–107 (99).
23. See in detail Woodward, *Balkan Tragedy*, pp. 129–30.
24. See Appendix, Table A9.
25. N. Malcolm, *Kosovo: a Short History* (London: Macmillan, 1998), p. 344.
26. Cohen, *Broken Bonds*, p. 84.
27. Lojže Peterle, speaking on 1 August 1990 (quoted in Cohen, *Broken Bonds*, p. 121).
28. Speaking on 26 August 1990 (quoted in Cohen, *Broken Bonds*, p. 115).
29. See Appendix, Table A14.
30. Udovički and Torov, ' Interlude', p. 93.
31. Tuđman's remarks at the first HDZ rally, held on 24 February 1990, became legendary: 'The NDH was not simply a quisling creation and a fascist crime; it was also an expression of the historical aspirations of the Croatian people.'
32. M. Križan, 'Kroatien unter Tuđman', *OE*, 47, 10/11, 1997, pp. 959–74 (961).
33. Except in (undefined) Serbian majority areas, where Cyrillic could be used side by side with Latin (Article XXI of the Constitution of December 1990, quoted in S.G. Meštrović [with Slaven Letica and Miroslav Goreta],

Habits of the Balkan Heart: Social Character and the Fall of Communism [College Station, Texas: Texas A & M University Press, 1993], p. 141).
34. On the role of the media in the Yugoslav wars, see chapters 3 and 4 of Mark Thompson's *Forging War: the Media in Serbia, Croatia and Bosnia-Hercegovina*, written for Article 19 The International Centre Against Censorship, and published in May 1994 in London.
35. See the instructive comparative study by V. Vujacic and V. Zaslavsky, 'Causes of Disintegration in the USSR and Yugoslavia', *Telos*, 88, summer 1991, pp. 120–40.
36. The role of the army is analysed by S. Sikavica, 'The Army's Collapse', in Udovički and Ridgeway, *Burn This House*, pp. 130–152.
37. After March 1991, positions became 'polarized' at the top of the army, and it was 'pushed further into Milošević's camp' (Sikavica, 'Army's Collapse', p. 137).
38. See the analysis by Sikavica, 'Army's Collapse', p. 139.
39. Interviewed in *Politika*, 28 September–4 October 1991, p. 7.
40. E. Štitkovac, 'Croatia: the First War', in Udovički and Ridgeway, *Burn This House*, pp. 153–73 (164).
41. This is the subtitle of Marcus Tanner, *Croatia: a Nation Forged in War* (New Haven: Yale University Press, 1997).
42. See H. Büschenfeld, 'Die Aussenwirtschaft der Nachfolgestaaten Jugoslawiens', *OE*, 46, 2, February 1996, pp. 174–84 (174).
43. Büschenfeld, 'Aussenwirtschaft', p. 183.
44. M. Križan, 'Kroatien unter Tuđman', *OE*, 47, 10/11, 1997, pp. 965–6.
45. I. Grdešić, 'The Dynamics of the Croatian Electorate', *SOE*, 5, 1993, pp. 289–300 (291).
46. Križan, 'Kroatien unter Tuđman', p. 965; *FT*, 16 June 1997, p. 2.
47. *FT*, 17 January 1997.
48. Bennett, *Yugoslavia's Bloody Collapse*, p. 234.
49. Addressing the Bosnian parliament in October 1991. See J. Udovički and E. Štitkovac, 'Bosnia and Hercegovina: the Second War', in Udovički and Ridgeway, *Burn This House*, p. 179.
50. In future references to Bosnia-Herzegovina the shortened form 'Bosnia' will be used to cover the whole territory, unless otherwise indicated.
51. Y.A. Jelinek, 'Bosnia-Hercegovina at War: Relations between Muslims and Non-Muslims', *Holocaust and Genocide Studies*, 5, 3, 1990, pp. 275–92.
52. Cohen, *Broken Bonds*, p. 246.
53. Pseudonym of Željko Ražnjatović, leader of the most notorious Serbian irregular force in Bosnia, 'Arkan's Tigers', who were trained and financed by the Serbian Ministry of the Interior in 1991, and carried out atrocities against Croats in 1991 and Bosnian Muslims subsequently (N. Malcolm, *Bosnia: a Short History* (London: Macmillan, 1994), p. 226).
54. Malcolm, *Bosnia*, p. 252.
55. The following outstanding studies have already been published on the Bosnian background: R.J. Donia and J.V.A. Fine, *Bosnia and Hercegovina: a Tradition Betrayed* (New York: Columbia University Press, 1994): F. Friedman, *The Bosnian Muslims: Denial of a Nation* (Boulder: Westview Press, 1996); W. Höpken, 'Yugoslavia's Communists and Bosnian Muslims', in A. Kappeler, G. Simon and G. Brunner (eds), *Muslim*

Communities Reemerge: Historical Perspectives on Nationality, Politics and Opposition in the *Former Soviet Union and Yugoslavia* (Durham, NC: Duke University Press, 1994); Malcolm, *Bosnia*; M. Pinson (ed.), *The Muslims of Bosnia-Hercegovina* (Cambridge, Massachusetts: Harvard University Press, 1993); and M.A. Sells, *The Bridge Betrayed: Religion and Genocide in Bosnia* (Berkeley: University of California Press, 1996).
56. As reported in *SWB YEE*, 17 February 1993, 1615/C1.
57. W. Zimmermann, 'A Pavane for Bosnia', *The National Interest*, 37, Fall 1994, p. 76.
58. Cohen, *Broken Bonds*, p. 244.
59. In 1993 the SDA (the main Bosnian Muslim party) changed its position on the term 'Muslim', replacing it with the previously spurned word 'Bosniak'.
60. See C. Lane and T. Shanker, 'Bosnia: What the CIA Didn't Tell US', *New York Review of Books*, 9 May 1996, p. 10.
61. M. Glenny, *The Fall of Yugoslavia*, 3rd edn (London: Penguin, 1996), pp. 206–7. The ethnic cleansing, massacres and death camps of 1992 have been described by Rezak Hukanović, a survivor, in *The Tenth Circle of Hell* (first published 1993), and by Roy Gutman, *Witness to Genocide* (Shaftesbury, Dorset: Element, 1993).
62. As quoted in R. Hukanović, *The Tenth Circle of Hell: a Memoir of Life in the Death Camps of Bosnia* (London: Little, Brown and Company, 1997), p. 56.
63. See Woodward, *Balkan Tragedy*, Figure 8.1, pp. 226–7.
64. S.K. Pavlowitch, 'Who is Balkanizing Whom? The Misunderstanding between the Debris of Yugoslavia and an Unprepared West', *Daedalus*, 123, 2, spring 1994, pp. 203–23 (208).
65. Cohen, *Broken Bonds*, p. 277.
66. On this see in detail the memoirs of Lord David Owen, *Balkan Odyssey* (London: Gollancz, 1995), Chapter 3 and in particular p. 102.
67. D. Rieff, *Slaughterhouse: Bosnia and the Failure of the West* (London: Vintage, 1995), p. 217.
68. Another 'protected area', Žepa, fell soon afterwards (28 July). The four that remained were Sarajevo, Goražde, Tuzla and Bihać.
69. The International Committee of the Red Cross gave a figure of 7079 persons missing after the fall of Srebrenica. David Rohde, in his careful study *A Safe Area. Srebrenica: Europe's Worst Massacre since the Second World War* (London: Pocket Books, 1997), pp. 348–50, accepts this as meaning they were killed by Serb forces.
70. The main ethnic minorities in Macedonia (1991) were: Albanians, 21.0 per cent; Turks, 4.8 per cent; Roma, 2.7 per cent; Serbs, 2.2 per cent.
71. These elections took place in three rounds, on 11 and 25 November and 9 December.
72. Later renamed Social Democratic Alliance.
73. See above, p. 88 for the election results in Macedonia.
74. H. Poulton, *Who Are the Macedonians?* (London: Hurst & Company, 1995), p. 178.
75. *Le Monde*, 21 March 1996, p. 3.
76. Bennett, *Yugoslavia's Bloody Collapse*, p. 208.

77. L. Madzar, 'Rump Yugoslavia Mired in Economic Problems', *RFE/RLRR*, 2, 39, 1 October 1993, pp. 45–9. See statistical appendix, Table A9, for the annual inflation figures.
78. In reply to a question by Mark Thompson (Thompson, *Paper House*, p. 138).
79. Woodward, *Balkan Tragedy*, p. 341.
80. *FT*, 13 March 1998, p. 2.
81. M. Rüb, 'Auf dem Amselfeld eskaliert die Gewalt', *Frankfurter Allgemeine Zeitung*, 3 March 1998, p. 10.
82. Malcolm, *Kosovo*, p. 355.
83. C.S. Leff, *The Czech and Slovak Republics: Nation Versus State* (Boulder, Colorado: Westview Press, 1997), p. 164.
84. M. Carpenter, 'Slovakia and the Triumph of Nationalist Populism', *CPCS*, 30, 2, June 1997, p. 209.
85. The deterioration in the position of the Hungarians in Romania in the 1980s was drastic; it has been analysed by G. Schöpflin and H. Poulton in *Romania's Ethnic Hungarians* (London: Minority Rights Group, 1991), pp. 17–18.
86. T. Gallagher, *Romania after Ceauşescu*, p. 64.
87. See above, Chapter 4.
88. Gallagher, *Romania after Ceauşescu*, p. 94.
89. See the detailed and thorough analysis of the ultra-nationalists in chapters 3 and 6 of Gallagher, *Romania after Ceauşescu*, as well as the brief account in J. Bugajski, *Ethnic Politics*, pp. 212–15.
90. The situation up to 1993 has been thoroughly examined by Bugajski, in *Ethnic Politics*, Chapter 8.
91. See above, Chapter 2.
92. D. Hall, *Albania and the Albanians* (London: Pinter Publishers, 1994), pp. 28–9; on Albanian ethnic organization see R. Qosja, *La Question Albanaise* (Paris, 1995).
93. Bugajski, *Ethnic Politics*, p. 276.
94. *FT*, 24 March 1996, p. 2.
95. A. Fraser, *The Gypsies* (Oxford: Blackwell, 1992), pp. 275–83.
96. D. Petrova, 'Get Out, You Stinking Gypsy!', *Transitions (OMRI)*, 4, 4, September 1997, pp. 14–21.

6 THE ECONOMIC UNDERPINNINGS: TEARING DOWN THE OLD, BUILDING UP THE NEW

1. *Transition Report 1995* (London: European Bank for Reconstruction and Development, 1995), p. 19.
2. See Appendix, Table A13, for the voting figures for communist parties and their successors in Eastern Europe.
3. The opinion polls for Eastern Europe over the period 1989 to 1993 have been examined systematically by Jakob Juchler in his comparative study *Umbruch in Osteuropa*; on pp. 163–4 he documents both the initially high support in Eastern Europe for the introduction of a market economy and the subsequent slippage (1991: Poland 56 per cent, Hungary 65 per cent,

Czechoslovakia 61 per cent, Bulgaria 62 per cent; 1992: Poland 56 per cent, Hungary 56 per cent, Czech Republic 55 per cent, Slovakia 51 per cent, Bulgaria 55 per cent).
4. Speech of August 1990 to American bankers, quoted by P. Wiles in 'Capitalist Triumphalism in the East European Transition', in H.-J. Chang and P. Nolan (eds), *The Transformation of the Communist Economies: Against the Mainstream* (London: Macmillan, 1995), pp. 46–77 (57).
5. B. Deacon, 'Social Change, Social Problems and Social Policy', in White et al., *Developments in East European Politics*, pp. 225–39 (235–6).
6. V. Tismaneanu, 'Truth, Trust and Tolerance: Intellectuals in Post-Communist Society', *P of PC*, March–April 1996, pp. 3–12 (7).
7. J. Lewandowski, 'Złudny wdzięk kuponovki', *Polityka*, 3 May 1997, pp. 42–4.
8. The question of restitution in agriculture is examined below, p. 118.
9. L. Balcerowicz, *800 Dni: Szok Kontrolowany* (Warsaw: Polska oficyna wydawnicza 'BGW', 1992), p. 64.
10. See B. Milanovic, 'Poland's Quest for Economic Stabilization 1988–91: the Interaction of Political Economy and Economics', *SS*, 3, 1992, pp. 511–31 (521).
11. S. Gomulka, 'Polish Economic Reform 1990–91: Principal Policies and Outcomes', *CJE*, 16, 1992, pp. 355–72 (366).
12. J. Kuroń, *Moja Zupa* (Warsaw: Polska oficyna wydawnicza 'BGW', 1991), p. 25.
13. K. Crane, 'Polish Foreign Trade in 1990 and the First Half of 1991', *PlanEcon Report*, 30 August 1991, p. 2.
14. *Zycie Gospodarczy*, 1, 1990, p. 2.
15. *Rocznik Statystyczny 1991* (Warsaw: Głowny Urząd Statystyczny, 1991), pp. 107, 117, 196, 244, 275, 380.
16. See the statistical appendices for economic indices. Caution is needed in relation to figures for GDP and industrial production, as firms had an interest in exaggerating production figures before 1989, and in minimizing them after 1989 for tax purposes (J. Winiecki, 'The Inevitability of a Fall in Output in the Early Stages of Transition to the Market', *SS*, 43, pp. 669–76.) There is also the general point that some 'goods' produced before 1989 did not in fact contribute to social welfare so their absence after 1989 was no real loss.
17. G.W. Kołodko, 'Transition from Socialism and Stabilization Policies: the Polish Experience', in M. Keren and G. Ofer (eds), *The Trials of Transition: Economic Reform in the Former Communist Bloc* (Boulder, Colorado: Westview Press, 1995), pp. 129–50 (135).
18. J. Winiecki, 'The Polish Transformation Programme: Stabilisation under Threat', *Communist Economies and Economic Transformation*, 2, 1992, pp. 191–213 (192–3, 196).
19. B. Slay, *The Polish Economy: Crisis, Reform and Transformation* (Princeton: Princeton University Press, 1994), p. 100.
20. A.H. Amsden, J. Kochanowicz and L. Taylor, *The Market Meets Its Match: Restructuring the Economies of Eastern Europe* (Cambridge, Massachusetts: Harvard University Press, 1994), pp. 114, 123.
21. Slay, *Polish Economy*, p. 107.
22. *The Economist*, 334, 7898, 21–7 January 1995, p. 76.

23. J. Freeman, 'Hungary: Utility Privatization Moves Forward', *Transition (OMRI)*, 2, 9, 3 May 1996, pp. 27–9; also *Transition (WB)*, vol. 6, 9–10, September–October 1995, p. 24.
24. See below, Chapter 8, for the impact of the corruption scandals on Hungarian politics.
25. *Keesing's, 1992*, 20 January, p. 38734.
26. *OECD Economic Survey, 1998: Czech Republic*, p. 51.
27. C.S. Maier, *Dissolution: the Crisis of Communism and the End of East Germany* (Princeton: Princeton University Press, 1997), p. 293.
28. H.-D. Brunner, 'German Blitz-Privatization', *Transition (WB)*, 6, 4, April 1995, pp. 13–14.
29. Maier, *Dissolution*, p. 295.
30. *FT*, 15 December 1994.
31. E. Conte and E. Giordano, 'Sentiers de la ruralité perdue', *Études Rurales*, 138–40, pp. 11–34(24).
32. C.M. Hann notes that in the village he studied in Hungary in 1992, 'the desire to re-establish private ownership rights was restricted to elderly members of families which had been well-to-do in the past' (C.M. Hann, 'From Production to Property: De-Collectivization and the Family–Land Relationship in Contemporary Hungary', *Man*, NS, 28, 2, 1993, pp. 299–320 [310]).
33. There is a useful sketch of the varying approaches taken in A.K. Kosminski, 'Restitution of Private Property', *CPCS*, 30, 1, pp. 95–106.
34. See T.W. Ryback, 'Injustice by Law', *Transitions (OMRI)*, 4, 2, July 1997, pp. 56–61 (60).
35. M.-C. Maurel, 'Recomposition des agricultures hongroise et tchèque', *RECE*, 26, 3, September 1995, pp. 53–89 (70).
36. S. Riedel, 'Bulgarien: Kontroversen um Agrarreformen', *SOE*, 43, 6–7, 1994, pp. 427–8.
37. S. Riedel, 'Bulgariens Landwirtschaft in der Transformation', *SOE*, 43, 6–7, 1994, pp. 384–402 (389); T. Meissner, 'Bulgarien nach dem Regierungswechsel am 25. Januar 1995', *SOE*, 44, 8, 1995, pp. 490–507 (492).
38. UNICEF, *Poverty, Children and Policy: Responses for a Brighter Future*, Regional Monitoring Report No. 3 (Florence: UNICEF–ICDC, 1995), p. 8.
39. Riedel, 'Bulgariens Landwirtschaft', p. 392.
40. W. Gumpel, 'Die bulgarische Wirtschaft – Chaos ohne Ende?', *SOE*, 46, 1–2, 1997, pp. 18–26 (25).
41. R. Begg and M. Meurs, 'Writing a New Song: Path Dependence and State Policy in Reforming Bulgarian Agriculture', in I. Szelényi (ed.), *Privatizing the Land: Rural Political Economy in Post-Communist Societies* (London: Routledge, 1998), pp. 260–4.
42. I. Harcsa, I. Kovách and I. Szelényi, 'The Price of Privatization: the Post-Communist Transformation Crisis of the Hungarian Agrarian System', in Szelényi *Privatizing*, pp. 214–44 (218).
43. Maurel, 'Recomposition', p. 59.
44. These figures are based on an index of 100 for 1979–81 average production (*United Nations Statistical Yearbook*, 41st issue, 1996, pp. 654–8).
45. Maurel, 'Recomposition', p. 86.
46. Kosminski, 'Restitution', p. 105.

47. *OECD Economic Surveys, 1997–1998: Romania 1997* (Paris: OECD, 1998), p. 159.
48. Despite warnings from economists, for example T. Ryczynski, 'The Sequencing of Reform', *Oxford Review of Economic Policy*, 7, 4, 1991, pp. 26–34.
49. L. Harris, 'Financial Fragility in the Transition to Market Economies', in Chang and Nolan, *Transformation* , pp. 177–202 (185).
50. See above, p. 117.
51. The resulting vulnerability of the financial sector was analysed by K. Brom and M. Orenstein, in 'The Privatised Sector in the Czech Republic: Government and Bank Control in a Transitional Economy', *EAS*, 46, 6, 1994, pp. 893–928.
52. J. Cook, 'Czechs Feel EU Pressure', *FT*, 4 September 1997, p. 2.
53. K & H Bank: *Kereskedelmi és Hitelbank Rt.* (Commercial and Credit Bank Ltd).
54. A. Lieven, 'Hungarian Banks Stronger after Braving Pain of Reform', *FT*, 11 September 1997, p. 2.
55. A. Robinson, in *FT*, 7 January 1997, p. 2.
56. Y. Golan, 'A Short Report on a Hungarian Long-Term Problem', *Environmental Policy Review*, 5, 1, January 1991, pp. 76–8 (77).
57. *Keesing's, 1993*, p. 39329.
58. *Keesing's, 1995*, p. 40516; *Keesing's, 1995*, p. 40741.
59. *United Nations Statistical Yearbook, 1996*, 41st edn (New York: United Nations, 1996), pp. 654–8.
60. A. Cornia and R. Paniccia, 'The Transition's Population Crisis', *Moct-Most*, 6, 1, 1995, pp. 95–129 (118).
61. See the essays in J. Klarer and B. Moldan (eds), *The Environmental Challenge for Central and East European Economies in Transition* (Chichester: John Wiley and Sons, 1997), particularly K. Georgievna and J. Moore, 'Bulgaria', pp. 68–9.
62. *United Nations Statistical Yearbook, 1996*, pp. 534–48.
63. M. Lavigne, *The Economics of Transition: From Socialist Economy to Market Economy* (London: Macmillan, 1995), Table 9.5, p. 236.
64. For foreign direct investment see EBRD, *Transition Report Update, April 1997*, Table 4, p. 12; for total capital flows see World Bank, *World Development Report 1996*, p. 136; for the proportion between the two, see Lavigne, *Economics of Transition*, Table 9.5, p. 236.
65. *FT*, 30 April 1996.
66. R. Kozul-Wright and P. Rayment, 'The Institutional Hiatus in Economies in Transition and Its Policy Consequences', *CJE*, 21, 1997, pp. 641–61 (645).
67. J. Kornai, *The Road to a Free Economy* (London: Norton, 1990), p. 22. Note, however, his wise qualification: 'Perhaps the role of government will be reconsidered at a later stage.'
68. This expression was coined by R. Kozul-Wright and P. Rayment. See above, note 66.
69. Lavigne, *Economics of Transition*, pp. 192–3, for 1993; the proportions for East Central Europe in 1997 are roughly the same (see *Cestat Statistical Bulletin*, 1997/4, Warsaw, 1998).

70. Amsden et al., *Market Meets Its Match*, p. x.
71. In fact in 1995 industrial output rose from its 1992 low point to 83.4 per cent of the 1989 figure, unemployment fell slightly rather than rising and GDP continued to rise (see the statistical appendices to this book). The MDF government, which had committed the minor civil rights violations referred to here, was in any case removed from office shortly afterwards.
72. On Klaus's readiness to 'violate his often-proclaimed principles' of rapid transition to the free market, without price controls or subsidies, see Wiles, 'Capitalist Triumphalism', p. 59.
73. M. Rutkowski, 'Labour Market Policies in Transition Economies', *Moct-Most*, 6, 1, 1996, pp. 19–38 (35).
74. T. Jelinek and O. Schneider, 'Time for Pension Reform in the Czech Republic', *Transition (OMRI)*, 4, 1, July 1997, pp. 77–81.
75. *FT*, 7 January 1997, p. 2.
76. On 17 May (*Keesing's, 1991*, p. 38214).
77. J. Varoli, 'Economic Reform Casts a Long Shadow in Russia', *Transition (OMRI)*, 3, 5, 21 March 1997, pp. 6–10. The EU figures are from Martin Walker, 'EU Victim of Growing Black Economy', *The Guardian*, 8 April 1998, p. 14.
78. As reported by an economic research company (SWB [Part 2. Central Europe, the Balkans], Weekly Economic Report, Third Series, EEW/0375/WA/5, 16 March 1995).
79. EBRD, *Transition Report 1995*, p. 27.
80. Juchler, 'Probleme', p. 903.
81. Z. Wilkiewicz, 'Arbeitslosigkeit und ihr Stellenwert in der polnischen Sozialpolitik', *OE*, 46, 1, 1996, pp. 64–79 (67).
82. A. Åslund et al., *Brookings Papers on Economic Activity*, 1996, 1, p. 221.
83. See Appendix, tables A7 and A8, for GDP levels.
84. See Appendix, Table A12.
85. See Appendix, Table A11.

7 THE SHOCK OF THE NEW: SOCIAL CONSEQUENCES AND COSTS OF TRANSITION

1. UNICEF (United Nations Children's Fund), *Central and Eastern Europe in Transition: Public Policy and Social Conditions* (New York: UNICEF-ICDC, 1994).
2. See Appendix, Table A12.
3. D.S. Mason et al., 'Increasingly Fond Memories of a Grim Past', *Transition (OMRI)*, 3, 5, 21 March 1997, Figure 3, p. 18.
4. Wilkiewicz, 'Arbeitslosigkeit', p. 68.
5. See Appendix, tables A8 (GDP per capita) and A11 (Real Wages).
6. See Appendix, Table A9.
7. This is clear from Table 4.2 of A. Glyn, 'Wasted Sacrifices', in Chang and Nolan, *Transformation*, pp. 113–35 (116).
8. *UN Statistical Yearbook: 41st Issue* (1996), p. 310.

9. L. Garrett, *The Coming Plague* (London: Penguin Books, 1995), pp. 500–5.
It should be added that AIDS has turned out to be a far smaller problem in transition countries than elsewhere. Deaths in 1995 in the whole region were 1 per cent of the world total, HIV infections 0.6 per cent. See J. Bongaarts, 'Global Trends in AIDS Mortality', in W. Lutz (ed.), *The Future Population of the World: What Can We Assume Today?* (London: Earthscan Publications Ltd, 1996), pp. 184–6.
10. See Appendix, Table A6 for life expectancy statistics.
11. J.-C. Chesnais, 'La récession démographique dans l'ex-URSS', *Population*, 52, 1, January–February 1997, pp. 234–40 (234).
12. *Transition Report 1995*, Chart 2.2, p. 23. See also Appendix 4.1 in the same publication.
13. See Appendix, Table A2.
14. See Appendix, Table A4.
15. A.-A. Guha, 'Blüms Last trüge er gerne', *Frankfurter Rundschau*, 6 December 1997, p. 7.
16. See M. Ellmann, 'Increases in Death and Disease', *CJE*, 18, 1994, pp. 329–55 (349); Chesnais, 'La Récession démographique'; A. Monnier and C. De Guibert-Antoine, 'La Conjoncture démographique', *Population*, 1994, 4–5 and 1992, 4–5; A. Cornia and R. Paniccia, 'The Transition's Population Crisis', *Moct-Most*, 6, 1, 1995, pp. 95–129.
17. See Appendix, Table A5.
18. For annual average population growth (in this case decline) see Appendix, Table A1.
19. The only countries where existing demographic trends *did* continue were Poland and the Czech Republic. Developments in the Czech Republic can be explained by government policy, which was aimed at limiting the costs of transition during this period; Poland is an anomaly for which no explanation has so far been offered.
20. Cornia and Paniccia, ' Transition's Population Crisis', p. 96.
21. Chesnais, 'La Récession démographique', p. 240.
22. It should be noted that changes in mortality, rather than the death rate as such, are in question here. Clearly, changes in the death rate may sometimes reflect changes in the age structure of a given population, rather than in the likelihood of dying; but the changes in life expectancy, a measure which is arrived at by holding the age structure constant, have run parallel to changes in the death rate in every case examined here.
23. Cornia and Paniccia, ' Transition's Population Crisis', Table 13, p. 120. Cornia and Paniccia assert that there was 'no particular decline in alcohol consumption in Eastern Europe', but their own figures do not bear this out. There were steep declines between 1989 and 1993 in Slovakia (from 3.4. litres per head to 2.2 litres), Lithuania (down from 6.0 litres to 2.5 litres), and Hungary (down from 11.3 to 10.6). One could well add Bulgaria, where consumption per head fell by 30.4 per cent between 1990 and 1994 (*Statisticheski Godishnik, 1995*, p. 113). Where alcohol consumption did increase was in the former Soviet Union. The Latvian increase was 37 per cent, the Russian increase 17 per cent. (See Goskomstat Rossii, *Rossiiskii Statisticheskii Ezhegodnik* [Moscow: Logos, 1996], p. 325.)

24. The Gini coefficient is used by sociologists to measure the extent to which the distribution of income among individuals or households diverges from equality. It is situated mathematically on a line from 0 (absolute equality) to 1 (absolute inequality). (Sometimes a scale of 1 to 100 is adopted.)
25. B. Milanovic, 'Income, Inequality and Poverty during the Transition: a Survey of the Evidence', *Moct-Most*, 6, 1, 1996, pp. 131–47.
26. L. Szamuely, 'Social Costs of Transition in Central and Eastern Europe', *The Hungarian Quarterly*, 37, winter 1996, pp. 54–69 (62). The World Bank's figures are actually higher. According to *From Plan to Market: the World Development Report, 1996* (Oxford: Oxford University Press, for the World Bank, 1996) Table 4.1, p. 69, Russia's Gini coefficient had risen to 0.48 by 1993.
27. See *From Plan to Market*, Table 4.1, p. 69.
28. Milanovic, 'Income, Inequality and Poverty'.
29. T. Cox, 'The Politics of Social Change', in White, Batt and Lewis, *Developments in Central and East European Politics*, pp. 216–33 (226–7).
30. For a comparative outline of Polish and Czechoslovak social policy, see M. Orenstein, 'The Failures of Neo-Liberal Social Policy in Central Europe', *Transition (OMRI)*, 2, 13, 28 June 1996, pp. 16–20. See also M. Castle-Kanerova, 'Social Policy in Czechoslovakia', in B. Deacon et al., *The New Eastern Europe* (London, 1992), p. 92.
31. J. Večerník, 'Changing Earnings Distribution in the Czech Republic: Survey Evidence from 1988–1994', *Economics of Transition*, 3, 3, September 1995, pp. 259.
32. J. Večerník, 'Anciennes et nouvelles inégalités économiques: le cas tchèque', *RECE*, 1996, 1, March, pp. 81–108 (100).
33. See above, Chapter 6.
34. See R. Lotspeich, 'Crime in the Transition Economies', *EAS*, 47, 4, 1995, pp. 555–89.
35. A. Jones and W. Markoff, *Ko-ops: the Rebirth of Entrepreneurship in the Soviet Union* (Bloomington, Indiana: Indiana University Press, 1991), p. 27.
36. Lotspeich, 'Crime', Table 1, p. 559; *Magyar Statisztikai Évkönyv 1996* (Budapest: Központi Statisztikai Hivatal, 1996), p. 206.
37. Lotspeich, 'Crime', Table 1, p. 559; *Rocznik Statystyczny, 1997* (Warsaw: Główny Urząd Statystyczny, 1997), p. 66.
38. E. Hankiss, *East European Alternatives* (Oxford: Oxford University Press, 1990).
39. J. Staniszkis, *The Dynamics of Breakthrough in Eastern Europe* (Berkeley: University of California Press, 1991).
40. I. Szelényi and S. Szelényi, 'Circulation or Reproduction of Elites?', *Theory and Society*, 24, 5, 1995, p. 629.
41. E. Fodor, E. Wnuk-Lipinski and N. Yershova, 'The New Political and Cultural Elite', *Theory and Society*, 24, 1995, pp. 783–800 (792).
42. V. Bunce and M. Csanádi, 'Uncertainty in the Transition: Post-Communism in Hungary', *EEPS*, 7, 2, spring 1993, p. 244.
43. Szelényi and Szelényi, 'Circulation or Reproduction', p. 620.
44. Szelényi and Szelényi, 'Circulation or Reproduction', p. 629.

45. T. Kolosi and Á. Róna-Tas, 'Poslední bude první? Sociální důsledky přechodu od socialismu k demokracii a trh v Mad'arsku', *Sociologický Časopis*, 28, 5, October 1992, p. 594.
46. M. Jones, 'Polish Elections', *Critique*, 26, 1994, pp. 165–70 (165).
47. J. Kurczewski, 'Poland's Perpetually New Middle Class', *Transition (OMRI)*, 3, 5, 21 March 1997, pp. 22–6 (23).
48. G. Eyal, I. Szelényi and E. Townsley, 'The Theory of Post-Communist Managerialism', *NLR*, 222, March/April 1997, pp. 60–92.
49. D. Ionescu, 'Romanian Corruption Scandal Implicates Top Officials', *RFE/RLRR*, 2, 30, 23 July 1993, p. 23. The person making the claim was Silviu Brucan.
50. V. Tismaneanu, 'Tenuous Pluralism in the Post-Ceauşescu Era', *Transition (OMRI)*, 2, 26, 27 December 1996, p. 9.
51. See J.A. Dérem, 'Le Monténégro tenté par la sécession', *MD*, September 1997, p. 4.
52. V. Shlapentokh, 'Early Feudalism: Best Parallel to Now', *EAS*, 48, 3, 1996, pp. 393–411.
53. Juchler, 'Probleme', Table 2, p. 903.
54. D.S. Mason et al., 'Increasingly Fond Memories', *Transition (OMRI)*, 3, 5, 21 March 1997, pp. 15–19 (15).
55. M. Myant, 'Czech and Slovak Trade Unions', in M. Waller and M. Myant (eds), *Parties, Trade Unions and Society in East-Central Europe* (London: Frank Cass, 1994), pp. 59–84 (63–4).
56. M. Cambalikova, 'The Emergence of Tripartism in Slovakia', in Á. Ágh and G. Ilonszki (eds), *Parliaments and Organized Interests: the Second Step* (Budapest: Hungarian Centre for Democracy Studies, 1996), pp. 197–200.
57. M. Orenstein, 'The Tripartite Council and Its Contribution to Social Peace', in Ágh and Ilonszki, *Parliaments and Organized Interests*, pp. 173–89 (173).
58. P. Rutland, 'Thatcherism Czech Style', *Telos*, 94, winter 1992–3, pp. 103–29.
59. Orenstein, 'Tripartite Council', p. 178.
60. Quoted by M. Myant, 'Czech and Slovak Trade Unions', p. 76.
61. A. Pollert, 'Trade Unionism in the Czech Republic', *Labour Focus on Eastern Europe*, 55, 1996, pp. 6–37 (17).
62. ČMKOS (Czech Republic): Českomoravská komora odborových svazů (Czech-Moravian Chamber of Trade Unions). This was the successor in the Czech Republic to the former all-Czechoslovak trade union federation ČSKOS.
63. SPR–RSČ: Sdružení pro Republiku – Republikánská strana Československa (Association for the Republic – Republican Party of Czechoslovakia), renamed SPR – Vlastenecká Republikánská Strana (SPR – Patriotic Republic Party) in August 1995.
64. See *Statistická Ročenka České Republiky 1996* (Prague: Scietia, 1996), p. 687.
65. M. Frybes, 'Le Syndicalisme en Europe centrale', *Cahiers Internationaux de Sociologie*, 95, July–December 1993, pp. 275–87 (280).
66. J. Pataki, 'Hungarian Government Signs Social Contract with Unions', *RFE/RLRR*, 2, 5, 29 January 1993, pp. 42–5.

67. Frybes, 'Syndicalisme', p. 275.
68. Frybes, 'Syndicalisme', p. 284.
69. J. Acsady, 'Shifting Attitudes and Expectations in Hungary', *Transition (OMRI)*, 1, 16, 8 September 1995, pp. 22–3.
70. M. Katzarova, 'Opening the Door', *The Nation*, 257, 4, 26 July–2 August 1993, pp. 148–50 (148).
71. Acsady, 'Shifting Attitudes', p. 22.
72. 1995 figures: Poland, 16.1 per cent of the female labour force unemployed, 13.6 per cent of the male; Czech Republic, 4.8 per cent of the female labour force unemployed, 3.7 per cent of the male; Hungary, 8.8 per cent of the female labour force unemployed, 12.5 per cent of the male. See *World Employment 1996/97: National Policies in a Global Context* (Geneva: International Labour Office, 1996), Table 4.2, p. 113.
73. Several of the contributors to the collection of essays edited by N. Funk and M. Mueller (eds), *Gender Politics and Post-Communism: Reflections from Eastern Europe and the Former Soviet Union* (London: Routledge, 1993), point out that the anti-feminist backlash was already apparent in the 1980s in Eastern Europe, during the communist epoch (op. cit., p. 4).
74. J. Stastna, 'New Opportunities', *Transition (OMRI)*, 1, 16, 8 September 1995, pp. 24–8 (26).
75. Susan Gal, quoted in G. Kligman, 'The Social Legacy of Communism: Women, Children and the Feminization of Poverty', in J.R. Millar and S.L. Wolchik (eds), *The Social Legacy of Communism* (Cambridge: Cambridge University Press, 1994), pp. 252–70 (253).
76. R. Panova, R. Gavrilova and C. Merdzanska, 'Thinking Gender: Bulgarian Women's Impossibilities', in Funk and Mueller, *Gender Politics*, pp. 15–21 (15).
77. See A. Čermaková, 'Gender, Společnost, a pracovní Trh', *Sociologický Časopis*, 31, 1995, p. 19; Stastna, 'New Opportunities'.
78. See on this point Z. Eisenstein, *The Color of Gender: Reimaging Democracy* (Berkeley: University of California Press, 1994), Chapter 1.
79. See S.L. Wolchik and A.G. Meyer (eds), *Women, State and Party in Eastern Europe* (Durham: Duke University Press, 1985), Section IV, *passim*, but in particular R.J. McIntyre, 'Demographic Policy and Sexual Equality: Value Conflicts and Policy Appraisal in Hungary and Romania', Chapter 16, pp. 270–85, and A. Heitlinger, 'Passage to Motherhood: Personal and Social "Management" of Reproduction in Czechoslovakia in the 1980s', Chapter 17, pp. 286–300. The following estimates of the percentage of married women of reproductive age in each country using modern contraceptives come from *People*, 16, 3, 1989, pp. 7–23: Bulgaria 8 per cent, Czechoslovakia 25 per cent, GDR 40 per cent, Hungary 30 per cent, Poland 2 per cent.
80. N. Funk, 'Introduction', in Funk and Mueller, *Gender Politics*, pp. 1–14 (11).
81. See M. Spencer, 'Post-Socialist Patriarchy', in B. Wejnert, M. Spencer and S. Drakulic, *Women in Post-Communism* (Greenwich, Connecticut: Jai Press Inc., 1996), p. 279.
82. A. Milić, 'Women and Nationalism in the Former Yugoslavia', in Funk and Mueller, *Gender Politics*, pp. 109–22 (113).

83. See S. Gal, 'The Abortion Debate in Hungary', *EEPS*, 8, 2, 1994, pp. 256–86 (256).
84. K. Verdery, *What Was Socialism, and What Comes Next?* (Princeton: Princeton University Press, 1996), p. 79.
85. See M. Fuszara, 'Abortion and the Formation of the Public Sphere in Poland', in Funk and Mueller, *Gender Politics*, pp. 245–7, for a detailed presentation of the debate of the early 1990s.
86. E. Hauser, B. Heyns and J. Mansbridge, 'Feminism in the Interstices of Politics and Culture: Poland in Transition', in Funk and Mueller, *Gender Politics*, pp. 257–73 (259).
87. *Keesing's, 1991*, p. 38207. The source is a speech in the Sejm by an opponent of the anti-abortion bill on 16 May 1991. The figure for legal abortion in 1990 was 59 417. Even in 1988 the number of legal abortions was only 105 333.
88. J. Juchler, 'Kontinuität oder Wende? Polen seit dem Wahlsieg der "Postkommunisten"', *OE*, 1, 1995, p. 68.
89. See Appendix, Table A6. There were exceptions: in the Czech Republic, Slovakia and Slovenia male life expectancy rose more than female.

8 THE MIDDLE YEARS: DRIFTING TOWARDS THE MILLENNIUM

1. G. Konrad, *Die Melancholie der Wiedergeburt* (Frankfurt, 1992), p. 279.
2. H. Tworzecki, *Parties and Politics in Post-1989 Poland* (Boulder, Colorado: Westview, 1996), p. 158.
3. The sense of surprise is lessened when one considers that the communist party in Poland had already surrendered to the peasantry and the Roman Catholic Church in 1956, thus abandoning a large part of the typically Stalinist endeavour to create a homogeneous society.
4. Tworzecki, *Parties and Politics*, p. 157.
5. T.G. Ash, 'Neo-Pagan Poland', *New York Review of Books*, 11 January 1996, p. 14.
6. Of Kwaśniewski's supporters 69.5 per cent were under 60, as against 58.7 per cent of his opponent's. These and subsequent opinion poll statistics are taken from J. Juchler, 'Machtwechsel – die Präsidentschaftswahlen in Polen', *OE*, 46, 3, 1996, pp. 267–83.
7. Of the people who identified themselves as 'left' 88 per cent voted for Kwaśniewski; 85 per cent of right-wingers voted for Wałęsa; but Kwaśniewski also won 52 per cent of the people who saw themselves as being in the 'centre' of the political spectrum.
8. Only 3 per cent of non-practising Catholics supported Wałęsa, 45 per cent of practising Catholics.
9. Juchler, 'Machtwechsel', p. 279.
10. See C. Bobinski, in *FT*, 28 August 1997, p. 2, and *FT*, 9 September 1997, p. 2.
11. The Minister of Finance, László Békesi, resigned over the issue, leading some foreign observers to describe this as a policy turn away from privatization and foreign investment. But his successor, the banker Lajos

Bokros, who also came from the ranks of the MSZP, pursued an identical policy.
12. *SWB EE* 2215 A/3, 31 January 1995.
13. *SWB EE* 2252 A/2, 15 March 1995.
14. This evaluation is based on the electoral statistics published in *Statistická Ročenka České Republiky* (Prague: Scientia, 1996), p. 687.
15. M. Lavigne, 'Le "Miracle tchèque" sauvé par les eaux', *MD*, October 1997, p. 10.
16. *Keesing's, 1997*, p. 41656.
17. These figures are taken from the 'Survey of the Czech Republic', *FT*, 1 December 1997, Supplement, p. 1.
18. *Právo*, 22 June 1998, p. 1.
19. This is view of V. Krivý, in 'Die Gründung des slowakischen Staates und ihre Folgen', *SOE*, 45, 3, 1996, pp. 197–218 (211).
20. K. Bartak, 'La Slovaquie, "mauvais élève" de l'Occident', *MD*, May 1997, p. 18.
21. Krivý, 'Die Gründung', p. 211.
22. Some of this increase is illusory, because it results from the division of Czechoslovakia; in 1993 the Czech Republic inevitably became Slovakia's biggest trading partner. But after 1993 the proportion of trade with the Czech Republic declined somewhat, while trade with other countries increased (1993: $5.5 billion of exports, $2.3 billion to the Czech Republic; 1996: $8.8 billion of exports, $2.7 billion to the Czech Republic.
23. I. Samson, 'Die Slowakei zwischen Annäherung an Moskau und Streben nach Westintegration', *BBIOST*, 2, 1997.
24. This is the EBRD October 1997 forecast; the *Cestat Statistical Bulletin*, 1997, 4 (Warsaw: ZWS, 1998) gives an increase of 6.5 per cent over 1996.
25. O. Hishow, 'Makroökonomische Politik und Reformfortschritte im östlichen Europa', *BBIOST*, 25, 1997, p. 9. See Appendix, Table A8. These are not purchasing power parity figures.
26. J. Gould and S. Szomolanyi, 'Bridging the Chasm in Slovakia', *Transitions (OMRI)*, 4, 6, November 1997, pp. 70–6 (72).
27. From the EBRD *Transition Report Update, April 1997*, Table 4, p. 12.
28. P. Havlik, 'East–West Comparison: Problems, Methods and Results', *Wiener Institut für Internationale Wirtschaftsvergleiche: Forschungsberichte*, No. 174 (Vienna, 1991), p. 37.
29. Gould and Szomolanyi, 'Bridging the Chasm', p. 73.
30. Juchler, 'Probleme', p. 903.
31. These are the 1995 figures (EBRD, *Transition Report 1995*, p. 206).
32. M. Križan, 'Zerbrechliche Hoffnungen: das Abkommen von Dayton/Paris und die Zukunft des Balkans', *OE*, 46, 4, 1996, pp. 315–30.
33. But see above, Chapter 3, for the alleged link between the Montenegrin bid for independence and quarrels over tobacco smuggling.
34. *Keesing's, 1995*, p. 41064.
35. See above, Chapter 4.
36. From a proclamation of 15 April 1991 issued by the Sofia Consultative Council of the SDS, quoted in R. Dimitrov, 'Bündnis oder "Bewegung"? Der Differenzierungsprozess der "Union der demokratischen Kräfte"', in Höpken, *Revolution auf Raten*, pp. 63–82 (69).

37. See the illuminating comments by J.D. Bell on the victory of the 'dark blue' faction within the SDS and their hostility, not just to former communists, but to 'pink blues' in their own ranks, who were usually former dissidents of the 1980s (J.D. Bell, 'Bulgaria', in White, Batt and Lewis, *Developments in East European Politics*, pp. 83–97 [92].
38. Namely the electoral law of 3 April 1990; the appeal of 8 October 1991 to the Constitutional Court; and the renewed appeal of 4 November 1991 to the Constitutional Court against the eligibility of DPS deputies. The appeal of November 1991 almost succeeded; the Constitutional Court refused on 21 April 1992 by the narrowest of margins to outlaw the DPS. See in detail S. Riedel, 'Die türkische Minderheit', *SOE*, 2, 43, 1993, pp. 100–24.
39. See above, Chapter 6.
40. Bugajski, *Ethnic Politics*, p. 236.
41. Riedel, 'Die türkische Minderheit', p. 115.
42. Riedel, 'Die türkische Minderheit', p. 117.
43. K. Engelbrekt, 'The Fall of Bulgaria's First Non-Communist Government', *RFE/RLRR*, 1, 45, 13 November 1992, pp. 1–6.
44. L. Troxel, 'Bulgaria: Stable Ground in the Balkans?', *Current History* (November 1993), pp. 388–9.
45. See Appendix, Table A10, and note 2.
46. For 1992, see F.M.A. Hassan and K. Peters, 'Structure of Incomes and Social Security in the Transition', *EAS*, 4, 1996, pp. 629–62 (634); for 1994 see R. Stokova and J. Deimel, 'Die Jugendlichen in Bulgarien – Gewinner oder Verlierer der gesellschaftlichen Transformation?', in *SOEM*, 36, 2, 1996, pp. 161–74 (162).
47. Höpken, 'Die unvollendete Revolution', p. xiv.
48. *From Plan to Market: World Development Report, 1996*, p. 136.
49. For comparison (mid-1996 figures): Hungary $1299, Slovenia $895, Czech Republic $586, Estonia $424, Croatia $268, Poland $265, Latvia $145, Albania $97, Lithuania $85, Romania $84 (*OECD Economic Survey 1997: Bulgaria* [Paris: OECD, 1997], p. 126).
50. H. Brahm, 'Macht und Ohnmacht der bulgarischen Sozialisten', *SOEM*, 36, 2, 1996, pp. 148–60 (156).
51. 1989–91 average: 6 672 000 tonnes; 1996: 3 328 000 tonnes (*FAO Quarterly Bulletin of Statistics*, 9, 3/4, 1996, pp. 14–15).
52. M. Venkova-Wolff, 'Bulgarien – auf dem Weg zur Demokratie?', *OE*, 4, 1997, p. 328.
53. Speaking on 29 May 1996 (*SWB EE*/2026/B/7, 31 May 1996).
54. The First Deputy Minister of Agriculture, Dimo Uzunov, made this claim on 6 August 1996 (*SWB EE*/2685/B/6).
55. *The Guardian*, 21 September 1996.
56. Ian Traynor, writing in *The Guardian*, 8 October 1996.
57. Venkova-Wolff, 'Bulgarien', p. 330.
58. *SWB*, Part 2, *Central Europe, the Balkans*, Third Series, EE/2604/B/5 (6 May 1996).
59. *SWB*, Part 2, *Central Europe, the Balkans*, Weekly Economic Report, Third Series, EEW/0435/WB/1 (16 May 1996).
60. *SWB*, Part 2, *Central Europe, the Balkans*, Third Series, EE/2620/B/1 (24 May 1996).

61. Romania's GDP began to rise in 1993 (successive increases were 1.3 per cent, 2.4 per cent, 7.0 per cent and 4.1 per cent). Real wages, after falling catastrophically in 1993 (by 54 per cent) stayed roughly constant in 1994 (−1.5 per cent) and rose substantially in 1995 (by 21.8 per cent). See the statistical appendices to this book.
62. A. Lieven, in *FT*, 9 April 1997, p. 2.
63. *Keesing's, 1998*, p. 42236.
64. P. Schubert, 'Albanien im Vorwahlklima', *SOE*, 2, 1996, pp. 138–53 (138).
65. *Koha Jonë* was founded in 1991 to provide a voice for democrats dissatisfied with the government propaganda put out by the official Democratic Party press. See L. Kim, 'The Free Press in Albania', *SOE*, 9–10, 43, 1994, pp. 570–5 (572).
66. *Eastern Europe Newsletter*, 7, 9, 27 April 1993. See also *Kohe Jonë*, quoted in *OE*, 1, 1994, pp. A50–1.
67. In July 1992. See M. Schmidt-Neke, 'Albanien vor einer neuen Wende? Das Verfassungsreferendum und seine Konsequenzen', *SOE*, 1/2, 44, 1995, p. 63–88 (66).
68. M. Schmidt-Neke, 'Die Albanische Parlamentswahlen vom 26.5.1996', *SOE*, 8, 1996, pp. 567–88 (567).
69. A. Gjonça, C. Wilson and J. Falkingham, 'Paradoxes of Health Transition in Europe's Poorest Country: Albania, 1950–1990', *Population and Development Review*, 23, 3, September 1997, pp. 585–609 (606–7).
70. Miranda Vickers and James Pettifer claim that the Kosovo problem played a vital and growing role in Albanian politics (*Albania*, p. 142). But although Berisha was prepared to 'play the Kosovo card' at election time, his main concern was to keep out of involvement there. Various minor parties of the extreme right (such as the Republicans) dreamed of a 'Greater Albania' including Kosovo, but they remained on the fringes of politics. Albania's fate in the 1990s has been determined by internal factors and also, naturally, by the global economic and political environment, not by the Kosovo question. This changed in 1999.
71. M.-F. Allain, 'L'Albanie, de Charybde en Scylla?', *Esprit*, July 1997, p. 58.
72. I. Warde, 'De la Russie à l'Albanie', *MD*, April 1997, pp. 22–3.
73. C. Chiclet, 'L'Albanie fragilisée', *MD*, July 1998, p. 10.
74. J. Kochanowicz, 'The Disappearing State in Poland', *Social Research*, 60, 4, winter 1993, pp. 821–34.
75. See R. Cooper, *The Post-Modern State and the World Order* (London: Demos, 1996).
76. E. Mortimer, 'Descent into Chaos', *FT*, 9 April 1997, p. 30.
77. See Jacques Sapir, *Le Chaos Russe: désordres économiques, conflits politiques, décomposition militaire* (Paris: La Découverte, 1996).
78. T. Brey, 'Trümmer, Chaos und kein Ende: Ehemaliges Yugoslawien', *OE*, 2, 43, 1993, pp. 139–44; similarly, X. Raufer and F. Haut, *Le Chaos Balkanique* (Paris: Table Ronde, 1992).
79. See Appendix, Table A7 for changes in the Gross Domestic Product.
80. *Hospodářské Noviny*, 20 August 1998, p. 1.
81. See *OE*, 12, 1993, p. 1183. There are a few exceptions to this rule, such as Andrējs Krastiņš, leader during Soviet times of the Latvian Party of

National Independence, who became Deputy Prime Minister in a coalition government formed on 21 December 1995, and Bronisław Geremek, the Solidarity veteran who became Foreign Minister in the Polish government formed on 31 October 1997.

82. B. Guetta, 'La Défaite des Héros', *Le Nouvel Observateur*, 16–27 November 1995.
83. J. Torpey, 'The Abortive Revolution Continues: East German Civil Rights Activists since Unification', *Theory and Society*, 24, 1, 1995, pp. 105–34 (105).
84. The question of elite survival has been discussed in Chapter 7 above.
85. H. Grabbe and K. Hughes, *Enlarging the EU Eastwards* (London: Royal Institute of International Affairs, 1998), p. 54.
86. M.A. Centeno and T. Rands, 'The World They Have Lost: an Assessment of Change in Eastern Europe', *Social Research*, 63, 2, summer 1996, pp. 369–402 (391).

Index

Abdić, Fikret 141
abortion 148–9
Acsady, Judit 146
advertising 57–8
Agrarian Democratic Party 72
agriculture: fall in
 production 128, 133;
 restitution measures 119–22;
 transition in 118–22
Ahmeti, Vilson 74, 182
aid programme 126–7
AIDS 133
Albania 14–16, 54, 72–5, 182–5;
 and Berisha see Berisha, Sali;
 and communist rule 15, 72;
 dealing with post-communists
 182; economy 73, 75, 183;
 elections (1991) 73;
 elections (1992) 74;
 elections (1996) 183;
 elections (1997) 184;
 ethnic conflict 15, 106–7;
 fall in agricultural
 production 133; Greek
 minority in 15, 106–7; and
 Kosovo 107; media 55;
 poverty 16, 59, 72; pyramid
 schemes 57, 184; strikes and
 protests 74, 75
Albanians 16, 18;
 in Kosovo 18–19, 83–4, 102,
 107; in Macedonia 100
alcohol consumption 135
Alia, President Ramiz 73, 74, 182
Alliance of the Democratic
 Left see SLD
Alliance of Free Democrats
 (SZDSZ) 22, 24, 25, 155
Alliance of Reform Forces 88, 99
Amsden, Alice 128
Angelov, Ivan 178
Antall, József 24, 25–8, 53
ÁPV Rt. (State Privatization and
 Holding Company) 156, 157

arms sales 129–30
Association of Workers
 (ZRS) 165
AWS (Solidarity Electoral
 Action) 153–4

Balcerowicz Plan 30, 113–16
Balkans 2, 14–16, 59–75, 110;
 economic backwardness 9–10;
 features 14; lack of open
 resistance 60; poverty 59;
 reasons for difference in
 transition from East-Central
 Europe 59–60; see also
 Albania; Bulgaria; Romania;
 Yugoslavia
Baltic States 2–3, 45–9, 76;
 see also Estonia; Latvia;
 Lithuania
banks 122–3
BBWR (Non-Party Bloc in Support
 of Reform) 145
Berisha, Sali 7, 73, 74–5, 106,
 107, 182–5; authoritarian
 rule of 53, 60, 75, 182–3;
 downfall 141, 184–5;
 reasons for failure 183–4
Berov, Professor
 Lyuben 172, 173–4
Bielecki, Jan Krzystof 31, 32
birth rate 134, 147, 190t
Bokros, Lajos 54, 156, 157
Boross, Peter 28
Bosnia-Herzegovina 77, 78, 87;
 elections and Census
 (1990) 88, 93–4;
 post-Dayton 167–8
Bosnian war 93–9; attempts
 at peace 96–7; brutality
 of 95–6; conflict between
 Serbs and Muslims 95–6;
 ending of and Dayton
 Agreement 98–9, 167;
 events leading up to 94–5;

NATO involvement 97, 98;
relations between Muslims
and Croats 96; Sarajevo and
Markale market place
massacres 97; US
involvement 97
Brazauskas, Algirdas 47
Breuel, Hanna 118
Brown, J.F. 50
Brozi, Judge Zef 54
BSP (Bulgarian Socialist
Party) 62, 173, 176;
control of media 177; and
DPS 106; and elections
(1991) 170; and elections
(1994) 174; forced out of
office 173, 177–8; pressure
on by SDS 63–4; and
Soviet coup 61
Bufi, Ylli 74
Bulatović, Momir 168
Bulgaria 21, 51, 53, 60–4,
169–79, 187; agrarian
crisis 120–1, 133, 176–7, 178;
banks 123, 177; and BSP
see BSP; constitutional
court 54; contraception 148;
economy 11, 131, 169,
171, 175–6, 177; elections
(1990) 62–3, 105; elections
(1991) 170; elections
(1994) 174; ethnic
conflict 105–6; features
of post-communist
politics 60–4;
female employment 147;
income distribution 136;
lack of foreign investment 173,
175; measures taken
to stamp out
communism 170;
media 55; nuclear
power 125; political
parties with monarchist
leanings 21; privatization 173,
174, 175, 176; restitution of
agricultural property 119–20,
171–2, 178; and Russia 61, 175;
and SDS *see* SDS;

shadow economy 130; trade
unions 63–4, 169; and
Turks 76, 105, 171, 172;
unemployment 132
Bulgarian Agrarian National
Union – Nikola Petkov
(BZNS-NP) 21, 62, 64
Bulgarian Socialist Party
see BSP

Čalfa, Marián 36, 37, 40, 143
Čarnogurský, Jan 40
CDR (Democratic Convention of
Romania) 70, 180, 181
CDU (Christian Democratic
Union) 20
Ceauşescu, Nicolae 65, 104, 179
censuses 77
Centeno, M.A., and Rands, T. 188
Centre Citizens' Alliance 31,
32, 33
Chirot, Daniel 9
Christian Democrats
(KDNP) 22, 158
Christopher, Warren 96–7
Čič, Milan 37
Ciorbea, Victor 180, 181–2
CIS (Commonwealth of
Independent States) 2–3,
45, 54, 126
CITUB (Confederation of the
Independent Trade Unions
of Bulgaria) 63–4, 169, 171,
174, 178
Civic Alliance 68
Civic Democratic Party
(ODS) 39, 40, 152, 159, 161
Civic Forum (OF) 36, 37, 38,
39, 187
civil society, concept of 54
CO_2 emissions 125
Coexistence (ESWM) 38,
103, 104
Cohen, L.J. 94
Comecon 4, 174
Communist Party of
Czechoslovakia (KSČ) 37
communists, former 186–7;
dealing with 49–52

Confederation of the Independent
  Trade Unions of Bulgaria
  (CITUB) 63–4, 169, 171,
  174, 178
Constantinescu, Emil 180
constitutional courts 54
constitutions 52, 53
contraception 148
Cornea, Doina 65
corruption 7, 122–3
Ćosić, Dobrica 101
crime, rise of 137–8
Croat Socio-Liberal Party
  (HSLS) 91
Croatia 10, 78, 83, 86–8,
  90–2, 168; abortion issue 148;
  elections (1990) 85; elections
  (1993) 91; elections (1995) 91;
  elections (1997) 169;
  exports 90; language
  issue 77; media 55;
  post-Dayton 168–9;
  re-integration of Eastern
  Slavonia into 90, 168–9;
  reasons for optimism 91–2;
  rise of opposition 91; secret
  police 90–1; separation of
  Krajina from 87–8, 89; Serbs
  in 16–17, 82, 85–6; Tuđman's
  stranglehold on 90–2; war with
  Krajina Serbs 89–90
Croatian Democratic Union
  (HDZ) 85, 91, 92, 94
Croats 16, 17, 79; in Bosnia 94;
  and language issue 81; war with
  Muslims in Bosnia 96
ČSSD (Czech Social Democratic
  Party) 43, 137, 159, 161, 162
Csurka, István 27–8
culture 14, 55–8
Cvetković-Maček Agreement
  (1939) 17
Czech Republic 43, 53, 158–62,
  186; banks 122, 123, 159–60;
  corruption scandals 42, 122–3,
  161; de-communization 51;
  early political stability 42,
  43, 158; economy 43, 160–2;
  elections (1996) 150, 159;
  elections (1998) 162; fall in
  family benefit 136; floods
  (1997) 160–1; increase in
  racism and xenophobia 161;
  nuclear power 124–5; political
  and social shifts 158–9;
  restitution of agricultural
  property 119; separation
  from Slovakia 41, 42, 103;
  smoking 58; trade
  unions 143–4
Czech Social Democratic Party
  (ČSSD) 43, 137, 159, 161, 162
Czechoslovakia 10, 20–1, 36–45,
  53, 128, 187; abortion issue
  148; arms sales 129–30; conflict
  with Slovakia 39–40, 42;
  dissidents 12; dissolution 41,
  42, 103; economy 11, 38–9,
  111–12, 165; elections 150;
  elections (1990) 37–8; elections
  (1992) 41; fall in agricultural
  production 133; female
  employment 147; impact of
  shock therapy economic
  reforms 39–40; income
  distribution 136–7;
  privatization 38–9, 112, 117;
  reasons for communists not
  playing major part in future
  political life 37; restitution of
  agricultural property 119;
  tension with Hungary over
  hydroelectric power
  project 124; trade
  unions 142–3; women
  politicians 146–7; see also
  Czech Republic; Slovakia

Dayton Agreement (1995) 99, 167
de Maizière, Lothar 20
de-communization 49–52
debt rescheduling 127
democracy, road to parliamentary
  democracy 52–5
Democratic Charter
  Movement 27, 54
Democratic Convention of Romania
  (CDR) 70, 180, 181

Democratic League of Kosovo
 (LDK)   102
Democratic National Salvation
 Front (FDSN)   69–70
Democratic Party (PDSH)   73,
 74, 75, 107
Democratic Union (UD)   32, 33,
 35, 152, 154
Dienstbier, Jiří   39
Dimitrov, Filip   170, 171
Dimitrova, Blaga   172, 187
diseases   133
dissidents   6–7, 12, 54, 55–6, 187
divorce   147
Dobrev, Nikolai   177
Dogan, Ahmed   172
DPS (Movement for Rights and
 Freedoms)   106, 170, 172
Drnovšek, Janez   93, 139
Dubček, Alexander   37
Dukanović, Milo   168
Dunai, Imre   117, 157
Duray, Miklos   103

East Germany (GDR)   2, 11,
 20, 23, 118
Eastern Europe: division   2;
 historical backwardness   9–11;
 main elements of
 post-communist   5–8;
 pre-transition   11–14;
 term of   1–2
Eastern Slavonia   90, 168–9
EBRD (European Bank for
 Reconstruction and
 Development)   126;
 Transition Report
 (1995)   109–10
economy   109–31, 185–6;
 assistance from the
 West   126–7; and
 banks   122–3; different
 approaches towards
 transition   109–11;
 divergences within Eastern
 Europe   11; effect on cultural
 decline   56; features essential
 for transition   109–10; impact
 of market forces   5–6;

initial impact of marketization
 and privatization   127–30;
 liberalization successes   131;
 links between stabilization
 programmes and excess
 deaths   134; and
 nomenklatura   140;
 pre-transition   13;
 problems with transition   131;
 protest vote against effect of
 reforms   110–11; shadow
 economy   130, 137; shock
 therapy versus
 gradualism   111–12; *see
 also* privatization
elections: fall in participation
 rate   150; performance of
 communist and post-communist
 parties in   198t
energy, supply of   124
environmental
 degradation   124–5
Estonia   45–6, 130, 132, 136
ethnic composition, former
 Yugoslavia   16, 199t
ethnic conflict   5; reasons
 for   78–9; *see also*
 individual countries
European Union (EU)   4, 7, 188

Falbr, Richard   144
family benefit, fall in   136
family planning   147–8
Fatherland Party of Labour   105
FDSN (Democratic National
 Salvation Front)   69–70
Federal Republic of
 Yugoslavia   101–2, 168
fertility rate   135
feudalism, reversion to   140–1
FIDESZ   158
Finland   46
FKGP (Smallholders' Party)   22,
 25, 26, 27, 121, 158
flag   77
food shortages   133
Former Yugoslav Republic of
 Macedonia (FYROM)   100;
 see also Macedonia

Freedom Union (UW) 154, 155, 161, 162
FSN (National Salvation Front) 65, 66–7, 68, 69, 104–5, 179
Funar, Gheorghe 77, 105

Gallagher, Tom 14
Gaulieder, František 54
Gavorník, Stefan 163
Gdánsk Shipyards (Poland) 128–9
GDP (Gross Domestic Product) 11, 13, 129, 132, 193–4t
GDR (East Germany) 2, 11, 20, 23, 118
Gegs 106
Germany 2, 7; *see also* East Germany
Gligorov, Kiro 100
Göncz, Arpád 25, 26, 27, 53
Greater Romania Party (PRM) 66, 105
Grebeniček, Miroslav 43
Greece 2, 100, 107
Grósz, Károly 23, 24
Group of Seven 126

Hadžić, Goran 169
Hall, D., and Danta, D. 64
Hankiss, Elemér 1, 23, 28
Havel, Václav 7, 36, 37, 38, 40, 43, 51, 53, 160, 187
HDZ (Croatian Democratic Union) 85, 91, 92, 94
health care, decline in standards 133
Homeland Union (TSLK) 47
Honecker, Erich 20, 49–50
Höpken, Wolfgang 63
Horn, Gyula 25, 28, 155, 156
Horthy, Admiral 28
Hungarian Democratic Forum (MDF) 21, 24, 25, 28, 116, 139, 156
Hungarian Democratic Union of Romania (UDMR) 66, 67

Hungarian Justice and Life Party (MIÉP) 28
Hungarian Socialist Party (MSZP) 23, 24, 25, 28, 29, 117, 129, 145, 155, 158
Hungarian Socialist Workers' Party (MSZMP) 24, 25; *see also* MSZP
Hungarians 1, 16; in Romania 66–7, 104, 180, 181; in Slovakia 103
Hungary 10, 14, 21–2, 23–9, 53, 57, 129, 147, 155–8, 180; abortion issue 148; admission to OECD 157–8; and Antall 24, 25–8, 53; anti-communist and nationalist measures 26; banks 123; concessions to communism 26–7; constitutional courts 54; crime rates 138; decline in agricultural production 121, 133; dissidents 12; economy 25–6, 111, 112, 128, 155–6, 157–8; elections (1990) 25, 150; elections (1994) 28–9; elections (1998) 158; fall in family benefit 136; and Nagymáros-Gabčikovo hydroelectric power project 124; and *nomenklatura* 23, 139; and nuclear power 124; pressure on Antall government from right 27–8; privatization 26, 112, 116–17, 156, 157; re-emergence of former political parties 21–2; relations with Romania 180, 181; restitution of agricultural land 121; 'roundtable' talks between government and opposition on transition 20, 21, 23, 24; shadow economy 130; Tocsik Affair (1996) 157; trade unions 144–5; unemployment 132, 157

HZDS (Movement for a Democratic
    Slovakia) 40, 41, 44, 45, 163,
    165, 166–7
Iliescu, Ion 7, 54, 65, 105, 180;
    economic policy 179; leadership
    style and methods of staying
    in power 60, 66, 71, 72;
    presidential elections 67, 70,
    180; reasons for defeat 180
IMF (International Monetary
    Fund) 109, 126; and
    Albania 75; and Bulgaria 173,
    175, 178; and Poland 31, 32;
    and Romania 71, 72
income: distribution 6, 13,
    135–6, 138; fall in real
    income 132–3, 138
Independent State of Croatia
    (NDH) 85–6
infant mortality 134, 191–2t
inflation 194t
investment, foreign
    investment 126–7
Izetbegović, Alija 94, 95, 97

Janos, Andrew 11
Jaruzelski, General
    Wojciech 12, 29, 30, 49
JNA (Yugoslav People's
    Army) 84, 87, 88, 89

Kadaré, Ismail 73
Kadijević, General Veljko 87
Kalvoda, Jan 122
Karadžić, Radovan 95, 97
Katyn massacre 52
Kauls, Alberts 49
KDNP (Christian
    Democrats) 22, 158
Klaus, Václav 41, 43, 51, 158, 187;
    and banking privatization 122,
    123; and dissolution of
    Czechoslovakia 42;
    downfall 112, 159, 161;
    economic policy 38, 39,
    111–12, 137, 160; and
    Havel 38; and
    trade unions 143, 144

KLD (Liberal Democratic
    Congress) 32, 33, 152, 154
Kochanowicz, Jacek 9, 185
Komárek, Valtr 38
Konrád, George 150
Kornai, János 127
Kosovo 10, 15, 82; and Albanian
    government 107; Albanians
    in 18–19, 83–4, 102, 107;
    economic backwardness 19;
    reintegration into
    Serbia 83–4, 101–2
Kováč, Michal 44, 53, 163
Kožený-Wallis affair 122–3
KPN (Confederation for
    an Independent
    Poland) 35, 152, 153
Krajina 91, 168
Krasts, Guntars 49
Krzaklewski, Marian 153
Kučan, Milan 84–5, 139
Kwaśniewski, Aleksandr 32,
    152–3
Kyrgystan 136

Labuda, Barbara 153
Landsbergis, Vytautas 46
languages, discord over 77
Latvia 45, 46, 47–9, 134
Latvia's Way 48
'leadership drift' 12
League of Communists 88
Lewandowski, Janusz 111, 115
Liberal Democratic Congress
    (KLD) 32, 33, 152, 154
life expectancy 133, 134, 149,
    186, 192–3t
Ligner, Jaroslav 123
Linz, J.J., and Stepan, A. 59–60
Lithuania 45, 46–7, 123, 134
Lithuanian Democratic Labour
    Party (LDDP) 47
Lopez, Alan 58
Lukanov, Andrei 61, 63, 64
lung-cancer 58

Macedonia 88, 99–101, 139
Mafia 6
Malcolm, Noel 93

market economy, impact of 5–6
Marković, Ante 80, 83, 88
marriage rate 135, 147
Mazowiecki, Tadeusz 30, 31
MDF (Hungarian Democratic
  Forum) 21, 24, 25, 28,
  116, 139, 156
Mečiar, Vladimír 7, 40, 44,
  53, 54, 55, 104, 162;
  authoritarian rule of 163–4;
  and dissolution of
  Czechoslovakia 41, 42;
  downfall and return
  to power 44, 45;
  reasons for
  success of 165–6
media, censorship of 7, 55
Meksi, Alexander 75
'Memorandum of the Serbian
  Academy' 82
Meštrović, Stjepan 17
Michnik, Adam 30, 187
Mihai, (former King of
  Romania) 21
Milanovic, Branko 5, 136
Milczanowski, Andrzej 51
Miller, Petr 136–7, 143
Milošević, Slobodan 7, 78, 94,
  168; aims 81–2; and Bosnian
  war 97, 98; control of
  media 55; and Kosovo 107;
  power of 101; and
  Slovenia 84, 87
minorities 76–108; see also
  ethnic conflict
Mladenov, Petur 61, 62, 63
Modrow, Hans 20
Moldova 3, 78
monarchism 21
Montenegro 18, 58, 89, 101,
  141, 168
monuments, public 77
Moravčik, Jozef 44–5
mortality rate 133–4, 135, 190–1t
motor vehicles 125
Motyl, A.J. 78
Movement for a Democratic
  Slovakia (HZDS) 40, 41,
  44, 45, 163, 165, 166–7

Movement for Poland's
  Reconstruction
  (ROP) 154, 155
Movement for Rights and
  Freedoms (DPS) 106,
  170, 172
MSZOSZ (National Confederation
  of Hungarian Trade
  Unions) 145
MSZP (Hungarian Socialist
  Party) 23, 24, 25, 28, 29,
  117, 129, 145, 155, 158
Muratović, Hasan 168

Nano, Fatos 74, 182, 184, 185
National Liberal Party
  (PNL) 21, 65, 67
National Peasant Party
  (PNTCD) 21, 65, 66, 67, 70
National Salvation Front
  (FSN) 65, 66–7, 68,
  69, 104–5, 179
Németh, Miklos 24
nomenklatura 6, 12, 138–40, 187
nuclear power 124–5

ODS (Civic Democratic
  Party) 39, 40, 152, 159, 161
ODU (Civic Democratic Union)
  (was VPN) 41
OECD (Organization for
  Economic Cooperation and
  Development) 157–8
OH (Civic Movement) 39, 41
Olszewski, Jan 33
OPZZ (All Poland Trades Unions'
  Alliance) 64, 145
organized crime 137–8
Ottoman Empire 9–10
Owen-Stoltenberg plan 97

Paris Club 31
parties, proliferation of 53
Party of Romanian National
  Unity (PUNR) 66, 105
Pashko, Gramoz 75
Pashovski, Slavi 177
Patriotic People's Front 25
Pavelić, Ante 77

Pavlowitch, Steven 96
Pawlak, Waldemar 36
PDP (Party for Democratic Prosperity) 99
PDSH (Democratic Party) 73, 74, 75, 107
PDSR (Social Democratic Party of Romania) 180, 181
Peasant Alliance (PL) 32, 34, 35
pensions 129
Peterle, Lojže 85
Petkov, Nikola 21
Petrus, Vladimír 143
Pilip, Ivan 160
Plesu, Andrei 56
PNL (National Liberal Party) 21, 65, 67
PNTCD (National Peasant Party) 21, 65, 66, 67, 70
Poland 10, 13, 21, 29–36, 55–6, 64, 151–5; abortion issue 148–9, 152; bank scandals 122; civil society 54; compromise (1989) 29–30, 151; contraception 148; crime rates 138; de-communization 50–1; divisions within 35–6, 151–2; economy 11, 29, 31, 34, 113–16, 128; elections (1991) 32–3, 53, 150; elections (1993) 34–5, 150; elections (1997) 150, 154–5; expenditure on culture 56; fall in agricultural production 133; GDP 11, 34, 114, 151; income distribution 13, 136; lack of intervention in Gdánsk Shipyards 128–9; 'Lustration Law' 33; and Mafia 6; political features 151; political features in (1997) 154; political situation before transition 12; poverty 136, 151; presidential elections (1990) 31; presidential elections (1995) 152–3, 187; privatization 112, 115–16; restitution of agricultural property 122; shadow economy 130;
'shock therapy' reforms 30, 31, 111, 114; and SLD see SLD; smoking 58; and Solidarity see Solidarity; survival of nomenklatura 139; trade unions 145; transformation of economy 113–16; unemployment 132, 151; and Wałęsa see Wałęsa
Polish Peasant Party (formerly ZSL) see PSL
Polish United Workers' Party (PZPR) 29, 30, 32
pollution 125, 135
Popov, Dimitur 64, 169
population 134–5, 189t
Potel, Jean-Yves 59
poverty 129, 136, 186
Pozsgay, Imre 24, 25
PPSH (Party of Labour of Albania) 73, 74
privatization 7; agriculture 118–22; banks 122–3; methods of 112–13; see also individual countries
PRM (Greater Romania Party) 66, 105
Proderon, Stefan 176
PSL (Polish Peasant Party) 33, 35, 36, 129, 149, 151, 153, 154; see also ZSL
PSM (Socialist Workers' Party) 180
Public Against Violence 37, 38, 39, 187
PUNR (Party of Romanian National Unity) 66, 105
pyramid schemes 57, 150, 184
PZPR (Polish United Workers' Party) 29, 30, 32

Radmilović, Stanko 80
Rakočević, Goran 58
Rakowski, Mieczysław 29, 30
Rašković, Jovan 86
religion, revival in 5, 57
rights 186
Rohwedder, Detlev 118
Roma 27, 76, 107–8, 161

Roman, Petre 68, 69
Romania 21, 50, 64–72, 179–82;
and 1991 coup in Soviet
Union 61; AIDS 133;
census (1992) 77; constitutional
court 54; contraception 148;
cultural decline 56;
demonstrations against FSN 65;
economy 11, 68–9, 70–2, 179,
181; elections (1990) 53,
67; elections (1992) 70, 105;
elections (1996) 181; ethnic
conflict 104–5; formation of
new parties 66; and FSN *see*
FSN; GDP 11, 68, 182;
Hungarians in 66–7, 104, 180,
181; language issue 77;
media 55; methods
undertaken by FSN to stay in
power 65–6, 67–8, 179;
migration of Romanians to
Transylvania 76–7; national
income 11; and
nomenklatura 140;
poverty 136; presidential
elections (1996) 180;
privatization 69, 181;
pyramid scheme 57;
relations with Hungary 180, 181;
restitution of agricultural
land 121; secret police 66;
shadow economy 130;
strikes 71, 72; trade
unions 71, 181;
unemployment 71, 132;
weakness and disunity of
opposition 67, 68; *see also*
Iliescu
Romanian Cradle (VR) 66,
67, 105
Romanian Ecological
Movement 66, 67
ROP (Movement for Poland's
Reconstruction) 154, 155
Rugova, Ibrahim 102, 107
Ruml, Jan 51, 161
Russia 6, 124, 141; arms
sales 129; attitude towards
ethnic Russians in other
states 78; and Baltic
States 45; and
Bulgaria 61, 175; collapse
of power 7; debt rescheduling
127; fall in male life expectancy
133; foreign investment
126–7; GDP 130; income
distribution 136; and
nomenklatura 140;
pollution 125; relations
with Latvia 48; shadow
economy 130; trade with
Slovakia 164
Rutland, Peter 143

SDA (Party of Democratic
Action) 94, 95
SDPR (Social Democracy of the
Republic of Poland) 32, 122
SDS (Serbian Democratic
Party) 86, 94
SDS (Union of Democratic
Forces) 60, 176; defeat in
(1990) elections 62–3;
election victory (1997) 172,
173; formation 61–2;
instability of rule 170–2;
measures taken to stamp
out communism 170;
reasons for defeat in (1994)
elections 174
Second World War 17
Serbia 10, 139; abortion
issue 148; elections (1990)
89; GDP 59; and Kosovo 19,
83–4, 101–2; post-Dayton 168;
rise of nationalism 82; *see also*
Milošević
Serbian Democratic Party
(SDS) 86, 94
Serbs 16, 79; in Bosnia 94;
in Croatia 16–17, 82, 85–6
shadow economy 130, 137
Sheehy, Patrick 58
Shlapentokh, Vladimir 141
Silajdžić, Haris 167–8
Simeon II(former King of
Bulgaria) 21
Skele, Andris 48–9

SKJ 84
Slay, Ben 116
SLD (Alliance of the Democratic Left) 34; elections (1991) 32–3; elections (1993) 35, 50, 149; elections (1997) 154–5; formation 32; instability of rule 151–2; and PSL 35–6, 153
Slota, Jan 104
Slovak Christian Democratic Movement 40
Slovakia 37, 43–5, 53, 77, 162–7; conflict with Czechoslovakia 39–40, 42; conflict with Hungarians 103–4; constitutional court 54; declaration of sovereignty 41; economy 164–6; effect of separation 43–4; elections (1992) 41, 104; elections (1994) 150, 165; ethnic conflict 59; failure in democratic consolidation 162–3; and HZDS see HZDS; language issue 77; and Mečiar see Mečiar; and media 55; nuclear plant 125; privatization 163; restitution of agricultural property 119; separation from Czechoslovakia 41, 42, 103; trade with Russia 164; trade unions 144; unemployment 40, 164; weakness of opposition 165–6
Slovenia 18, 83, 84–5, 92–3, 127, 139; declaration of independence 87; elections 92–3; exports 92; orientation towards the West 92; shadow economy 130
Smallholders' Party (FKGP) 22, 25, 26, 27, 121, 158
smoking 57–8
SNS (Slovak National Party) 44, 103, 104
Solidarity 33, 112, 139, 145; and abortion issue 148; and AWS 153; battle with communist leadership 12, 29; coming to power 20, 29–30; decline 54; and elections (1991) 32; and elections (1993) 35; establishment of political party 32, 54; recovery of and defeat of post-communists 153–4, 187; splits within 30–1, 145; victory in (1989) elections 30
Solidarity Electoral Action AWS 153–4
South-Eastern Europe see Balkans
Soviet Union 3
Štěpán, Miroslav 50
Stoica, Ion 57
Stolojan, Theodor 69
Stoyanov, Petur 177
stress, psychological 133
Suchocka, Hanna 33
SZDSZ (Alliance of Free Democrats) 22, 24, 25, 155

Tanev, Georgi 120
Teller, Edward 124
Third Yugoslavia 101–2, 168
Tito, President 19, 80
Tocsik Affair (1996) 157
Todorova, Maria 14
Tőkés, Bishop László 66, 68
Topol, Jáchym 56
Torgyan, József 27, 158
Torpey, John 187
Tosks 106
trade 128, 195–6t
trade unions 142–6
Trenchev, Konstantin 63
Tuđman, Franjo 7, 79, 85, 89–90, 90–1, 94
Turks, in Bulgaria 76, 105, 171, 172
Tymiński, Stanisław 31, 150–1

UD (Democratic Union) 32, 33, 35, 152, 154
Uhl, Petr 187

unemployment   5, 131, 132, 136, 146, 147, 197t
Union of Democratic Forces
  see SDS
United States   7, 97
UP (Union of Labour)   35, 154
USRP (Social Democratic Union)   35

Văcăroiu, Nicolae   50, 70–1
Vance-Owen Plan (1993)   96–7
Vasile, Radu   182
Videnov, Zhan   54, 175, 176, 177, 178
VMRO-DPMNE   99, 100, 101
Vojvodina   82, 102
VPN (renamed ODU)   40, 41

wages   131; changes in real   196–7t; fall in   132–3
Wallis, Václav   123
Wałęsa, Lech   21, 32, 50, 51–2, 145; conflict with parliament   52, 152; defeat in presidential elections (1995)   152–3, 187; eccentricity   33, 36; setting up of Centre Citizens' Movement   30–1
Weiss, Peter   45
West: economic divergences between Eastern Europe and   11; influence on Eastern European culture   55, 56–7; investment and aid in transition countries   126–7
Wolff, Larry   1–2
women, effect of transition   146–9
World Bank   31, 109, 126, 173

Yeltsin, Boris   7, 48, 51–2, 78, 98
Yugoslav War (1991)   17, 87–90
Yugoslavia   10; collapse of and reasons for   79–90; elections (1990)   84–5, 88–9; ethnic problems   16–19, 79; *nomenklatura* in former   139–40; shock therapy programme   83; transferring of sovereignty to republics   18; *see also* individual countries

Zeman, Miloš   43
Zhelev, Zhelyu   53, 60, 63, 172, 178–9, 187
Zhirinovsky, Vladimir   142
Zhivkov, Todor   61, 170, 179
Zieleniec, Josef   161
Zimmermann, Warren   94
Zogu, King Ahmed   15
ZSL (United Peasant Party)   30; *see also* PSL